LEAVE THE LAND YOU LOVE
LOVE THE LAND WHERE YOU LIVE

LEAVE THE LAND YOU LOVE
LOVE THE LAND WHERE YOU LIVE

DO AN DUC TRI

authorHOUSE®

AuthorHouse™
1663 Liberty Drive
Bloomington, IN 47403
www.authorhouse.com
Phone: 1-800-839-8640

Published by AuthorHouse   05/10/2013

ISBN: 978-1-4772-7407-1 (sc)
ISBN: 978-1-4772-7406-4 (hc)
ISBN: 978-1-4772-7405-7 (e)

Library of Congress Control Number: 2012917994

Contents

Flying Birds

PROLOGUE

September 8, 1980

Fifteen long months of anxious waiting in refugee camps were finally over. Boarding the early flight on that glorious morning to the country of our choice, my family and I ended five nightmarish years of being "liberated" in the native land we all loved so much.

Seeing us off at Hong Kong's sumptuous Kai Tak International Airport that morning were our Hong Kong friends and refugees from the local transit centers. Feeling much attachment, they heartily embraced each of our family members. In heartrending tearful whispers, the friends we were leaving behind mumbled into our ears their wishes for our good luck and happiness in the new world.

Sunk in deep thought during the twelve-hour-long flight across the Pacific Ocean to the West Coast of the United States, I mulled over innumerable incidents that had happened in the past tragic years: the appalling demise of our beloved homeland, the abuse and persecution of loved ones during the years that followed, the hopeless vision of the world with no future that the liberators repeatedly proclaimed, our life-and-death escape, and our perilous crossing of a turbulent ocean on a tiny wooden boat in search of freedom. Heading eastward from Hong Kong to San Francisco, the flight was taking my family to an unimagined future. Many great promises and potential opportunities were lining up along the avenue to this new future.

For the first time in my life I contemplated with amazement the glorious sun rising above the eastern horizon twice in a single day. A third sunrise in my heart enlivened the new world I was entering.

High above the endless cushion of colorful clouds on such a beautiful autumnal day, the aerial navigation offered me a singular opportunity for insight into the two opposing worlds I had experienced: the dark world in which my compatriots, my family, and I had tragically lived, versus the new, bright world in which we would happily embark on a new life. It was a long story flooded with countless sufferings and brimful of splendid hopes.

Whether or not my recollection may evoke in you any of your own reminiscences, I am pleased to invite readers to join me in patiently looking back over countless eventful memories.

BIRD NEST

1. Yuletide angel

Spring, 1975.

Nature was so wonderfully inspiring. Filled with glorious sunlight, the spring of the Lunar Year of the Cat began its glowing days with so much colorful scenery. Many delightful social events and festivities enlivened this part of our beloved Vietnamese homeland.

The sweet scent of wildflowers wafted through the air evoking graceful reveries and preventing them from sinking into forgetfulness. Ribbons of white clouds wandered about the sunny blue firmament way up high. The wind mildly breathed its first warmer breeze, signaling the coming of a pleasurable summer.

Resplendent features of the Lunar New Year celebration permeated the city streets. Sweet melodies praising the coming of spring were on the broadcast waves. The whole bustling city was animated with the happiness of the most popular national holidays. In brilliant costumes and stunning jewelry, devout faithful flocked to temples and churches. Radiant city residents poured in great numbers to the local entertainment centers. Mirthful faces filled the public places and private homes. Everyone in the largest northern metropolis of the Republic of Vietnam enthusiastically took pleasure in new releases of humorous color movies featuring the country's celebrity comedians. With joyful smiles on beaming faces, city residents, during the gleaming time of the New Year, rejoiced in their prosperous and peaceful lifestyle. The future seemed bright and rosy with the promise of exciting days to come.

Da Nang had been my beloved city since I moved from my birthplace to live there in the summer of 1964. Approximately one hundred miles north of Da Nang is Quang Tri, my hometown. I was born in the remote countryside of Trieu Thuan Commune, where I made so many sweet childhood memories. I lost my dad when I was too young to remember. I had a sister about two years older than me. She was as weak as a reed in the wild wind. While I was growing up, my sister was the only sibling available to provide me companionship.

On our first school days, during World War II, my sister and I, together with a few kids in the hamlet, went to the private home of a village tutor about two miles from our home to learn the alphabet. Wintertime was damp and windily bitter. The whole area was covered in an endless cold drizzle. Too timid to show its face to the cold, the sun tightly wrapped itself in layers of cloudy blankets behind a dull curtain of fine rain. The days were short and dreary.

The road home, soaked with rainwater and made mucky by trampling cattle, often was too muddy for tiny kids to wade through. Running homeward, we boys would cheer as we competed against each other to jump over the slippery mounds of a potato field that undulated alongside the boggy road. The race warmed us up in the wintry environment. My poor sister tried strenuously to climb over the slick potato field, mound by mound. When I looked back from the end of the field, she was several hundred yards behind. Other kids kept running and cheering. Giving up the race, I went back to help her. Carrying my sister on my shoulders, I resumed the homebound jumps.

It was the final days of World War II. Allies' B-29 bombers kept carrying out air raids on nearby Japanese barracks. Upon hearing the deafening roar of the incoming bombers, my quivering sister in her shivering fear clung fast to my neck as we ran to the shallow bomb shelter dug along the backyard's bamboo hedge. She was horrified by the continuous bombings. Her health declined precipitately. As a lamp goes out for lack of oil, she passed away that summer when cicadas were crying on the moody slender willow standing in the corner of the garden under the simmering sun.

Japanese fascists left. Vietnamese Communists rolled over the country. Under the horrible reign of the Communists, no school or teacher was available anymore. At night, guerillas carrying machetes hunted through every home. They caught and beheaded renowned people. They plugged the blood-tinged heads of their victims onto bamboo poles erected along roadsides, to instill fear. Stuck to the bloody heads were pieces of paper with scribbled words accusing the victims of crimes, with words such as *Traitor, Betrayer,* and *Landlord.* Those new Vietnamese terms were unfamiliar to the local villagers' parlance at the time. I asked my mom about the meaning of those terrifying designations; mom could not give me a precise explanation either.

Much older than I, my only big brother was an active opponent of Communism. Most of the young intellectuals of my brother's age fled the area. Some of the youths were captured and killed on the spot. The most notorious murder was that of the Vo family's brothers. The brothers lived in the neighboring Trieu Dong Commune. In March 1947 Bui Tin, the Communist killer, came with his comrades. Dragging the Vo brothers[1] out of their home, Bui Tin repeatedly stabbed the brothers with his machete. He kicked their dead bodies into the Vinh Dinh canal. Years later Bui Tin was promoted to the rank of colonel and became Editor in Chief of the Vietnamese Communist Nhan Dan newspaper.

A former classmate of the local youths, Mr. Tao, was a resident of neighboring commune. He knew well the younger generation in my commune and their political propensities. Not long after the Communist seizure of power, early one morning, Mr. Tao came, bearing the rank of captain, imposingly riding on a horse and followed by his platoon to the village church.

The previous day, on a splendidly sunny morning, the local youths had organized a public ceremony honoring the Vietnamese forefathers. Captain Tao and his platoon arrived as we kids were on our way to our daily tutoring class. Mr. Trung Duong, our teacher, disappeared to his hiding place upon Tao's coming; with no class that day, most of us kids curiously gathered at a corner of the churchyard. The Communist captain had his men cordon off the area and rake our Trieu Thuan Commune for young gentlemen.

Most of the blacklisted people could not escape or hide themselves in time. Mr. Ngoan who was the local Chinese medical practitioner and my mom's cousin, my uncle Long Duong, and tens of the local youths[2] were captured. They were trussed up, led away, and killed or jailed at unknown sites. Of the tens of young men captured by Tao, only two of them came back after years without news.

My uncle Long's wife, mourning her missing husband, suffered severe dementia. She wandered aimlessly until she was completely lost. My uncle Long's sister, who lived by herself, had to foster his two orphaned children.

My big brother was out of town on a business trip when Tao came. After returning from his excursion, my brother was apprehended at a city hotel and sent to a prison far away.

Our village teacher ran away for his safety. Without teacher or schooling, children were wandering around looking after cattle or amusing themselves in the muddy fields. My mom assumed the task of teaching me to read and write. Later on, a very young man in a nearby hamlet took the risk of holding a class in his kitchen. Mom sent me for his teaching.

During the cold drizzle season, mom wrapped me up in a raincoat woven of palm leaves and a conical hat. On the two-mile walk to class, mud flooded to my little knees. Clay clung to my skin as if glued. Arriving, tired out, at the teacher's hut, the other kids and I looked as if we were wearing clay boots. We set our feet beneath the water dripping from the porch roof to gradually wash off the unwanted boots of clay. Cleaned away, clay boots left behind the bare, shivering tiny legs. On windy and rainy days, copybooks were wet through, ink pots dirty, and clothes soggy. But in our innocent childhood, as a fugacious breeze, the hardships suddenly came and quickly went away.

Years later, my brother fortunately was liberated by the Allied forces. After a short time hiding at home to recuperate from exhaustion after his prolonged detention, he left our politically unsafe countryside home. Settling down in the imperial Citadel of Hue, he joined the Chieu An organization under Governor Phan Van Giao. So afraid of the possibility that I might be killed or indoctrinated by the Communists, my mom heartbrokenly sent me away to Hue to live with my brother. Mom stayed back alone.

Governor Phan Van Giao was later assassinated by the Communists. His Chieu An organization was dissolved by the next governor Tran Van Ly. Before leaving Hue to move to the Central Highlands, my big brother sent me to a private boarding school in Tam Toa, a village near the city of Dong Hoi in the northern province of Quang Binh.

Dong Hoi is several hundred miles north of my hometown. Tam Toa, in the Dong My commune, was a small village lying alongside the northern bank of the famous Nhat Le River and about a mile north of the Dong Hoi downtown. Running by the side of the city, the one-hundred-mile Nhat Le, which means "River of Heavenly Tears," embraced a sumptuous old parish church. Not far from the church was a prestigious school. The private middle school was named Mateo Phuong after a local Catholic martyr.

When the 1951-1952 school year started, I entered sixth grade at Mateo Phuong. Far away from my lonely mom, my remote birthplace, and the countryside ambiance, my uprooted childhood was more sad than happy. The boarding school turned its backside to the glamorous Nhat Le River. Watching romantic scenes of the river from the second floor of the boarding school in the afternoon breeze, the displaced little boy was lost in melancholic feelings.

The city of Dong Hoi was not very prosperous, and suffered greatly during the war. The boarding school was a short walk from the Tam Toa parish church. At times I would stand in its shadow, pensively looking northward along the broad road. The road looked so spacious, well paved, and somehow lonely, in the eyes of a child away from home. Although short, it was the main street of the Dong My Commune. Far beyond the boulevard lay the quiet airport. Imposing mansions lined the two sides of the boulevard. I was too young to remember the name of the splendid road. The great Vietnamese poet Han Mac Tu was baptized in 1912 in the parish church at the south end of the road. The road might have been named Han Mac Tu Avenue.

As young and unsophisticated as I was, I was chosen to sing occasionally during a ceremonial mass and regularly on the nightly broadcasting sessions. Reverend Father Ai Do was in charge of the musical program. Reverend Father Phuong Nguyen was the eloquent preacher undertaking speeches. However, as a little boy staying up so late into the night to listen to lengthy sermons, I could not help but fall asleep. Somebody had to wake me up when it was time for me to sing.

One of my sweetest memories of the old days in Dong My was of Christmas Eve, 1953. Strictly speaking, it was not the Christmas celebration but the little angel appearing on the Yuletide Eve that struck my inner chord. Its echo kept ringing for the rest of my life.

In the cold winter ambiance, the parish church on that Yule night was splendidly decorated with a multitude of flickering candles. Adorned with multicolor lanterns, a beautiful manger on the left hand side of the sanctuary was captivatingly trimmed with tiny murmuring streams and lively man-made bird songs.

Clad in warm clothes against the chill of the night, I was among the choir singing on the unforgettable night. Church bells rang melodiously. The midnight ceremony was about to start. The church was gradually filled with splendidly dressed parishioners. Young children were wide-eyed in amazement at the glorious beauty.

The manger was the main attraction. Upon the bell signaling the beginning of the night ceremony, to everyone's surprise a pretty little live angel hesitantly appeared at the splendidly decorated sanctuary. She was about nine years old. The angel tottered around, looking for a way to climb to her high position on the manger. In fact, behind the manger a three-step stairway was cleverly hidden behind several layers of fake mossy rocks. The angel planned to step on the stairs from behind the manger. She was to sing the Vietnamese version of Gloria to announce to the shepherds and to the congregation the birth of the bambino Jesus. The innocent little angel seemed not to be able to find the hidden steps. She then tried and failed to get on the platform from the front side. The angel's long dress and her small body kept her from climbing up. It was higher than her little shoulders. Her eyes glittered on her rosy face as if she were about to cry. The first notes of the Gloria started sounded on the harmonium. Poor little angel! Seeing her in a desperate situation, I wished she could flap her little wings to fly onto the platform.

The little angel turned around as if she were looking for human help. I felt nervous for her. My singing friends gave me, the youngest boy in the group, an encouraging look. Was that because I was about her height and age? Looking around with some brief hesitation, I naively left my singing rank and rushed across the sanctuary to the manger. Standing there, she looked so innocent and beautiful in her angelic dress. With her rosy lips and sparkling eyes in the twinkling of thousands of candles, she was an extremely cute angel.

Hesitantly taking the angel's tiny trembling hand in mine, I silently led her to the stairs in the back where she stepped onto the stool sheepishly without looking to see who had helped her up. I heard some applause from the church attendants as the radiantly beautiful angel reappeared high on the manger in the glorious rays of the spotlight.

The parish church and my childhood school had been built on the northern bank of the Nhat Le River. The river was a historic line of demarcation. In 1630 General Dao Duy Tu erected a ten-mile-long military brick wall along the river's northern bank. Enforced with troops, the great wall prevented the invading troops of the northern Lord Trinh from coming against the southern Nguyen Lord's territory. Originating in the Dau Mau mountainous area in Le Thuy District, rippling waves of the Nhat Le River break onto the sandy shore of Dong My village before its flow reaches the immense Eastern Ocean. My childhood time spent along the Nhat Le River was not as long as I wished. It was wartime. The little boarder boy would not have much time or opportunity to get to know the local people and all the fine scenery of the area. As time flew, the 1953 Yuletide event sank deep into my unconscious.

In July 1954, the Geneva Treaty was signed. It cut Nhat Le River, Dong My village, Tam Toa hamlet, and my boarding school away from the free world. I was among the refugees going southward, leaving behind so many regrets and attachments. My boarding school was ravaged during the following years of hellish war. And so was the ancient church and Dong My village. The remainder of the bombarded church was kept as a distressing war vestige.

1954 was such a damaging year. After leaving Dong Hoi to resettle in Hue, I was struck by a deadly typhoid fever and was bedridden for months before being accepted into the special ninth grade. The class was occasionally opened to refugee boys at the Nguyen Tri Phuong Public Middle School. Attending the school only for the second semester of the ninth grade, I was fortunately nominated to represent the school in the area's math and English competitions. At the same time, the teacher-songwriter Hoang Nguyen sent me to represent the school in the Vietnamese Literature contest. The school's headmaster, however, warned me not to compete in more than two subjects. Having taken part in the Vietnamese and English matches, I was selectively awarded the First Class Honors Prize in English competition.

After graduating from middle school, I attended the famous Quoc Hoc High School. Founded in 1896, it was at one time called Khai Dinh Lycee. Quoc Hoc was a public boys' school. However, when I was in twelfth grade, in the 1957-1958 academic year, the girls' public high school, Dong Khanh, sent their twelfth-grade girls for coed with my class. The classroom, a huge space on the second floor, swarmed with more than a hundred students. When I graduated from the Hue University years afterward, I started my teaching career in a remote village close to Thuan An beach and then in my Quang Tri hometown.

Another fatal year in the history of the young republic was 1963, marked by the Vietnamese coup d'état. I left my troubled hometown not long after the disastrous event to intentionally hide myself further south. The political turmoil, however, nailed me down to Da Nang City instead. As the 1964-1965 academic year started, following the recommendations of my friends, I landed a teaching job mainly at the private Sao Mai High School. Later on I held teaching positions at the private Sacred Heart girls' high and the nearby Nguyen Cong Tru semi-public high.

A two-story L-shaped institution, Nguyen Cong Tru High was named after a Vietnamese poet. Turning its back to Nguyen Thi Giang Street, the school's frontage looked out to the short Le Thanh Tong Avenue. The refugees originally coming from Tam Toa in the North had steadily established themselves in the new Tam Toa Ward in the Second District of Da Nang. Many students from the Tam Toa refugee settlement attended the nearby Nguyen Cong Tru High. The twelfth-grade classes I was teaching were up on the second floor. Eleventh-grade classes, where I gave lessons in dissertation style and Vietnamese literature, were on the first floor next to the teacher conference room.

Upon leaving my instruction sessions on the second floor to go down to the teacher conference room, I kept being jocularly blocked at the staircase by boisterous twelfth-grade girls. Hoai Tam was the leader of the teasing group. Lien Chinh, Huyen Vy, and Thu Hoai were among the more active girls of the group. They were always posing intricate humorous questions to poke fun at their bachelor teacher.

"Dear teacher! Tell me whether the eleventh-grade girls are more beautiful?" Hoai Tam tricked me into her entanglement.

"You're the most beautiful fairies I've ever seen."

"Smart flatteries. Then tell us why you keep biking up the Tran Cao Van Road with that eleventh-grade girl?" Hoai Tam continued her attacks.

"You go there to teach the girl the dissertation technique. Don't you, teacher?" Lien Chinh started her mocking allusion.

"Oh, I know. I know. In his dissertation technique lessons, the teacher says that the body has three points." Some girl behind Lien Chinh added.

"Press hard on the two upper points!" Hoai Tam loudly said with a teasing stare.

"And go deeper into the lower point!" Huyen Vy added with no hesitation. The whole group of girls burst out laughing noisily at the double meanings.

"I give in. Girls, you know the points and the technique to handle them so well. I'm sure you must have skillfully carried it out."

"Teacher, that's what you've taught us to do."

That kind of back-and-forth baiting enlivened the teaching days of a bachelor, but it also caused me much embarrassment. One evening after class when I took my bicycle out of the rack and was about to ride home, the twelfth-grade girls, who kept their bikes at the same rack reserved for the teachers, rushed at me. Seeing that I was alone, one of the girls, with a deceptively innocent air, sang the first verse of a Vietnamese song that began, "Honey, you're not with me this evening . . ."

Another girl directly posed the question, "Where's yours, teacher?"

I could not keep silent. "Why do you girls keep throwing out innuendoes against her?" I said, and to satisfy the girls' curiosity added, "I know which girl you're talking about. She's my uncle's daughter."

"Uncle? How distant is he?" Hoai Tam asked.

"He's so distant that a missile couldn't reach him, isn't that right?" Lien Chinh said.

"Love shortens the distance." Huyen Vy or some other girl added, poking more fun at my response when I had fondly thought my explanation might clear up their inquisitiveness.

I had no close relatives living in Da Nang City to spend long weekends with. Sometimes a group of us teachers would gather at the home of a teacher named Vinh Linh, and I enjoyed these assemblies of friends. Otherwise, I had nowhere to turn other than to visit the family of my uncle. He was only a distant relative—so distant that I did not know how he was related to my family. All I knew was that my mom told me to address him as uncle and advised me to visit his family as often as I could. In fact, the uncle had passed away before I came to Da Nang. The widow was mourning the premature loss of her husband.

My dad had passed away as well. No children were by my mother's side; in such an anguished situation, my mom felt the emptiness of a lonely life and could comprehend the uncle's widow's state of mind. Seeing my reluctance to visit the uncle's family, my mom strongly urged me to pay frequent visits to the forlorn widow in her grief.

"Son, she may be a distant relative, but you know, even distant, a relative has some diluted blood of ours."

"Mom, you've told me: a drop of diluted blood is much superior to a bowl of cold water."

I understood the uncle's widow's sad situation. I loved my mom and did not want to behave contrarily to her wishes. However, to avoid being the subject of ridicule and widespread misconception, I tried not to bike to her home along with the eleventh-grade student anymore.

In her distress, the uncle's widow had abandoned her profitable fish-processing business. Away from her Tam Toa birthplace, having settled down in an alien area far from her relatives, the distressed lady felt it very meaningful to have someone pay her even a short visit. The twelfth-grade girls made it into a puzzling love story to amuse themselves, and fought with feigned jealousy to win back their bachelor teacher.

It was a Friday evening. The year of 1965 was drawing to an end. Away from my hometown on an evening at year's end, I deeply sensed the great emptiness in a world without close relatives. Reluctant to be back at my rented lodgings to see the owner's family enjoying a weekend get-together, I roamed around the city on my bike for a while after my evening class. I normally came to my teaching sessions without any book or document or anything else on hand, except when there were previously collected and already corrected students' papers to distribute to the class. After years on the teaching stand, all the details of the instructional materials came to my mind's eye as vivid as an open book.

After the last class session of the day, I often took a leisurely bike ride in the open. On that weekend evening at year's end, the streets were mostly empty and boring. Everyone was hurrying homewards as the daylight dimmed. After stopping for a short time by the Han River, as the sun went down and the riverbank became deserted, I reluctantly biked to the home of the distant uncle to pay another visit to his family.

Facing the local market, the home of my uncle stood about five yards back from the Tran Cao Van Road. I hesitatingly stepped up two stairs from the road and crossed the narrow front yard, and I was at the open front door looking into the home. In the twilight of the living room I was struck by surprise. An amazingly pretty girl about twenty-some years old greeted me as I stepped in. I had never seen her during my previous visits. I stayed silent for some seconds trying to revive my memory. There was something familiar as if I had met this girl somewhere, maybe a long time ago. Her rosy lips and sparkling eyes resurrected something vague from my subconscious.

"Hello Ms. Unknown! Did I ever meet you?"

"I don't think so," the girl sharply replied.

"You remind me of someone I've met somewhere sometime."

"Teacher! Are you daydreaming? Did you mistake me for one of your girls? Who told you my name is Ms. Unknown?" The girl retorted in a lively and seemingly familiar way. I had not taught her at any time, but following the Vietnamese tradition, the girl addressed me with the title of teacher.

"Sorry, young lady. I didn't have the honor of knowing your name. But your rosy lips and sparkling eyes remind me of a little Yuletide angel I've seen somewhere."

"Really? Interesting coincidence! Where did you see the Christmas angel? In your dreams or in the real world?"

"Give me a break! I'm trying to revive my memory. Maybe it was when I was a stranded little kid."

"That's interesting! When I was a little girl, I used to play the role of an angel during Christmastime."

"Wow! Was it you who stood on a manger stool and sang to the shepherds?"

"How did you know?"

"Now I remember everything. It's you. Once I helped you climb on the stool that was too high for you. Don't you remember?"

"Oh, yeah! You were a little boy singing in the parish choir, weren't you? It's such a long time ago. How do you know it's me?"

"Your tiny hands. Your attractive lips and sparkling eyes. Now, you're such a grown-up angel, but your lovely lips and eyes haven't changed. I should say they're much more beautiful, even more attractive!"

"My sister kept mentioning you. Now, here you are. I didn't expect you to be an old acquaintance."

"Really? Your sister talked about me? I hope your sister didn't say anything bad behind my back."

"My sister was right. You're handsome. You're speaking so gracefully. No wonder the twelfth-grade girls at school keep chasing after you. Did any of them win you over? Did you fall in love with any of them?"

"It's only because of my unfortunate destiny that I kept being bullied by those wild beauties."

"What? Unfortunate destiny? No way. You're so lucky in love."

"Oh, my God! I'm succumbing to your witty repartee."

I was enchanted by the lovely girl. The unexpected encounter revived so many long-lost memories, yet at the same time it left some new, unexplained impression on me. The interchangeable images of the innocent angel of the old days and the loquacious beauty of today kept coming back to my mind during the day and showing up in dreams at night.

I stopped visiting the uncle's family after the surprise meeting with my childhood acquaintance. By doing so I hoped I might elude the haunting image of the angelic beauty.

2. Beach-nesting birds

The hellish Vietnam War stamped a disastrous social stigma on our country. Besides the loss of innumerable human lives, the brotherhood conflict turned many a lover into an inconsolable unfortunate who waited in despair for the homecoming of his or her partner. A Vietnamese folk song tells the heartbreaking stories of family separation due to the unending wars:

> *For her enlisted son's homecoming*
> *At Ai Tu Bridge the mother sat endlessly waiting.*
> *Stood watching out for her husband-warrior's return,*
> *On Vong Phu peak the spouse into a boulder turned.*

Ai Tu in Vietnamese means "love for son." The humble Ai Tu sandy area in my Quang Tri hometown lies on the northern bank of Thach Han River along Vietnamese National Highway 1. At the crossroads of the national highway and the waterway, columns of naval forces and the infantry of Lord Nguyen Hoang in the eighteenth century were vehemently marching into battle. Legend has it that at the northern end of the bridge spanning Thach Han River, a poor mother saw her son off to the battlefields and then sat, languishing, waiting for his homecoming, until she turned to stone.

Vong Phu, which means "waiting for husband," is the name of a mountain in Lang Son province whose rocky peak resembles a woman holding a baby. It is believed to be the petrified Lady To Thi, who stood tirelessly watching and waiting for her husband to return home at the end of the war.

The eighteenth-century poet Dang Tran Con (1715-1745), in his epic "Song of a Soldier's Spouse," exalted the agonizing situation of a wife from the day she bids farewell to her husband-warrior. She watches her husband, a cuirassier, riding away majestically on a white horse. After the wrenching farewell, she goes back to her empty room and begins to imagine his perilous life on fierce battlefields. Once her romantic image of a hero on the day of separation gradually discolors, a terrible fear of her husband's fate during the threatening battles starts causing her own constant suffering.

> *The warfare turbulence once having started,*
> *Rosy cheek beauties in distress engulfed.*

Countless tales of desperate people waiting in vain for reunion with a relative were everywhere in legendary folk songs and in the country's classical literature. Such things were an undeniable everyday reality in our war-torn motherland that we love so much. In the whirlwind of war, many times I also got caught up in the turbulence. But there was still a lot of luck brought to me. It may hurt some people who have suffered by the war when I say that the horrible warfare in some instances opened advantageous windows that somehow led me into happy encounters. It is a rather lengthy story.

Graduated from Hue University in 1959, as I have recounted, I first taught in my hometown only several miles from the famous Ai Tu Bridge. The political turmoil later drove me away from my birthplace on my way southward. When I reached Da Nang, the so-called Peoples National Rescue Forces (PNRF), a self-established anti-governmental movement, cut the city off from the central leadership. Dr. Nguyen Van Man, mayor of Da Nang, and Colonel Dam Quang Yeu, the military commander of Quang Da Special District, joined the rebels against the central government. At the request of the district commander, Captain Dzu moved the 11th Ranger Battalion from Quang Nam to Da Nang, and occupied the First Corps Headquarters, the city radio station, the Police Department, and local Military Armed Services. The PNRF stationed the post of their command of operations at the provincial Buddhist Phap Lam Temple on Ong Ich Khiem Street. The year 1966 was an eventful one. In five months, four First Corps commanders—Nguyen Chanh Thi, Nguyen Van Chuan, Ton That Dinh, and Huynh Van Cao—were successively replaced.

Stationed in Da Nang, Lieutenant General Lewis William Walt, the United States Marine Corps (USMC) commander in the five northernmost provinces of South Vietnam, sided with the PNRF against the Vietnamese central government. He officially made known his decision to retaliate if the Vietnamese central government raided the PNRF. The political and military situations were extremely heated. Schools, businesses, and markets were intermittently closed as a result of the pandemonium.

During the first week of April, the central government began its military campaign to take back the city of Da Nang from occupation by the rebellious PNRF. Prime Minister Nguyen Cao Ky flew to Da Nang to negotiate with Lt. Gen. Walt so the USMC would not intervene in the PNRF defense. On June 3, 1966, three thousand Vietnamese Marine Corps and parachutists entered the city. Businesses and schools were all forced to close. Homes were closely shut leaving deserted streets with garbage uncollected.

Temporarily out of work, I decided to get away from the possible dangers of the brotherly conflict in Da Nang; I rode, among terrified passengers, on the last bus to the nearby ancient town Hoi An.

The historic city was only twenty miles south of Da Nang. In the eighteenth century, Hoi An was known as Faifo and was the busiest commercial port of the region. Missionaries came to Faifo to learn the language before going deeper into the country. For centuries, merchants from Asia Minor, Japan, and China had flocked there for trade and commodity exchange. While waiting for the favorable wind stream of monsoon season to sail back to their home countries, wealthy Japanese and Chinese traders built Faifo into the historic ancient city. Some married the local residents and stayed permanently. They associated themselves into their various ethnic groups and built their own temples. Japanese and Chinese cultural traces have turned the ancient city into a famous resort. Thu Bon River rolls in a wavering flux through the ancient city before emptying into the East Ocean several miles away.

My plan for one day out of the embattled city of Da Nang unexpectedly would become a full week confined in the ancient town of Hoi An because of a newly imposed martial curfew.

I had no acquaintance in the city. Stumbling around that first afternoon, in the unfamiliar environment, I was looking for an inn or somewhere to stay during the military curfew. The ancient city was graceful, but it became a scary place for me in that warfare atmosphere. At the time, local tourism had not been widely developed. Inns and hotels were hard to find. Residents of the town hurried home and shut their doors early. Streets became deserted in dim light. The ancient town seemed to draw back into the distant past as the sound of military movements echoed and the sun hastened down behind rows of ancient houses.

I reached the corner of a road leading to the famous roofed pagoda bridge, and if I had been one or two steps ahead, I might have rushed hard into two lovely bike-riding girls in health-care uniforms. It was amazing to see them on the street so late. They looked worry-free. Each rode with one hand on the steering handlebar, the other hand keeping her white skirt from flying pleasantly in the evening breeze.

"Lovely angels! Sorry! I almost crashed into you," I burst out upon head-on confrontation. The bike-riding girls, one shorter and one taller, stopped and looked at each other in surprise.

"Who's this? Do you know him?" the shorter girl asked her taller companion.

The lovely taller girl did not answer her comrade but stared at me for a moment. "Heavens! What are you doing here so late?" she asked me, with the clear voice of a singer and a radiant smile. Her last word rang high in the air, expressing her interest and astonishment. Her long right foot rested hesitantly against the ground as if she was ready to come closer to me.

"Sorry, young ladies. But I didn't know your beautiful names to greet you both." Pointing to the taller, smiling girl with hair floating in the wind I tried to explain to her friend. "This is the third time I've seen this lovely beauty in a thirteen-year span. How stupid I am for not knowing her name."

"I'm Tan." With an amused look, the shorter girl introduced herself. As I barely opened my mouth to greet her, the short, lively girl interrupted me to say:

"If you guys know each other, you'll both keep talking. It's late. I have to go." With a witty look to her friend, Miss Tan tried to retire from the scene.

"Hi, Miss Tan! Very nice to know you. Please keep us company!"

"You both stay. I'm going," Miss Tan replied, and rode away.

Without preventing Miss Tan from leaving, the taller girl, showing her high interest in the surprise encounter, started storming me with an endless string of questions:

"Why are you here? They imposed curfew, how did you get here? How will you get back? Where are you staying? Did you come with somebody else? Have you eaten anything yet?"

"Oh, my dear! May I stop you so I can answer your string of questions?"

"OK. Answer my questions!"

"Thanks, Miss who?"

"You've named me Miss Unknown once. Don't you remember?"

"Sorry. But such a lovely angel as you must have a very beautiful name. Don't you?"

"U.A. Unknown Angel. Satisfied?" she improvised in a mocking tone.

"OK. M.A."

"What did you say? Did I hear M.A?"

"Yes. M.A. Short for My Angel!"

The girl did not argue against my naming her "My Angel," but looked at me with astonishment. I kept talking for fear she might stop me and say something else.

"Dear My Angel, I came for a one-day visit to the ancient town. And then the curfew was imposed, preventing me from going home."

"Who has compelled you to come here?"

"It's by good fortune!"

"Don't lie to me. Are you chasing after some girl?"

"No girl here but My Angel."

"Huh! Go back to your twelfth-grade girls!"

"How come? I'm looking for somewhere to stay overnight or until the curfew is over. Are you working here, in this wonderful town?"

"Don't throw me a red herring." She paused. "Am I working here? Yes, but it's a temp assignment. Tell me, where are you staying?"

"I'm still looking."

"I'm staying with relatives. Didn't you find an inn? It's late. All the doors are closed. How about if I ask my relatives to let you stay?"

"It would be wonderful if I could stay with my beautiful angel." I hesitated as soon as I'd spoken. A slip of the tongue had betrayed my joy at the girl's invitation. I attempted to cover up my feelings by retreating from her advances: "The city is so charming. I may stay somewhere and find someone to guide me around so I can contemplate the city's stunning sights at nighttime."

"May I join you on the night tour? I'd like to see the hidden beauties of the town, too. Please!"

I could not resist her repeated appeals. I'd tried to extinguish my suddenly quickened feelings—unsuccessfully. The night fell. And the love story started. The unplanned week in Hoi An was but happily spent with the lovely angel by my side. Maybe I had been struck hard by the love-storm. However, readers, do not let your imagination wander too far, please! Let me tell you what actually happened.

On the first magical night in the romantic Hoi An, although I was close to such a beautiful angel for the first time, a delicate distance was discreetly honored. The intimate, magic word "love" was not spoken, though the scenery, with its Japanese traces and its old Chinese establishments lit by flickering night lights, offered such a poetic ambiance for the first-time lovers. City streets were deserted. The Thu Bon River behind the inn where I stayed was quietly drifting in the sparkling moonlight. Sitting next to each other by the charming riverbank, each of us felt in our own heart that something was evolving. We spent successive nights at each other's side, until the poetic river witnessed our most magical moments together, away from the fratricidal gunfire.

It was not hard for me to find out where the lovely angel was working in the small town. Military curfew had not been enforced in the tourist heaven. The charming angel had to report to work during my stay. Knowing that I would sit in the coffee shop at the corner, earnestly waiting for her at the end of her working day, she changed her outfit from the health uniform to a very captivating dress.

The evening atmosphere in Hoi An on the following days was bright and delicate. When she came out of the office, the lovely angel stopped to look left and right at the roadside, hesitated for a moment, and then quickly crossed the asphalt road and headed toward the coffee shop with hasty steps and a happy look. Knowing that I had no bike, she walked instead of biking as usual. Miss Tan, her amicable workmate, might have guessed what her friend was up to, for she did not come along with her. We went for a short walk after having coffee. In the peaceful Hoi An, not many people were on the roads during the rush hour. Strangers were easily recognized. Some passersby threw an inquisitive look at both of us. The angel seemed very happy. She paid no attention to the passersby.

We stopped at a shop serving local delicacies.

"Don't you have to go home for dinner?" I hesitantly asked.

"You want to send me home, don't you?" She looked a little bit somber.

"Oh no, dear. I'm just wondering if your relatives are waiting for you. I'm glad you didn't leave me alone."

After having a good dinner together, we sat silently, looking passionately at each other. The sun had turned off its evening light to go for a night's rest. Some shops switched on their decorative lanterns, which turned the ancient town as sparkling as the stars in the night sky. We left the restaurant to take another short walk. Most of the evening, I chose to spend sitting in the moonlight at the south riverbank of the Thu Bon River listening to my angel's heartfelt confidences.

Born in Dong My, she had to bid farewell to her birthplace and childhood memories on Nhat Le, the River of Heavenly Tears, in July 1954, when she was but an eleven-year-old little girl. With her refugee parents she escaped from the coming of the Northern Communists to the city. The heartbreaking separation took place after the Vietnamese Communists and their Red Chinese allies defeated the French on the Dien Bien Phu battlefield. They forced the defeated France into signing the Geneva Treaty to divide Vietnam into two parts against the protest of the nationalist government.

After several sleepless nights on the high seas, on board a steamship, the poor little angel and her displaced family landed at Da Nang. Stayed for weeks in crowded, makeshift quarters, the family finally had no choice in the foreign city other than to settle down on the designated sandy beach where a multi-unit settlement for the newly arrived refugees was hurriedly built. The freshly established hamlet was named after the refugee home village of Tam Toa in the city of Dong Hoi.

Speaking of her traumatic childhood experience, the lovely angel apprehensively confided, "After sounding its long siren, the steamship eternally cut me off from the landscape of my childhood memories. My mom cried bitterly all throughout the expedition. During the sleepless nights under the starry skies in a salty atmosphere, sitting drowsily next to a pile of smelly hides on the exposed deck and listening to the endless murmur of the waves, I thought of myself on the boundless ocean to be like a poor small child being kicked out of her own cradle onto a road, and stumbling to an uncertain future."

"Darling, it sounds so sad," I vaguely responded, deeply immersed in her tragic confidences.

The dew was falling. Breeze from the Thu Bon River turned the atmosphere chilly. She did not protest when I suddenly put my right arm around her slender shoulders. She leaned in. Having for the first time a beauty in my own arms, I felt the blood was flooding my heart, and my heart was racing. I moved closer to her, and she resumed her sad story.

"I was just a ten-year-old girl. The separation from my birthplace left a never-healing scar inside me." She looked into the darkness. Swallowing her sobs, she continued to relate her melancholic memory. "There are no more unforgettable Yuletide nights. As you well know, during Christmastime, dressed as a little winged angel, I was chosen to stand next to the crib of the newborn Jesus to sing to the shepherds. No more meandering lanes leading to neighboring gardens."

"Darling, you must miss your birthplace so much."

"Back there, after afternoon classes my friends and I used to enjoy all kinds of juicy fruits and beautiful flowers under shady trees. Long gone are those poetic childhood days!"

"My dear!" I interrupted her confidences to insert my equivocal comments. "You were born on the Dong My side of the River of Heavenly Tears, Nhat Le. Maybe you're destined to lead a floating life as a running river, full of tears. You may shed many tears in your whole life."

"During my childhood years, each time my mom flew away from home on her trading trips, I missed her so much. And you know, as a child, I couldn't help crying bitterly, especially at sunset."

"Darling! It's surprising, the places you come from are one way or another related to tears."

"Do you mean I'm nothing but a tearful girl?"

"Oh no, darling! But don't you know a girl's tears are the sharpest sword that pierces the human heart?"

The little angel stole a quick glance at me in the dark. I imagined there might be some teardrops on her beaming eyes as she unfolded her string of dark childhood days.

"Darling! Your birthplace was Nhat Le, meaning the River of Tears. And you also have Le Thuy, meaning Tears District. I believe that other parts of Le Thuy District are named Le Xa, or Shedding Tear Ward, and Chau Xa, which also means the ward of Shedding Tear, and so on."

She looked deeply contemplative. From a boat floating on the Thu Bon River, an oil lamp was flickering and an oar quietly crunching. Sweet sounds of the country girls selling local products resonated as echoes of distant dreams.

"Darling! Your parents must have given you a designated name. I imagine it must be a beautiful and significant one," I said suddenly, cutting off her introspective line of thought as I tried to learn her name, which so far she had kept from telling me.

"They named me after a mythical bird."

"Anything related to tears? Is it Nightingale, or Oriole?"

"Those are real, not mythical birds."

"Then Eagle. Isn't it?"

"No. Eagle is another real bird. Can you think of any mythological one?"

"Oh. I know it, my dear!"

"Know what?"

"You're a wonderful Phoenix! Aren't you?"

The Vietnamese have a love of four sacred mythical animals. The first three are Dragon, Unicorn, and Turtle. The Dragon is believed to have personalized into the first forefather of the Viet people under the name of Lac Long Quan who had espoused the fairy Au Co. The legendary Lady was pregnant with one hundred fetuses and gave birth to the first hundred ancestors of the Vietnamese. The Turtle, as recounted in the country's legend, provided King An Duong Vuong with the technique to build the ancient Co Loa citadel during the king's founding of the new nation. The mythical Turtle also equipped the king with the miraculous crossbow that was capable of destroying invaders en masse to protect the newly established dynasty. The turtle currently living in Hoan Kiem Lake in Hanoi is believed to be a descendant of the legendary Golden Turtle.

The fourth fabulous creature, Phoenix, is referred to in the Christian Bible and is also highly revered by different civilizations. The immortal bird has been engraved as the noble emblem of numerous organizations and great nations.

When they named her after the mythical bird Phoenix, the parents of the little angel probably could not have anticipated that the lovely personified Phoenix would lead such a wandering life full of adventures.

"Sweetie! Phoenix is the symbol of power and nobleness."

"I know." She paused, and then abruptly whispered into my excitement, "But don't you want me to be your little angel instead?"

Thrilled at her revelation, I stammered nervously and replied, "Sweetie ! I do! I do! You are My Angel, darling! You'll always be my little angel! Won't you?"

"I will."

At these intimately exchanged confidences, we had our first amorous kiss to seal our eternal commitment, that night, on the bank of Thu Bon River, in the ancient town of Hoi An, with the witness of the radiant moon far on high.

I could not know how long we were in such an ecstasy. It must have been quite a while. The moon over our heads was dimmed by a big flying mass of clouds and then reappeared bright and brilliant.

"My Little Angel!"

"But don't call me My Little Angel in front of others!"

"Then I abbreviate it into MyAn. OK?"

She did not respond. After thinking a moment, I continued, "Dear honey! MyAn doesn't sound Vietnamese. How if I nickname you My Le (Mee Leh) instead?"

"My Le? What does that mean? How come?"

"My Le is the abbreviation of Dong *My* and *Le* Thuy, the two designations of your birthplace. Does My Le sound good to you?"

"Huh!"

"My Le in Sino-Vietnamese also means Beautiful Tears."

"Beautiful Tears?"

"You know. The Sino-Vietnamese term My Le is also an adjective which simply means Beautiful. My Little Angel, you're so beautiful, physically and emotionally! You came from a place having many names with *My* and *Le*. From now on I'll name you My Le. That's right, My Le. It's wonderful that we came up with such a meaningful and beautiful name. OK? My little angel?"

"Darling! You've upset my life by turning it in a new direction. And now you rename me into a different person!" she stated matter-of-factly without any direct objection, after a short silence.

"My dear! You know, once being crowned, the new king gets a new name. And so does a new queen." In the dim light, she stared at me with wide-open eyes without saying anything, as if she were expecting something.

"Honey! Tonight you're crowned to be my beautiful queen. My Le is my queen's title." Tightening my hold of her, I lifted her and felt her weight. Her heart beat strongly against my chest.

"No matter what your real name is, in public life or on official papers, from now on you'll be the little My Le I love!"

With tight embraces, we passionately kissed to seal the intimate appellation and our everlasting love.

During unforgettable high school years in the refugee settlement, My Le was an admired singer and a gifted talent show actress, chosen by the Da Nang Culture and Information Office. Public audiences highly appreciated her vivid and sincere performances. Each time My Le appeared in public, her presence warmly stirred the spectators. Long legged and slimly built, My Le in the limelight had a soft and inspiring voice in a delicate body. On the school athletic team, however, the slim singer turned out to be an active and competent player.

"My classmates characterized me as a tomboy," My Le admitted. "I ran fast. I liked to climb rope."

"Honey! I can tell. Long legged, you must be a good runner!"

"I was a good high jumper too. Interestingly, in talent shows I often played the roles of boys."

Having gone through a nightmarish childhood in wartime, My Le turned out to have a strong character. After graduating from high school, she lost her beloved father. Without the main breadwinner, the financial status of her family was impaired, so My Le decided not to go on to higher education. It broke her heart to leave home and her mom to attend the health-care technical college in Saigon. Upon graduation as a certified lab technician, My Le rushed back home to work close to her mother.

The ancient town of Hoi An where we started our meaningful relationship was such a memorable watershed to me. Thu Bon River did not stop flowing incandescently in my memory's fairyland. The war between brothers had given the stranded visitor and his angel a golden opportunity, leading the two of us to our life of unending love.

With the blessings from our two mothers, My Le and I were united in marriage on Sunday, January 1, 1967. We made our new home in the village of Tam Toa, a small refugee settlement along the coastland of the lovely Da Nang Bay.

Peacefully perching by the murmuring waves that rippled along the sandy beach, our family's wooden beach home, which we built a couple of years later, looked out to the busy Tien Sha Harbor across the rippling Da Nang Bay. About fifteen miles to the north of our home, the towering Hai Van Pass extends some thirteen miles over the lofty mountain. Encircled with whistling sea pines on the verge of the serene bay, our tiny home sat nicely on a two-acre plot of sandy land.

Through resplendent rays of the setting sun and out of the living room windows facing the undulating bay, onlookers would be amused to bend their gazes on white flying seagulls. In the immensity of the celestial space the birds, silently stretching their unwearied wings, scanned the surface of the calm bay. From the seemingly limitless Eastern Ocean, fishing boats sailed home with their day's catch. On the vast horizon, tiny boats were but small growing dots alongside gigantic ocean liners fuming into the busy harbor.

Danang and its Bay

Stretching to the southeastern boundary of the half-moon-shaped Da Nang Bay, the busy Tien Sha Harbor was ensconced at the north end of the Son Tra peninsula. The bay extended north to the Hai Van pass with its peak standing some sixteen hundred feet high over the deep blue ocean.

From the lofty Son Tra crest, known as Monkey Mountain to the Americans, the local television station began its daily evening shows with the lovely Vietnamese song "Golden Autumn." Since then, each time the Golden Autumn is sung, it resuscitates in me serene memories of my peaceful years in my lovely homeland. The local television was first broadcast from a flying airplane. The station was then established on Son Tra peak in the fall of 1967, when My Le gave birth to our firstborn child. In my heart the song "Golden Autumn" consequently became a wholehearted reminder of the unforgettable time of our family. Though far from home, the whole home ambiance and emotional memories vividly arise in my mind as this love melody resounds. Our adorable princess arrived several months before we bought the piece of land and built our wonderful beach home in this scenic ambiance.

We gave our newborn little daughter the name Huong Giang. Huong Giang, or Perfume, is the name of an inspiring river that flows through the imperial city of Hue. The river has been admired as the emblem of the central part of our homeland. Central Vietnam consists of tens of provinces stretching from Thanh Hoa in the North, through the cities of Hue and Da Nang, to the southernmost province Binh Thuan. Both My Le and I were from this war-ravaged and disaster-stricken stretch of land we hold dear.

During my high school and college years in the imperial city of Hue, I had the privilege of enjoying the mountainous and coastal scenery of the province Thua Thien as I crisscrossed every part of the ancient capital city and spent poetic nights on gondolas admiring the hypnotic charm of the famous Perfume River and its surrounding splendors. We hoped our firstborn, Huong Giang—born in this land of famous writers, poets, and heroes, with beautiful landscapes and historic sites—would inherit the essence of this glorious central region of our motherland.

On the very day of the Lunar New Year in 1968, North Vietnamese Communists broke the truce agreement to start their Tet Offensive in the early hours of January 29. Quang Tri, Hue, Saigon, and many other urban localities were under simultaneous surprise attacks by the northern troops. Thousands of innocent people were brutally massacred or buried alive in a series of mass trenches around the City of Hue. On our trip to pay tribute to the lonely paternal grandma of Huong Giang on the Lunar New Year occasion, My Le, I, and our three-month-old daughter, got trapped in the city of Quang Tri under unfriendly fire for two long, terrifying weeks.

During the reign of terror of the 1968 Tet Offensive attack, my seventy-three-year-old mother, with great sorrow, joined the simple country fellows and ran away from her home in the remote Quang Tri countryside. Mom had led a peaceful, solitary life there for years after my dad passed away. Old age, poor health, and loneliness mom joined the panicked refugees on the escape trail. Fortunately, Mom got out of the fighting safe and sound. Her home became permanently occupied. She could not go back there anymore. Mom had to stay with our family in our beach home with an endless memory of her cherished lost birthplace.

Two years after the birth of his sister, our first son arrived, to the delight of both My Le and my mom. My Le and I gave our charming son the name Nhi Ha. Nhi Ha, or Red River, is the grandiose water body flowing through the northern part of our country. The river brought silt from far upstream to build up the North Delta where our ethnic Vietnamese ancestry had formed the original part of our nation thousands of years ago. In the heart of the North Delta, the first Vietnamese dynasties had successively built historic capitals Co Loa, Me Linh, Long Bien, Thang Long, and Hanoi. It was in this primitive region of the S-shaped country that our founding fathers had bravely fought to drive away waves of northern invaders and to build the foundation of our fatherland. Nhi Ha or Red River serves as the symbolic representation of the northern part of our country.

Five years later, on a sunny day in the spring of 1974, our youngest boy was born. My Le and I named our little boy Ky Nam. In 1834, Vietnamese King Minh Mang officially named twenty-one newly established provinces of the southern part of our country "Nam Ky." This southern region is the wealthiest and most developed territory of the country. The famous Mekong River with its rich water-borne sediment had built up this prosperous South Delta of the country. In the 1960s, Saigon in the heart of this delta was internationally known as the "Far East Pearl." Designating our little boy the name of Ky Nam (in lieu of Nam Ky), we dreamed of our son inheriting the fullness of this southern part of our glorious fatherland.

My Le and I were deeply inspired by the famous Vietnamese song "Symphony of Three Rivers" by Pham Dinh Chuong. In the symphony, the three rivers, Nhi Ha, Huong Giang, and Mekong, representing the three parts of the country, were personalized as the three sisters. The magnificent lyric of the symphony goes like this:

> *The three sisters are the three parts (of the country)*
> *Love has joined them.*
> *They meet each other in the graceful Eastern Ocean.*
> *Promises made*
> *To have combined waves propagated to all corners of the world,*
> *To fight for the people's freedom*
> *And the country's everlasting well-to-do.*

Happily coexisting in our wooden home on the Da Nang Bay beach were three and a half generations. My mother was one of the generations. My Le and I were the second. Our three children were the third. Readers may wonder about the mentioned half generation. Do you want to know what the half generation was? Our brother-in-law, Captain Ton Ha, a pilot, in one of his stops at a Da Lat resort, had brought home on his helicopter a lovely German shepherd puppy. He named the puppy Kino. When Captain Ton Ha was away on his combat missions, Kino stayed with us. It was so sad that Captain Ton Ha got killed on one of his missions in 1972. The orphaned German shepherd Kino, which had turned into a huge canine, snuggled with us as a close component of the warmhearted family.

3. Secondary job

The family of six beach-nesting birds (plus the German shepherd) was leading a peaceful life in such a scenic environment.

Hiding from the nearby noisy urban area, our beach home was lying low at the south end of a two-hundred-yard asphalt walkway. The shadowy lane was just wide enough for a rolling car. Neighboring houses lined both sides of the short lane, which opened its north end to the broader Tran Cao Van Road.

During the blossoming days of the 1975 spring, the garden surrounding our beach home was bountifully covered with a fruitful orchard. It was the first season the orchard yielded its prolific outcome. The sweet fragrance filled the air, from the morning dew till the caressing afternoon breeze.

Living less than half a mile from us, our children's maternal grandma, or BaNgoai[3] in Vietnamese, had settled down in a one-level home after fleeing the Communists in the city of Dong Hoi in 1954. On the Tran Cao Van Road connecting Tam Toa village to the downtown of Da Nang, maternal grandma's home was the first one into the refugee hamlet. The Catholic small ward of Tam Toa was sandwiched between two non-Christian ones: Thuan Thanh on the east side and Thach Thang on the west. A significant number of Tam Toa's residents were fishermen. Resettling right on the shore of Da Nang Bay, they had the benefit of continuing their traditional occupation as they had before being uprooted from their native town in the North.

Shrouded in the shade of swinging palms, BaNgoai's home faced the busy market across the Tran Cao Van Road. Built on the western bank of a tiny canal, the home was less than a half mile from the bustling railway station. Through the window of her living room, we could watch the train going back and forth and the pedestrians crisscrossing the road. The palm trees cast their slender shadows on the spacious shed connected to Grandma's home along the babbling little stream.

Having had eleven children, BaNgoai nonetheless had an empty nest. Grandpa had passed away years ago. Most of Grandma's children resided far away in the South. One of her younger sons, Uncle Su, was drafted and became a member of the local military security forces. A young bachelor, Uncle Su Duong (subsequently referred to as Uncle Su) was the only son who stayed with lonely Grandma day in and day out.

Our children's paternal grandma, or BaNoi in Vietnamese, was much older than BaNgoai. The eighty-year-old BaNoi was very healthy. She loved to work a little bit around the orchard during her daily free time. She happily looked after our two toddlers, while Huong Giang attended the Sacred Heart grammar school on Yen Bay Street in the heart of downtown Da Nang. The school was run by the Sisters of St. Vincent de Paul. Nhi Ha later entered kindergarten at the same institution. Both of them started their first piano lessons with the Sisters there.

To have more space for our German shepherd Kino to run freely around, we put up a head-high barbed-wire fence around our two-acre piece of land and a decorative iron front gate next to a red flowering oleander. A young live-in maid took care of the miscellaneous chores of our family nest.

Working for the Vietnamese First Region Public Health Center, My Le at the end of a work day shopped for fresh food at the market in front of BaNgoai's home. My Le preferred to let BaNoi fix the delightful dishes for dinner. The way BaNoi cooked resulted in a slightly salty but delicious menu we all loved and easefully enjoyed.

I was busy teaching at several private schools in the area. It was a privilege that so many schools invited me to lecture at their institutions. My teaching schedule was therefore overfull to the point where I had to turn down several teaching offers. On my way to school in the morning I gave Huong Giang and later Nhi Ha a ride on my blue Vespa LX 150 to the Sacred Heart grammar school. My teaching sessions lasted late into the evenings.

Major Anh Kiet, the then director of the Da Nang Port Authority, was a close friend of ours. His two young children were also attending the Sacred Heart grammar school. In the late afternoon, Major Anh Kiet's personal driver, while picking up the major's children from school, would give our two children a ride to the major's residence. Major Anh Kiet's lady housekeeper might give Huong Giang and Nhi Ha some evening treats. Our children enjoyed the company of the major's young kids. When I was done with the late classes, I would come to take the two of them home. Managing the Da Nang Office of Air Vietnam, Major Anh Kiet's lovely wife used to arrive home quite late as well. And so did the major. We hardly saw the major and his wife at their residence during weekdays. Eventually, the driver hauled us over to enjoy the company of the major's family at the Tien Sha Harbor.

Before escaping from the city of Dong Hoi, BaNgoai had a very profitable business in seafood processing, while My Le's father was the Director of Meteorology of Dong Hoi City. Several times a year, Grandma chartered Cosara flights, the then civil airline of Vietnam, to transport seafood products from Dong Hoi to her customers in Hue. In the new refugee settlement, Grandma mourned the loss of Grandpa and felt too tired in her old age to engage further in the seafood business. My Le and I tried to pick it up where Grandma left off, as a secondary but good moneymaking activity.

The fish-processing business was busy from the last days of winter and into the new spring. In the 1975 season, anchovies and tiny shrimps were so abundant they keep us busy for several months.

The spring of 1975 was not over yet. Anchovies and shrimp were still fully available. However, our seafood production had reached its full capacity, so our processing was completed for the season. Rows of twenty-liter containers of shrimp paste lined the small warehouse and would be ready for sale soon. Basins full of salted anchovies were well fermented and would be ready for sauce extraction in a very short time. The subtle aroma of the products wafted through the cool evening breeze.

As the sunny days of the marvelous spring brought vitality to the flowers and trees, we looked ahead with much delight to the lucrative outcome of our investment.

4. Magic coincidences

The recollection of our family bird nest has brought me to several interesting number-related coincidences about which I would like to quickly speculate before going into reminiscences.

As you may know, numbers were invented thousands of years before Christ. Numbers were found in the Hindu sacred texts, the Vedas, even when they were simply oral texts (2000-500 BC). Pythagoras and his followers paved the way to the observation of numbers and gave numbers their mathematical computing values. St. Augustine of Hippo (354-430) wrote, "Numbers are the universal language offered by the deity to humans." Many people got addicted to specific strings of digits. They attributed mysterious or sacred meanings to them. The Egyptian number 7 is considered the symbol of perfection and completeness. Many believe that numbers can be a real code cracker of their life experiences.

I do not believe my life is linked to any specific numerical signature. However, I have experienced some coincidences that seriously startled me. It may be thought provoking to name some of my number-related experiences. Readers may draw conclusions of their own.

In my life, by coincidence I guess, many events and realities, social and personal, have been related to specific numbers. The two numbers that our family has had intriguing relations with so far are 3 and 9.

Number 9, or a string of digits which adds up to 9, such as 1+8, 2+7, 4+5, etc., is widely believed to be a blessed representation. Many friends of ours paid a special fee to the office of Vehicle Administration to have the sum of the string of digits on their car license plate be exactly 9. Some are very happy to have the string of digits of their home address added up to a perfect 9.

I do not believe in numerology. However, in real life my family and I had unhappy experiences during the years in which the last two digits add up to number 9, for example 1945 where 4+5 = 9. I name those years "nine-added years."

I was not in this world in the years of 1918, 1927, and 1936 to recall any event, happy or disastrous, that happened during those years. Later on, however, so many catastrophic episodes came into being in the "nine-added years" I have lived through.

In the year 1945, the 38th Division of the Imperial Japanese Army under Commanding General Tsuchihashi, after having invaded our fatherland, caused a very terrible hunger among our countrymen. The whole of Vietnam became deeply submerged into famine. Millions of people died of starvation. To alleviate the misery of local compatriots, My Le's parents generously cooked behemoth pots of rice porridge to distribute for hunger relief. In August 1945, Japan was defeated after two atomic bombs were dropped on Hiroshima and Nagasaki killing some 170,000 people.

In September of that nine-added year, Viet Minh, the precursor of the Vietnamese Communist movement, started its thirty-year-long guerilla war. It was the sinister year when Viet Minh caught my mom's cousin Ngoan, my uncle Long Duong, my big brother, and tens of local youths to kill them or jail them indefinitely. My mom cried all her tears, and deep into the night ran around every prison site without finding any news of my ill-fated brother. The then Communist chairman of the central part of the country, Mr. Tran Huu Duc, was one of our villagers and a family acquaintance. To pull the wool over my mother's eyes when she turned to him as a last informative resource, the chairman reassured her that it was for my brother's security that the government had temporarily put him in a safe place and he would be home soon. My brother was liberated only years later when the Allies came. Mr. Ngoan and my uncle Long Duong never came back.

My Le in 1945 was less than two years old. Her parents brought her and her siblings to a slim sampan and the whole family fled from her birthplace to a remote countryside location to hide away from the fighting. For a two-year-old girl, it was even sadder to leave the peaceful nest to go down-at-heel. Though a small child, she could not forget the mournful scene. Huddled in the cold roofed skiff, watching the endless drizzling rain in the gloomy sky, she felt her heart sink in infinite melancholy.

The 1954 nine-added year was the worst year for my country, my family, and me. In the summer of 1954 my elder brother was killed on the Central Highland. My mom passed out at the tragic news of his sudden death. And in July '54 my beloved country was unmercifully divided into two parts under two antagonist regimes by the Geneva Treaty, contrived by the Vietnamese Communists. Millions of people fled from the Communist-occupied northern part of the country via the "Operation Passage To Freedom" (OPTF) program. Thousands of others, deceived by the Communists posing as relief agencies come to transport them to the OPTF, ended up being moved to remote deserted areas. Plunged in grief, they paid for their credulity by being detained away from populous regions for the rest of their miserable lives.

In the summer of that sinister nine-added year, little My Le and her family were among those who were uprooted from their birthplaces to adventure in search of freedom. It was the year I was cut off from my childhood friends and classmates, when I left the school on the Nhat Le River bank in Dong Hoi to move south. That summer of '54, I was struck by a deadly typhoid fever and bedridden for months. My backbone became permanently bent and my voice deformed. Once recovered from the tropical disease, I had lost the first half of my ninth-grade schooling. As a refugee student I had to drag my feet to three different schools to finally complete my second half of ninth-grade at Nguyen Tri Phuong Middle School.

Then came the disastrous South Vietnamese 1963 coup d'état.

Under the protectorate of the US ambassador in Saigon, Mr. Henry Cabot Lodge, with the blessing of the US president John F. Kennedy and with US$42,000 paid directly to the coup plotters by the then CIA chief in Saigon, Lucien Conein,[4] on November 2 of that nine-added year, the founder and first president of the Republic of Vietnam and his brother were brutally massacred. The First Republic was overturned. Thousands of military and civil personnel serving the First Republic were either killed or put in jail. The '63 coup d'état created the chain of social and political disorders and repeated government toppling which resulted in the final total debacle of our Republic. Because of the '63 coup d'état, I was almost killed by the local guerillas and I had to run away from my hometown and my lonely mother to migrate southward.

In the year 1963, My Le lost her beloved dad. She cried bitterly for the massacre of the Vietnamese president and for the early death of the head of the family, whom she loved and relied on.

Nine years later, in the nine-added year 1972, my hometown was invaded by the Communists. The ancient citadel of Quang Tri was turned into rubble. My Aunty Thanh, suffering from her tuberculosis, managed to leave her lonely way of life in the remote countryside of Quang Tri to join the escapees southwards. On their road of escape, tens of thousands of refugees from my hometown were brutally gunned down by the artillery regiment under the inhuman command of Communist Colonel Nguyen Viet Hai. Hundreds of killed escapees, some with babies still alive and clinging to their parents' fetid bodies, lined the horrid highway. The nine kilometer strip of the deadly escape road, along the Vietnamese National Highway 1, has been infamous in our wartime history ever since. It has been called the "Horror Highway."[5]

It was also in the nine-added year of 1972 that our brother-in-law Captain Ton Ha got killed on his mission while his wife Uyen, who is My Le's sister, was pregnant with her first baby. Our nephew Tam Giao was born months later and would never see his ill-starred pilot-father.

We do not feel happy with the number 9. Too many disasters were related to the nine-added years we have lived through. Our prayers are that the next nine-added years will be disaster-free for our family, our homeland, and the whole world.

Another number has turned out to be significant: the number 3. I hope it will stay that way. But first, let me get into some details.

From a theological viewpoint and in the religious doctrines familiar to our Asian world, such as Christianity, Buddhism, Confucianism, and Taoism, we can see that 3 is the most revered number.

Christians believe in the Trinity, *Three* Persons in one God: Father, Son, and Holy Ghost. Buddhism preaches the doctrine of *Three* Bodies of Buddha: Rupakaya or his physical body, Sambhogakaya or the salvation body, and Dharmakaya or the transcendent body.

Taoism has the theory of *Three* Essential Elements, which consist of Heaven, Earth, and Human. In Confucianism, male persons have to follow *Three* Bonds which establish the relations between two subjects of the three main social pairs: King and Subject, Father and Son, and Husband and Wife. Females have to keep *Three* Accomplices: she should follow her father at home, her husband in marriage, and her son if her husband died.

Ancient Greek mythology attached number 3 to Jupiter, which later became the supreme deity of the Roman gods. Jupiter symbolizes perfection and strength.

I am in no way enough of a theologian or ambitious enough to go into a philosophical discussion of these abstract 3-related conceptions. While number 9 relates more to the tragic fate of our nation, I privately invite readers to take the time to look at the number 3, a number of more personal significance in my case.

Geographically speaking, my S-shaped fatherland Vietnam consists of *three* regions: North, Central, and South. North Vietnam is a populous delta created mainly by Nhi Ha or the Red River. Central is a very narrow stretch of land flanked by the rocky mountains on the west and the Pacific Ocean on its eastern side. Nam Ky or South Vietnam is a much bigger fertile delta accreted by the Mekong River. Normally, the three regions were under *three* different governors. During the French colonization era, Vietnam was known with *three* regional names: Tonkin for the northern region, Annam instead of Central, and Cochinchina for the southern part of the country. For years, our country was symbolized on the national colors by *three* red stripes on a yellow background.

For me personally, number 3 seemed to be a figure of fate. In our beach home, *three* generations of our family were under the same roof. Our marriage produced a total of *three* kids. We gave them the three names Huong Giang, Nhi Ha, and Ky Nam. The aliases were taken from the symbolic appellation of the three main regions of our motherland.

I was out of school for a long period during the war. Village teachers had been either arrested, chopped to death, or driven to run away from the Communist persecutions. After I had been illiterate for a while, my mom sent me to Hue for primary education. Out of the remote muddy countryside of my childhood, I became an elementary school boy in the imperial city. I lived with my elder brother in an area named Tam Toa, which means *Three* Courthouses. The Three Courthouses composed of three main imposing buildings accommodating the ancient royal

Supreme Court. The Three Courthouses were located several hundred meters behind the Citadel Gate Thuong Tu within the royal citadel and next to the monumental flagpole.

Interestingly, my lovely My Le was born in another place that was also named Tam Toa[6], meaning *Three* Edifices, in the Dong My Ward of Quang Binh Province. After we joined our lives in matrimonial love, My Le and I settled down in our beach home in the new Tam Toa, or *Three* Edifices, this time in the refugee settlement in Da Nang City.

After being "liberated" by the Communists in 1975, we lived under *three* political entities: Party, State, and People, governed by the *triple* policy "Party leads, State manages, and People owns."

Apologies for such a long digression. I know that in Egyptian mythology number 3 was considered the symbol of plurality. The esoteric meaning of number 3 could happen to be a real code cracker in our circumstances. Corresponding to Mars, number *three* represents Luck, Talent, Versatility, and Joviality. Number 3 typically symbolizes reward and success in most undertakings. The *3-related-people* are characterized as highly intuitive and intelligent. Being miraculously attached somehow to number 3, I fool myself in the hope that the lives of my beloved family and my own may coincide with plurality, prosperity, and happiness. That is simply a wish of mine.

5. Rising typhoon

Established about 610 miles north of Saigon, our Da Nang City during the previous century was the second largest city of the Republic of Vietnam. About five miles away from the National Highway 1 and lying serenely along the lovely Han River banks, Da Nang was sometimes called "shelled city" by the GIs. The reason was that the Communist forces repeatedly rained missiles on it from all angles during the intense days of the Vietnam War.

Originating in Quang Nam Province, the Han River meanders around the Marble Mountain and ripples leisurely through the city center. The river spreads itself out into the spacious Da Nang Bay, winding on every side of Tien Sha Harbor. Finally the calm stretch of water empties itself into the immense Eastern Sea.

Da Nang is a recently developed city. Prior to 1000 AD, Da Nang was the central part of the Champa Kingdom. Its former capital city Indrapura (860-986) was in the neighborhood of the current City of Da Nang. Located in a remote forested valley some forty miles west of Da Nang, the ruins of Champa temples and royal tombs in its twin sanctuaries My Son and Tra Kieu (Simhapura) were in their forgetful sleep for centuries.

In 1650, the French missionary Alexandre De Rhodes drafted a map of the region and gave our ancient city the name of Cua Han, meaning the mouth of the Han River. In 1858, French troops landed in Cua Han, and in 1889 the colonists gave the city the name Tourane. No information was given to clarify the date the port city was officially renamed Da Nang. The name, after unconfirmed interpretation by several scholars, could be a Vietnamese adaptation of the Champa word *da nak*, which is translated as the "opening of a large river."

Danang City before 1975 - viewed from left bank of Han River

As the Vietnam War grew intense, the Air Forces Base on the west side of the city became the country's most active airport. The air base was also the headquarters of the First Vietnamese Air Forces Division. During the Vietnam War the base was described as the world's busiest airport,[7] reaching an average of 2,600 air traffic operations daily.

The twinned Da Nang Bay and Tien Sha Harbor on the north side of the city were home of the First Coastal Zone Fleet under the command of Rear Admiral Ho Van Ky Thoai. Tien Sha was a busy seaport for commercial ships, the military fleet, and oceangoing liners.

Under the administration of a military officer, in 1975 the Port Authority had its last days managed by Major Anh Kiet, a close friend of our family. The Port Authority administrative office was on the west bank of the Han River while its loading zone was at Tien Sha Harbor.

Da Nang was also the home base of the Vietnamese First Corps. Its last commander in chief, Major General Ngo Quang Truong, was also in charge of the Military Region 1. The region covered fives provinces.

Lying north of Da Nang were Quang Tri, Thua Thien, and the Hue Municipality. Stretching southward of Da Nang City were Quang Nam, Quang Tin, and Quang Ngai provinces. Three Army divisions took defense of the northernmost border territory.

The US XXIV Corps took Da Nang as its headquarters during the Vietnam War. Its Panama Intelligence Center sat hidden on the summit of Son Tra Mountain next to Tien Sha Harbor.

In his memoir, *Strange War, Strange Strategy*,[8] Lieutenant General Lewis William Walt, US Marine Corps commander in the five northernmost provinces of South Vietnam, wrote an impressive narrative of his encounter with a Da Nang little girl. The girl's father, a Vietnamese Marine, was killed by the Communist guerillas. The girl brought a gold watch she had found to the general, who returned it to its US Marine owner. Lt. Gen. Walt wrote that the eleven-year-old girl grew up in a war-torn city but she learned from her father and other soldiers to lead a noble life with pride and self-esteem.

On summer evenings, city residents loved to stroll leisurely along the west bank of Han River under the shadowy line of trees in the cool evening breeze. Seagulls extended their wings on the undulating waves alongside the sailing ships as far as the open ocean.

March, 1975. It was the end days of a wonderful spring. Looking forward to a fun-filled summer, high school students were preparing themselves for the coming final exams. Twelfth graders were exchanging warmly heartfelt lines in their yearbooks before bidding farewell and departing on a multitude of walks of life, taking with them unforgettable memories of their youthful school years.

Located at the corner of Doc Lap Boulevard and Le Dinh Duong Street, Sao Mai was the most notorious private institution among the local fifteen high schools. Students at Da Nang schools were of a blend of political backgrounds. Some of them had close relatives in the North Communist Vietnamese regime and its military forces. One of my students at Sao Mai, Miss K.N. Vo, was the daughter of Mr. Vo Chi Cong, the onetime president of Communist Vietnam (1987-1992). Classes at most Vietnamese private high schools were very crowded. Typically, more than eighty students were jostling in a single classroom.

Teachers had a hard time remembering the names of all the students, even in a single classroom.

It was a cloudy day when the war news grew gloomier and gloomier. Communist troops were advancing against our Central Highland. The minds of students and faculty alike were heavy with anxiety at the dark vision. In one of the twelfth-grade classes at Sao Mai High where I was lecturing, from a bench toward the back of the classroom a tall student raised his hand for a question:

"Professor! What will happen if the Communists come here?"

In daily life, students—boys or girls—normally addressed their instructors by simply saying "Teacher." The word sounded less adamant and much friendlier.

Questions the students posed to me in those days commonly sounded very political. For example ten years ago on March 8, 1965, 9th Marine Expeditionary Brigade, the first group of US Marine Corps commanded by Brigadier General Frederick J. Karch, had landed on Nam O beach on the northern side of Da Nang Bay. The event drew different reactions in the local society. A leftist student had voiced a patriotism-related question:

"It is said that we've lost our country. Isn't it true, teacher?"

Knowing the implication of the question and the political trends of the questioner, instead of directly replying I swerved from the politically heated controversy. To divert the attention of the current student assembly to another area I asked them to consider the following scenarios:

"If a person is ashamed of his Vietnamese birth name of Mit or Xoai and renames himself as Robert, Henry, or anything that sounds foreign instead, he has negated his Vietnamese identity, hasn't he?

"If the person, instead of proudly proclaiming that he is a Vietnamese, sidesteps to say 'I'm Japanese' as unfortunately did a Vietnamese lecturer at the University of Hue when he was asked in his 1959 Colombo Plan trip to New Zealand, the person has denounced his Vietnamese nationality, hasn't he?

"If the person does not like the Vietnamese folk songs or traditional costume but prefers the rock and roll, the hippy dress, he has thrown away the Vietnamese heritage. If, without any regrets, he disposes of the garments, cotton or synthetic, made by the local Sicovina Textile Company to put on the pricey garments imported from Italy or

Germany or anywhere else overseas, this person has nullified his love for his country, hasn't he?"

The whole class stayed silent during my lengthy reasoning. Some girls in the front rows stole a look at the back of the room. The questioning student tried to avoid being the center of attention of his classmates. After a short pause and in the yielding atmosphere of the class, I rounded up my conclusion:

"By negating his Vietnamese identity, denouncing his Vietnamese nationality, throwing away his Vietnamese heritage, nullifying his love of the country, the person has actually and totally lost his Vietnam, hasn't he?

"If each and every one of you here behaves the same way, nothing of Vietnam will be left. The homeland has, in that way, been totally lost from your hearts and minds."

My view of the issue did not satisfy leftist inquirers. However, most of the young listeners showed their appreciation with hand clapping and smiling faces.

That day, by solemnly calling me 'Professor' the inquirer put himself on an adversarial footing, showing an opponent's point of view toward me and a favorable taste for the unfolding military atmosphere under the winning Communist advance. To the harsh question raised in such a way, I answered with the following prediction:

"If the Communists do come, people of my generation will either get a terminal bullet each, or spend our last days in concentration camps. As for your generation, you may become fighters in the front line on battlefields in Cambodia or Laos for the establishment of the United Indochina."

Having a strong conviction in the noble cause for which our Republic of Vietnam and its Allies were fighting, I had high hopes we would withstand firmly and invincibly the invasion from the North Vietnamese regime and its Communist allies. I was badly troubled by the tragic news that Mr. Henry Kissinger was negotiating with Peking to let the Communist North Vietnam take over the Republic of Vietnam. In return, the United States was able to withdraw honorably out of the Vietnam War. However, the insulting news did not diminish my confidence in the future of the land we loved and dearly defended.

But I was wrong, and the tragic outcomes did happen.

Kontum, Pleiku, Ban Me Thuot, and the whole Central Highlands of the country, territory of the II Corps, one after the other succumbed to the Communist 1975 invasion. Thousands of refugees escaping to the lowland were unmercifully killed by the invading troops' fire. General Pham Van Phu, the commander in chief of the II Corps and Military Region 2, killed himself. Multiple commander deputies and their men fought heroically and were killed in the battles.

On March 17, 1975, Brigadier General Pham Duy Tat organized a counterattack against the enemy's 64th Regiment, but his troops were repeatedly beaten back in their attempts to keep Route 7 open for a safe retreat. By the early hours of March 18, the North Vietnamese 64th Regiment had blocked all the routes around Tuna Pass, while the 48th Regiment and elements of the North Vietnamese 968th Infantry Division began closing in on Cheo Reo from three different directions. The loss of Ban Me Thuot marked the first swift victory of the invaders. The subsequent evacuation from the Central Highlands started the deadly withdrawal and cost the II Corps Tactical Zone more than 75 percent of its combat units.

Aside from the losses of military territory and its defending fighters, millions of civilians who took part in the unplanned evacuation also suffered the consternated consequences of the Communist coordinated attacks along Route 7. Of the estimated four hundred thousand civilians who initially took part in the dreadful march, only a handful of them reached their destinations in the lowland region. As a result of the dismayed retreat, Route 7 has been known as the "convoy of tears" ever since.

That was when, anticipating the overall victory of the northern 1975 invasion, the leftist student had the nerve to draw his classmates' attention and challenge my conviction by vehemently voicing his political question.

March 1975 had not yet come to an end. However, Reverend Father Vu Nhu Huynh, headmaster of Sao Mai High, gathered the teaching body to distribute the monthly salary ahead of time. The reverend took the occasion to warn us seriously about the warfare situation.

"Due to the unfavorable unfolding situation, each of you should take swift action for the safety of yourself and your loved ones, before it's too late."

March 26, 1975. In the northern part of the Republic, under the advance of three Communist army divisions into the territory of Military Region 1, Forward Forces under General Lam Quang Thi, reinforced with a Vietnamese Marine Corps division, stood firmly against Communist attacks. For unknown reasons, I Corps commander General Ngo Quang Truong was summoned to Saigon and ordered to abandon the First Military Region. Stupefied by the tragic order, General Thi hastily withdrew his Forward Forces in an unplanned way that had fatal consequences. The unexpected retreat pushed most of his men to Thuan An beach, cutting them off from all access to combat. If they had been able to use the National Highway 1, the main Vietnamese North-South route, which was safely guarded by the Vietnamese Marines Corps Division for retreat, South Vietnamese Frontline Armed Forces might possibly have been able to reassemble, slow down, and even block the advance of the enemy. Quang Tri, Thua Thien, and Hue consecutively fell under the Communist invasion without heavy fights.

The first flux of refugees hurried for their security into our Da Nang City. Local people started hoarding food supplies. Rice markets closed. Local activities drew to an end. Schools, offices, markets, businesses, all were closed or became deserted. People were running hysterically to and fro looking for a means to get out of the embattled locality.

South of Da Nang, Brigadier General Tran Van Nhut, commander of the Second Infantry Division, withdrew his forces from Chu Lai to Ly Son Island, leaving Quang Tin and Quang Ngai fronts wide open.

Streams of refugees from north and south of Da Nang were pouring in by the hundreds of thousands. They carried their disabled elders on their shoulders and little babies in baskets along with their odd and poor belongings. They came by day and by night. They came running, by car, by boat, by bicycle, by walking, by ox-drawn cart, by trampling on each other. They came over the lofty Hai Van pass, through the immense Da Nang Bay, along multiple winding treacherous streets converging to Da Nang City. They came leaving behind their dead or dying relatives along the escape routes. Everyone, city residents as well as incoming refugees, looked terrified and disoriented. No one was able to help any other.

Trying to stop people from running away from them, the Liberation Army, a local insurgent group backing the North Communists, fired at the fleeing mass with automatic rifles, grenade launchers, mortars, 75mm recoilless cannons, and any other available weapons.

Situated on Da Nang Bay beach looking north to the Hai Van pass, at night our home received unending beams of lights from the incessant convoy of refugee cars and trucks slowly coming down from the towering pass. The dazzling rays streaked the bay waters, illuminating our home and garden. Under the gleaming streaks, people who had just arrived in the late evening from nowhere were able to set up tiny makeshifts on our front court, in the backyard, along the sandy beach, on any piece of available ground, for calming down their trembling elders and terrified children. People came from nowhere. People were everywhere. Everyone moved silently under the reign of the dreadfulness that was polluting the dreary atmosphere.

The fluxes of refugees were so voluminous. Local authorities and charity organizations ran out of hands, resources, and means to help. Refugees were settling themselves down everywhere, anywhere they could find a small space for their displaced families. They lay on the sides of streets, against tree trunks alongside the roads. They camped in the gardens of neighboring homes, in the open space of the markets, under bridges and overpasses, beneath abandoned trucks, and under the tattered roofs of devastated shanties. Emaciated toddlers looked out from awry makeshifts with terrified gazes.

Some teachers, volunteers, and I worked the whole time to empty the classrooms of the neighboring school for hosting the incoming refugees. Tens of emptied rooms could not provide enough space for the engulfing flood of tattered escapees. We could not find blankets and food for these disoriented crowds.

Exhausted by extending a helping hand to relatives and miserable country fellows, My Le and I did not have time to think much about our own endangered situation. We began worrying about our status when the flux overwhelmed our capabilities and the approaching Communist firing alarmed us.

A friend of ours and a mother of three children, Mrs. Dieu Nguyen, was the director of the Air Vietnam office in Da Nang, while her husband managed the Port Authority. In such a chaotic situation, both of them stood fast to their posts of duty. Mrs. Dieu was at the station twenty-four hours a day to provide air tickets and flight information to the nervously fleeing crowd. Her hands were tied when the airport was heavily damaged by the enemy missile attacks and forced to close. Mrs. Dieu and her husband kept in close communication with our family during the panic of the city. We admired their sense of responsibility. We counted on these reliable figures and were not so panic-stricken as to rush ourselves into the terrified escaping flood.

With the urgent protection of the US Marine Corps, the local US consulate closed its office on Bach Dang Boulevard and left, taking along the families of Vietnamese who had been working with them. The precipitate withdrawal of our US ally was an ill omen signaling the inevitable debacle of our beloved city. People were hysterically running away. Our neighbors rushed to board any available motorized wooden boat to sail perilously to the South on the high seas. Friends of ours strongly begged us not to stay another day in the endangered city.

Now that II Corps was eliminated, I Corps's front lines disintegrated. Hue was captured on March 25. Neighboring Quang Tin and Quang Ngai provinces fell to the Communists. Captain Vu Khac Can, chief of staff at Quang Ngai military district, killed himself rather than run away from his post or surrender to the captors.

Should we join the exodus? Should we leave Da Nang for Saigon?

6. Birds flying in disarray

Da Nang was hemmed in by the northern troops. Refugees kept pouring by the thousands into the paralyzed city, while residents tried their best to leave everything behind and run away from it. Everyone raced to Tien Sha Harbor, the last possible gate out of the besieged city.

When we came to his residence on Wednesday, March 28, Major Anh Kiet was on the phone. He lengthily tried to convince President Nguyen Van Thieu to come to Da Nang. The city was in chaos. The presence of the South Vietnamese president in the city must be the last hope to pacify the minds and hearts of people. His physical presence might restore the local government activities, revitalize the residents' confidence, and strengthen the military defense.

We were all so nervous, while the major behaved so calmly. Being a relative of the Republic president, however, Anh Kiet was but a low-level officer working at a secluded civil base. The major might not have been well informed by the higher level of local authority of the unexplained order of the president to abandon the First Military Region. Military commanders in the region had either killed themselves or withdrawn their troops from battlefields and dismissed them. Seeing the unavoidable downfall, some commanders had ordered their soldiers to go home and take care of their endangered families.

We came again to Major Anh Kiet's home the next day to see only his housekeeper there. His wife and children were all long gone. The lady housekeeper told us that the major had moved to his command post at Tien Sha Harbor. By the order of the central government, the major was to assume the responsibility of organizing the orderly transfer of refugees to the South by provided oceangoing fleets.

Our six-member family unexpectedly grew to eleven refugees. Besides the two frail grandmas, our three small children, Uncle Su, My Le, and myself, two straying nuns and a old crippled cousin unexpectedly joined us in the very last critical minutes.

The cousin, Mr. Quang Hoang, had left his family in Saigon to come to Da Nang to finalize his disability retirement process. And Da Nang collapsed. In his despair, the enfeebled cousin had nowhere to turn, other than to us, for possible assistance. His mindset was lamentable. He trembled incessantly. His disability became aggravated. He kept thinking of his inevitable permanent separation from the rest of his family, left in Saigon. Having run away from Quang Ngai battlefield, one of his children also came to our home seeking help. Once he had seen his desperate, quivering father, the son silently fled away with his wife without notifying us, leaving Mr. Quang Hoang in our care.

It was not the best solution, but My Le and I had no other option than to find a last minute survival exit for our family. Northern forces started raining 120mm missiles into the air base and the densely populated areas of our city. Local Communist guerillas under the title of Liberation Army appeared here and there. They fired at the fleeing masses to deter panicked people from running into and out of our embattled city.

To attempt escape from the approaching northern troops by way of the high seas was very risky. But staying back under the Communist domination was a much riskier option. It was life threatening to be under Communist capture. Running off to Saigon? If our Da Nang fell, in my calculations, Saigon's last days were numbered.

Trying to calm down the members of my newly extended family, I asked them to think:

"Once the free-world allies withdraw their support and leave the Republic of Vietnam to the mercy of the Communist bloc, the Republic cannot withstand by any means."

Everyone mused but had no reaction to my assertion. I went on:

"Fleeing Da Nang for Saigon in this case was similar to 'the ant's running around the edge of a bowl' as our Vietnamese saying goes."

"But we cannot get stuck here," Brother Quang Hoang retorted in a trembling voice as he shuffled incessantly in the old armchair in a corner.

"To effectively run away from the Communists, there's no other way than to escape to the free world," I said, giving voice to my thoughts. No one had any additional comment, so I broke the stifled silence: "Unfortunately, our Republic is surrounded on all sides by Communist countries and the boundless Pacific Ocean. We have no means to overcome those terrible obstacles. Our hands are bound."

One of the two nuns was a younger sister of my mother. In everyday life she was always in a contemplative mood. The terrifying future woke her up. She responded, "Three of my brothers[9] one after the other were shot to death by the Communists. I don't want to be next."

"Aunty! You're a nun," I assured her. "They won't do you any harm."

"They will. They will." My aunt argued by bringing up the facts: "Reverend Ho was my old parish priest. What did he do to have been buried alive by the Communists in the Tet Offensive in 1968?"

"It's terrible! Two of my cousins[10] have also been murdered by the northern capturers," My Le said, adding to the list of Communist atrocities. "My dad's brother, Reverend Father Nguyen, was jailed to his death. His only crime was to stay back with his poorest faithful in the remote Communist occupied area after the 1954 Geneva Treaty."

"My older son was imprisoned indefinitely by the Communists until he was liberated by the Allies." My mom broke her silence to add to the dreadful litany.

"Please stop your tragic stories. I know. We have either to leave or to die. But how? Anybody have any suggestions?"

The recitation of victims in the family revived the lethal days under the Communists' 1968 invasions. Thuyet Ngo, my cousin's son, a high school student, was killed and mass-buried by the Communists when they came to Hue in the Tet Offensive in 1968. In that New Year Offensive, three of my classmates[11] were among 5,000 civilians brutally killed in Hue in less than a month. In 1954, after taking over North Vietnam, the Communists organized the so-called Land Reform. Thousands of innocents were brought to the People's Tribunals, accused of fabricated crimes, and killed. There were more than 172,000 victims of the People's Tribunals officially reported by the Vietnamese

Communist historian Dang Phong.[12] Family members stood up against each other and even killed their relatives without any mercy.

"Eight of my children are in Saigon." BaNgoai cut short my thinking by calling everyone's attention to her motherly anxiety and concern. "I must join them. If anything disastrous happens, I must be with them."

It was impossible to anticipate what would become of us if we escaped. But we had better cling to the hope of some light at the end of the dark tunnel. Stay with the Communists? Past events had taught us how to predict the future. There was no other choice than to join the fleeing masses. "Don't let the grass grow under your feet," I said to myself. We had to run before it was too late. When being asked if she would join our escape, our live-in maid decided to stay back and wait for her parents whose fates she did not know. Unable to wait any longer, we entrusted our home to our maid and left.

Paying an unusually high amount of money to the owner of a motorized wooden sampan moored at the quay along the Han River bank, we rode the evening waves to race alongside of countless escapees rushing apprehensively toward Tien Sha Harbor, although we did not know what to expect over there. Rocked excessively in the small boat, we hoped to board a ship in time, before the gloomy sunset. Gathering its last rays, the dooming sun was about to hide its dreary appearance behind the dark western mountain ridge.

The airport, mercilessly hit by missiles, had long been closed. The last plane leaving Da Nang air base was a Boeing 727 operated by World Airways. The fugitive plane was overwhelmed with people seeking to flee our beleaguered city. Military and civil airplanes were all grounded. All routes out of the city were blocked by heavy firing from the Liberation Army. Those who had luckily escaped other fallen cities en route to the South finally were caught or killed along the escaping roads.

It was Thursday evening, March 28, 1975.

Thankfully spotting a mammoth ocean liner, we hurried the owner of our hired boat in the fervent hope of being able to meet the incoming rescue ship. Getting close to the vessel that loomed ten stories high above our heads, our shaky sampan was the target of repeated warning shots from the liner's deck. Our boat was kept from approaching it. Our hopes dashed, we turned away. To sail the short distance to the piers at

Tien Sha Harbor we had to empty our pockets to pay the boat owner. Multiple floating barges overloaded with refugees were anchored at the harbor with uncertain hopes under the cloudy evening sky.

With little kids, elderly mothers, and a crippled cousin, we stumbled with difficulty through the bustling crowd to reach Major Anh Kiet at his communication post. Exhausted, we distracted the major from his work by complaining about being fired at and not being able to board the anchored ocean liner. The major calmed us down with his lengthy explanation:

"Those seagoing ships used to have heavy loads in their bottom level to keep them well-balanced. Now, to prepare enough room for tens of thousands of expected refugees, the ships have emptied their loads and become so floating that any approaching vessel may dangerously disturb their balance in a very risky way. Secondly, approaching boats may or may not be friendly ones; they have to keep them away."

"Don't we have several ships for evacuation?" My Le anxiously asked.

"We do. However, refugees must first board the barges at the piers. Tug boats will guide the barges to the ship. The refugees will then be hoisted up to the deck. Tonight we'll ferry loads of refugees to several evacuation ships."

"Dear Major!" My Le said. "The other day, when the raging masses overcrowded the Air Vietnam office, we found your wife still in her workroom. She kept a ticket in her pocket and battled her way through the crowd to hand it over to us. We'd asked her for a ticket for our Uncle Thua Hoang to fly to Saigon." My Le had changed the subject to indirectly mention the tenacity of Major Anh Kiet's wife to her post of duty. "This afternoon, I didn't see her and the kids anywhere. Are they safe?"

"The airport was bombed. Air Vietnam couldn't fly anymore. None of the airplanes, civil or military could use the airport. My wife's hands were bound."

"Fortunately, my uncle got out on the last flight," My Le told the major, with a happy tone. My Le got seasick easily, even on a short trip. Recovered from seasickness and from the consternation of our desperate rush to the sea, and with her worry about our boat being fired at finally subsided, she could think of others' troubles.

"The airport was closed. My wife had to ask for help from the MACV [US Military Assistance Command, Vietnam] to fly the kids from the MACV combat airfield in Non Nuoc to Saigon. She's just phoned to inform me the kids are now with their grandpa in Taiwan."

"Very good for them."

"And do you know what? She asked me to let her return to Da Nang," Major Anh Kiet told us.

"How come?" My Le said, surprised. "Why would she do that when everyone is trying to run away from here?"

"You know, I couldn't agree to her desperate request." While constantly attending to the electronic control station, Major Anh Kiet explained to My Le, "My wife's in Saigon. Her being here would only hinder my tasks."

"Dear Major! How long does it take an evacuation ship to reach Saigon?" My Le interrupted.

To this inquiry Major Anh Kiet warned us, "You should know that all ships were ordered to unload the refugees only at Nha Trang Bay. No evacuation ship's allowed to reach Saigon. And you should know the sea travel will be very risky for the kids and for you as well. Mass robberies by desperate people may happen during the journey."

Defeated II Corps' military forces attempted to reassemble around the lowland in Nha Trang. Mingled with hundreds of thousands of refugees coming down from Central Highlands were local Communist insurgents. They did their best to spread chaos in the region while the northern forces were closing in. Nha Trang was no more a safe refuge. It was on the verge of downfall.

At the Major Anh Kiet's communication post we met Mr. An, Director of the Administration and Finance Department of the Da Nang Port Authority where the major was the General Administrator. Mr. An looked old and depressed in his dark wrinkled outfit. We did not see his family around. In his escape to the harbor, Mr. An had brought along the major's salary payment in cash. When Mr. An handed VN$90,000 over to him, the major said, "Please keep the amount for yourself. When you're in Nha Trang you may badly need it to feed your family."

"It's your March salary. I cannot keep it," Mr. An argued.

"I know, but I'll stay here." Major Anh Kiet said, revealing his intention. "I don't need money. You see piles of rations on the quay. They're enough to feed us for months if not years."

"But—"

"Did everyone get their salaries? Are they safe?" Major Anh Kiet interrupted Mr. An to ask.

"Sir, I couldn't know much of our coworkers' status. Most of them got their money and disappeared days ago. I was the last to leave the office."

Thousands of our fellow Da Nang refugees were clustering at the harbor. Night slowly fell. Many people secured their spaces on the uncovered barges in the hope of being hauled first onto early evacuation ships. Others scattered all over the quay. Here and there prayers rose from the subdued crowd. My Le and I brought our children and relatives into the hangar closest to the quay. Many early arrivals were lying there terrified and exhausted. Massed body heat and the humidity of early summer filled the stuffy hangar. Besides bags, suitcases, and personal belongings, many bewildered escapees had brought along some of their family furnishings, such as electric fans, radios, bikes, and so on, that they held dear. Those furnishings turned the crowded hangar floor into a messy space in the dim illumination of late evening.

It was about nine o'clock.

The *SS Pioneer Contender* freighter sailed into the harbor to pick up refugees as planned. The agitated crowd noisily called to each other to prepare to board the incoming ship. The night was dismally dark. Mingling among the escapees were Communist forward reconnaissance agents. They signaled their artillery stationed on the mountain peaks across the bay to adjust their coordinates. Spotting the flashing lights of the incoming ship, the Communist artillery catapulted their first rounds of 122mm missiles, darting horrendous whistling rays of fire in the sky over the crowded quay. First rockets hit the hangar we were in. After the dazzling flares of successive exploding missiles, the whole area fell into complete darkness. Screaming rang out all around, occasionally overwhelmed by thunderous explosions and the earsplitting bluster of debris raining down.

None of our three children responded to our repeated panicked calls. Afraid they had been killed, groping about in darkness with her trembling hands, My Le blindly touched Nhi Ha next to her on the ground. My Le burst out crying "Oh my son!" when hot blood touched her fingertips. No word or cry from Nhi Ha. He lay motionless. My

Le was terrified that Nhi Ha was gone. Tumbling onto Nhi Ha and clasping him tight in her arms, panic-stricken, My Le felt, to her relief, Nhi Ha's breath and weak heartbeat against her breast. He had been hit on his left side by the first rocket splinter. When we found Huong Giang and Ky Nam, they were both alive but too numbed with fear and stifled by smoke to move.

Early rounds of missiles stopped. Major Anh Kiet crept into the petrified crowd to give emergency help. He found us among the horror-stricken refugees lying paralyzed on the floor in darkness. Fumbling in the murk, the Major temporarily bound up our son's bleeding wound by flashlight. "You should go back to the city as soon as possible," he advised us sternly.

"Major! We want to board the earliest evacuation vessel."

"You shouldn't! Get out of here. Hurry up before the next rounds of missiles."

At about 9:30 pm on March 28, 1975, the I Corps commander convened an urgent meeting at Tien Sha Bay for reactive operations. Among the available battlefield commanders, besides Major General Ngo Quang Truong, were Rear Admiral Ho Van Ky Thoai, General Lam Quang Thi, Lieutenant General Bui The Lan, and Major General Nguyen Duy Hinh.

General Truong called Saigon to seek military orders from the Joint Chiefs of Staff and from the president of the Republic. At 10 pm, to the stupefaction and devastation of the whole assembly, the I Corps commander notified the generals of Saigon's fatal order: abandon Da Nang!

After leaving the meeting of the assembled battlefield commanders, Major Anh Kiet quickly briefed us on the order from Saigon, the desperate departure of the last military commanders, and the dangerous situation.

Flabbergasted at the central government order, the downcast and bewildered generals left the meeting room and toiled up over the Son Tra peak to reach the other side of the peninsula.

Da Nang air base was totally disabled. Brigadier General Nguyen Van Khanh, commander of the First Air Force Division had left the air base on a helicopter to Tien Sha, missed the meeting session of commanders, and strove to climb up the hilly slopes and over the rocky mountain in the dark in the hope of catching up with other generals.

The chief of staff of First Air Force Division dismissed his subordinates and killed himself. One of the commanding pilots of the 219th Helicopter Squadron loaded his family on a Huey. Once airborne, the pilot opened a grenade to explode the plane and kill the whole load.

Struggling hard to reach the other side of Son Tra mountain, Rear Admiral Thoai was looking for any of his stranded warships. General Ngo Quang Truong found an unused life buoy on the rocky beach. With help from Colonel Tri and Major Phuong, General Truong swam to the landing ship LST 404 moored thousands of yards offshore.

Reaching us, Major Anh Kiet firmly assured us he would stay to fulfill his responsibility to evacuate the escapees. He asked us to leave the death place immediately.

After spending hours in total darkness amid the sprawling ruins and slimy dead bodies, we had tossed away all bulky items and left the traumatizing scene. With fumbling steps we had left the devastated hangar and were several thousand feet along the serpentine road. But the terrible night was not over yet. As Major Anh Kiet had predicted, Tien Sha Harbor got hit by the rain of Communist missiles again. Explosions rocked us continuously. Our escape road trembled under our feet. Our terrified children hunched themselves in our arms, trembling violently.

I double checked the members of our group and asked them to form a straight line. Broken personal equipment got abandoned along the roadside. Uncle Su picked up a damaged yet manageable bicycle and put little Huong Giang on it to push along. Uncle Su led the line, followed by the two nuns. The crippled cousin was next, followed by the two grandmas. Carrying our one-year-old trembling Ky Nam in her arms, My Le walked in front of me. With the five-year-old wounded Nhi Ha wrapped in a towel and hung across my chest, I was at the end of the line, making sure none of the family fell behind or got lost or killed without our knowing. Each person followed the previous one at a distance of about two yards, so that in case we were hit by a missile, the whole group would not be killed all together in one single shot.

Hundreds of victims dying of missile injuries lay on the meandering road along the foot of Son Tra Mountain. The snaking single-lane route connected Tien Sha Harbor to the main road leading to the downtown. Over the treetops, dawn began shedding its dim light. The lane winding around the mountain base was still covered in darkness. On the broken bicycle, Huong Giang was still alert enough to point to wads of cash blowing away from victims on the roadside. Nhi Ha and Ky Nam were too scared to move or say a word. The two grandmas were at the exhaustion point. We were so anxious to know whether we could make it out of the deadly road alive. The shivering crippled cousin fell to the ground each time he heard a rocket explosion, and we had to help him up to continue the walk. We were doing our utmost to leave the deadly area but, mentally and physically exhausted, we could only go ahead at a very slow pace, commending our fate to chance.

The presiding judge of the local court, too old to carry his trembling mother, leaned dumbfounded against a protruding rock, looking with silent desperation at passersby.

Upon seeing us on his way out of Tien Sha port, Captain Cuong, chief of the local office of military security, encouraged us, saying, "Don't give up! If you want, follow me. Just follow me. I have a million dollars in my shoulder bag. We can buy our escape to the US Seventh Fleet. Come on."

With kids, elderly relatives, crippled cousin, injured Nhi Ha, and personal weariness, we could not keep pace with the active young captain. Countless wounded people lying along the road desperately asked passersby for help. Seeing them in such a miserable and terrified state, our hearts were broken. Being in the same tragic situation, we were exhausted trying to flee from the bombed area. We felt so sorry that we were unable to extend a helping hand to the innumerable dying victims as missile explosions kept shaking the ground, followed by flaring-up fires. We could not even know whether we would survive to reach somewhere safe or not.

We could hear handgun firing as, after hours of walking away from the deadly seaport, we finally approached the main road leading to the Da Nang downtown. Armored tanks were abandoned here and there. Military uniforms, forsaken weapons, and dead bodies were scattered across the road. Stranded children, some crying, some silent with exhaustion, lay next to their dead parents.

It was not morning yet. Wearing red bands on their arms and carrying the red and blue flags of the National Front for Liberation of South Vietnam, some youths were driving around on military trucks in the early hour, ignoring the dead and the dying on the road, loudly singing "As if Uncle Ho Were here On the Great Victory Day." The Communist-supporter youths were calling up the dead, the dying, and all city people to welcome the incoming Communist troops.

The chorus "As if Uncle Ho Were here On the Great Victory Day" marked the painful early hour of Good Friday, March 29, 1975, in which Da Nang was taken over.

7. Stragglers

Hours after we had left the shattered Tien Sha Harbor, our weary, staggering group spotted the steeple of a church at the end of the long, dreadful escape trail. We left the fleeing crowd on the asphalt road and turned onto a winding path to go to the isolated parish church off the life-threatening avenue.

Miraculously, we found an abandoned refuge at the back of the secluded church. Our worn-out group needed at least a short pause. I asked everyone to sneak into the tiny shelter for a fleeting rest. It was musty and somewhat stuffy, but in such a terrifying situation no one paid any attention to the unfavorable smell of the cramped shelter. In our situation, it was a refuge whether it was safe or not. The dark place seemed to be an abandoned, empty storage room.

My Le gave the last drop of bottled milk to our wounded Nhi Ha. With no food in his mouth since yesterday noon, wounded and bleeding, Nhi Ha must be very thirsty. However, he refused to take it. Nhi Ha looked so downcast. My Le appeared paralyzed with fear as she gazed constantly at him. I could not tell whether our son was bitterly suffering because of the wound or he was terribly scared of the situation. His temporarily covered wound was not bleeding anymore, and we worried that there might be life-threatening inner lesions. Wearied by anxiety about our children and our unknown plight, we could not act but had to wait for the first rays of the doomsday sun to cope with our current impasse.

Full of anticipation of misfortune for the male adults of our group, My Le and the grandmas pushed Uncle Su and me to go and find a way out to the waiting evacuation ships. The grandmas were whispering their imperative demands while looking slyly around as if some invisible one were stalking us. Several of the ships intended for refugee transportation were still lingering miles from shore. Everyone in our group was so alarmed that the Communists would either subject Uncle Su and me to their collective bloodbath, as had happened during the infamous 1968 Tet Offensive, or put us indefinitely in a concentration camp for hard labor and ill treatment until we died of exhaustion.

As a military security sergeant, Uncle Su faced a direct imminent threat. We insisted he find a way to leave before it was too late. We were so terrified. Pictures of tortures and killings lurked in everyone's mind. No one wanted to witness the terrible things that might happen to the uncle or me. Local pro-communist insurgents might come any time soon to take control of the area and inflict terror.

Maternal Grandma cried bitterly, demanding Uncle Su not stay a minute longer. Reluctantly, Uncle Su sneaked out before the first sun rays gilded the tops of the pines lining the sandy shore. Sporadic firing could be heard. Lines of fugitives were converging from different directions to this part of the beach. Everyone was hoping to reach the evacuation ships that appeared vaguely as ghost vessels on the horizon.

Both grandmas prayed loudly, in tears. We all were praying in our hearts that Uncle Su might be saved before the Communists took control of this secluded section. We expected the northern Communists or at least the local insurgents to show up anytime soon. The firing and shelling were intermittent, meaning the main battle was long over. Now was the time when insurgents were hunting for locals to kill for their personal revenge, as they had done during the 1968 Tet Offensive.

We packed our remaining personal items to leave the vulnerable shelter. Nhi Ha clung hard to me. I could feel his faint heartbeat. Huong Giang clung to BaNoi. My Le picked Ky Nam up. Our enfeebled cousin seemed unable to summon his last bit of strength to stand up on his trembling legs. BaNgoai looked puzzled to the point her limbs were shivering as contemplated the cousin's bad condition. No capable extra hands were available to help. We were hesitantly ready to leave the temporary refuge.

Beyond everyone's expectation, Uncle Su came back to light.

Uncle Su had met Captain Cuong at the seashore. The captain, together with some people Uncle Su did not recognize, boarded a small boat to reach the barge crowded with refugees out on the high seas. The SS *Pioneer Commander*, the SS *Pioneer Contender*, the SS *American Challenger*, and the US naval vessel USNS *Miller* were staying way offshore in the last hope of picking up stragglers from lighters and barges. The sea looked indifferently calm at sunrise.

Escapees on flatboats, once they had gotten close to the two-story-high ships, had to cling to a cargo net as they were hoisted aboard the cargo ships and naval vessels. Terrified, trembling, hustling one against other, many missed the hauling nets to drop dead into the deep ocean water before the horrified eyes of desperate relatives. Despite having witnessed horrific scenes of panic refugees at the sea, Uncle Su hurried back to petition all of us to join the fleeing people who were bearding the lion in his den to reach the waiting evacuation ships.

Assessing the capability of our group to assume this great danger, My Le and I decided against the perilous undertaking. Our group consisted of three little kids, one of them suffering from a bleeding wound. The crippled cousin was hardly able to keep himself balanced on solid ground; how could he bite the bullet? The two very frail old grandmas badly needed mental and physical support. The two straying nuns in their embarrassing religious dresses did not utter a single word but silently followed every step we went.

Even if we tried our best, the three of us—Uncle Su, My Le, and I—would not be capable of climbing up to the evacuation vessels while struggling hard against the bustling crowd to help the other eight members of the group. How could we manage to get onto an evacuation ship and withstand the hardship of a desperate sea-going escape? Furthermore, Nhi Ha needed to be operated on as soon as possible, before it was too late. He could not survive, untreated, being exposed to a long, risky journey on the rough high seas.

BaNgoai was crying. She wiped away her tears and burst out, "Go. You both go. Get out of my sight!"

"But—"

"Don't say anything." Grandma stopped Uncle Su from finishing his sentence. "You both leave if you want to be my sons!"

"But this is the land I love, the people I cherish." Uncontrollably raising my voice, I spoke out what my heart compelled me to say. "My children, my wife and you moms, you're the dearest people I love. I won't leave you. Uncle Su may leave. I won't!"

After a couple of undecided minutes, Uncle Su made up his mind. He took the danger and chose to stay with BaNgoai and us, rather than leave everyone behind in that nightmarish situation. Grandma could not force him to leave and could not bless his decision to stay, either. We felt unhappy and anxious about Uncle Su's fate, for fear of the dangerous days to come.

The whistling sound of the missiles had stopped tearing the airspace. Gunfire calmed down. And a dreary day began. Coming out of the hiding space, Uncle Su and I explored the perilous environment while looking for some means to bring the family out of the unfamiliar location. Should we go back to the city? Would our home site be safe to return to? Had it not been occupied or burned down? Is the carnage going on there? Did the Communists actually take over everything? How could we manage to overcome such a long distance to get home from where we were? Lots of dreadful unanswered questions assailed our minds. Although we were hysterically confused, nowhere else but home could be our destination in this desperate situation. We had better cling to our last hope to get back to our residence as soon as possible. It must be tens of miles away, and we had no means of transportation but our weary legs. We had to walk our way home. There was no other option.

Wounded, old, and worried, our group walked in apprehension for several hours toward the center of town. Panicked people were fleeing in the opposite direction. Pushing the broken bicycle with Huong Giang on it, Uncle Su had to help the crippled cousin as well. Dead tired and mentally incapacitated, we had not gone far when our group had a stroke of good fortune.

With an empty commercial truck he had found abandoned, Reverend Father Thai, pastor of our Tam Toa parish, took the risk of driving among relinquished tanks, sprawling weapons, and unfriendly fire. The priest went about picking up the exhausted, the wounded, the dying, and the stranded children along the road leading to Son Tra peninsula. It was a miraculous rescue when our hearts were in such a desperate state.

On the magical truck we slowly rode back and forth in multiple directions through the chaotic city to pick up the needy and deliver the riders to their destinations. We spotted here and there various types of armed people, some in olive or yellowish uniforms, most in civilian outfits, with guns and bags on shoulders. Most of them were young men and women in their early twenties. They looked astray. They posed for pictures, defenselessly, as if they were on a picnic excursion. Those with military uniforms were northern regular army that had just come out of the jungle. Sharp amazement appeared on their juvenile faces. They looked up with disbelief at the tall and spacious buildings standing along the city avenues. Others pointed with great bewilderment to the ransacked shops along the streets, where all kinds of looted merchandise they had never seen before was scattered all over the pavement. They neither paid any attention to nor intervened with our back-and-forth driving. Some fired shots to the sky as we drove by. They might have taken us to be people who were cheering their arrival. In some areas, curious children poured out onto the streets, climbing on abandoned tanks or waving to the newcomers. Scattered around were disoriented refugees who looked confused and terrified.

With our hearts fluttering wildly, we reached home about noontime to brokenheartedly witness our home and the neighboring houses being ransacked. People from remote hamlets were energetically hauling away belongings from the homes, right in front of the owners' eyes.

Our beach home was wide open. The TV set was long gone. The sewing machine could not be found anywhere. The refrigerator had disappeared from the kitchen corner. The gas stove did not wait for our return to say its farewell. Bedroom shelves had been rummaged. Tiled floors were blurred with muddy footprints. Half of our shrimp-paste barrels had been carried away. Several more people came with carrying tools ready for hauling away bulky furniture or even doors and windows in their final loads. The streets were crowded with people carrying away heavy burdens of household items. Most of the looting people who came to our home were relatives of our live-in maid. We had entrusted the young maid, who chose not to join the fleeing mass but waited to hear from her parents, with the task of safeguarding our home while we were away. She had notified her relatives to come pillaging.

Looters also broke into local department stores, big and small retail shops, other vacant private homes, closed government offices, and the nearby rice depot. Roads were scattered with garbage and looted items. Rice from the ransacked warehouse was spread along the roads for miles.

Numerous escapees had come from afar but could not flee; they were still hanging around. Many of them were looking with amazement at the multitude of looters hurrying back and forth with burdens laden with pillage. Some of the refugees simply moved into the deserted homes of families who were gone. Everything was in havoc. Military uniforms and weapons left behind by former soldiers in their run from the Communists were seen here and there along the roadside, around our backyard, and on the secluded beach.

There appeared at some street corners armed people, some in uniform, others in civil outfits. The local people, especially left-behind male city dwellers, stayed strictly hidden behind closed doors, trying not to expose themselves to the plunders and scrutiny of those who had just come out of the jungle. City residents hided and tried not to be first victims of a mass killing everyone expected to take place as it had happened when the Communists came to towns in the 1968 Tet offense.

After a few days on the suspense watch, My Le and maternal Grandma risked taking our poor wounded Nhi Ha to the medical center along Quang Trung Boulevard for an operation before it was too late. Keeping out of sight, Uncle Su stayed behind closed doors with the crippled cousin at Grandma's home. I shut myself in with Huong Giang, Ky Nam, and BaNoi and guarded our home from being looted further. The two Sisters left our group and simply disappeared.

The medical center on Quang Trung Boulevard was deserted. None of the resident physicians was available. There was neither electricity powering the hospital nor any attending nurse. No running water. The atmosphere at the hospital was gloomy and dismal. No one to tend the bedridden patients. No anesthetic facilities, but innumerable dying patients in the emergency and waiting rooms looking helplessly for urgent care. Medical equipment and materials were scattered around.

On Quang Trung Boulevard along one side of the healthcare center, small groups of people were parading. With loud speakers they were noisily welcoming the liberators. In one of the deserted operation rooms, My Le miraculously found the lone surgeon Hanh Phung in his civic outfit. The surgeon was a resident physician at the nearby military medical center Duy Tan. In the dim room, Dr. Hanh Phung examined Nhi Ha. No X-ray machine was available to scan the wound. Not a single nurse was around to help with surgery tools. The surgeon took a bold and urgent decision to operate on the left flank of Nhi Ha with neither general nor local anesthesia. Without sterilized garments, My Le held both of Nhi Ha's hands and Grandma held his outstretched legs to keep him from moving on the dark operation table. Little Nhi Ha withstood the traumatic painful surgery with neither tears nor screaming. The surgeon took out a rocket splinter over an inch long that had been clinging very close to his heart.

CAGED BIRDS

1. New days

We counted our days into April. Normally, April was full of vitality: nice weather, multicolor flowers blossoming everywhere, the sky lit by caressing sunny rays.

Those beautiful and precious days belonged to the remote past. The occupied Da Nang City silently struggled to slowly recuperate after its March 29 debacle. Not many city residents but stranded escapees were seen on the garbage-filled streets. Everyone looked dismal, with anxious expressions on their faces. The shooting had stopped in this northern part of the Republic. We were looking with hope for the survival of Saigon and the southernmost part of the Republic, which were battling to survive. The winning northern invaders were fighting hard to advance southward.

After taking over all facilities of the former government in Da Nang City, the new victors made every effort to keep the local population under their full control. They had conquered the territory. Now they fought the political battle to win the hearts and minds of the defeated residents and to revive the daily city life to create a seemingly normal appearance. The winners were attempting to make a good impression on those residents who had failed to run away from them.

Schools were a mess, cluttered with broken tables and benches, mounds of stinking garbage, and myriad flies and mosquitoes. City streets were strewn with rubbish. Shops were closed. Front doors of private homes were tightly shut. Small groups of welcoming youths with flags and loudspeakers were seen every day on the streets. They shouted slogans cheering the winners, exhorting people to join their parade.

Numerous refugees who had converged to the city were still around, without getting any help. Some simply settled themselves in vacant homes. Others attempted to move their families back to their original localities. This was a difficult endeavor. Buses, railroads, and other means of transportation had stopped being in service. All roads into and out of the city were vigilantly guarded. Passersby were thoroughly inspected by armed people. The majority of the population who had missed the opportunity of fleeing were still in search of ways to escape, over the high seas or by land, to leave Da Nang City for Saigon.

It was announced that the Military Management Committee (MMC) was in charge of the so-called "Copper-Walled" Da Nang City. While the northern military forces were gathering all their strength in the attempt to capture Saigon, local city supporters to the Communist conquerors assumed the roles of the temporary government. Having been a teacher and Communist ally at Sao Mai High, Mr. Te Tran took over the local Educational Administration office. The headmaster of the Phan Chu Trinh Public High School had light-footedly fled overseas. Mr. Dong Trinh was the self-proclaimed new principal. Former local teachers Ngoc San, Thanh Xuan, Dac Loi, and Thanh Nam, who were sympathizers of the victors, paid home visits to their fellow teachers who had failed to escape. They did their best to canvass these tardy educators to stay and serve the new regime.

The regional Educational Administration requested that teachers of all levels should report back to their schools for reopening the classes. Employees of other establishments were directed to be present at their posts of duty as well. Arrests and terrorism had been predicted but had not happened yet. The underlying endeavor of the winners was to appease Da Nang residents' panic mentality against the new occupation and to reassure them that nothing had changed; that life was going on; that the liberation forces were taking care of people.

All day and night, loudspeakers at every street corner blasted deafening military rhythms. Left behind, we burned in our hearts and minds to know what was happening to the rest of the Republic of Vietnam. Eight brothers and sisters of My Le resided in the embattled Saigon. Grandma and all of us desperately worried about their survival. BaNgoai could not eat or sleep for anxiety about the fates of her far-away children. Throughout the day and night Grandma was bemoaning the unknowing state of being cut off from her children. We apprehensively anticipated the possibility of a permanent family separation. Would Saigon withstand the invasion? Would we ever see our siblings again?

The British Broadcasting Company and Voice of America were the sources of information every left-behind person relied on for breaking news. Via our shortwave radio, they gave us an intermittent awareness of what was happening to the rest of the Republic and the remainder of the world.

Their reports outlined a very messy and confusing picture. News was tragic and gloomy and sometimes contradictory.

Multiple Communist infantry divisions from Cambodian jungles poured into the Fourth Military Region of the Republic. Sharing a border with the neighboring Cambodia, the southernmost region of the Republic covered sixteen provinces: Kien Tuong, Dinh Tuong, Go Cong, Kien Hoa, Kien Phong, Sa Dec, Vinh-Long, Vinh Binh, Chau Doc, An Giang, Kien Giang, Phong Dinh, Chuong Thien, An Xuyen, Bac Lieu, and Ba Xuyen.

The IV Corps commander, Lieutenant General Nguyen Khoa Nam, and his deputy, Brigadier General Le Van Hung, sternly defeated the advancing Communist troops on every battlefield. Knowing the US secret plan to withdraw and abandon the Republic, the American advisors to the two commanders repeatedly offered them a chance to evacuate. The two generals refused each of the offers. They decided not to abandon their men and the country but to stay and defend it to their deaths.

Conflicting feelings invaded our hearts and minds. We wanted and wished Saigon to withstand the enemy. At the same time we did not want to be left indefinitely in the Communist bloc, separated from relatives in the free world. News of a defeat in a Republic battle inflicted a further wound in our hearts. At the same time the downfall stirred up the hope that we could reunite with our relatives in the South.

Communist forces from the captured Second Military Region closed in to the lowland. They put heavy pressure on the Third Military Region. The heart of the Republic covered Saigon and eleven provinces: Phuoc Long, Binh Long, Binh Duong, Long Khanh, Binh Tuy, Phuoc Tuy, Bien Hoa, Tay Ninh, Hau Nghia, Long An, and Gia Dinh.

The military and political situation of the Republic was deplorable. While the Communists were advancing, anti-government movements increased, precipitating the debacle of our Republic. US forces retreated to their Seventh Fleet or to Guam. The US embassy packed up to leave. The French ambassador in Saigon, Mr. Jean-Marie Mérillon, was trying desperately to work out a last-minute solution for the Republic.

Communist troops, converging from every battlefield, were advancing further southwards. In the meantime, having completely taken over Da Nang, the Military Management Committee was consolidating its position. The propaganda system of North Vietnam hurriedly set up a new campaign to win the confused hearts and minds of Da Nang citizens.

With a personal long pocket filled with dried cooked rice on his shoulders, Mr. Thieu Son Hoang, a Doctor of Philosophy before the war, came unpredictably to BaNgoai's home. A distant nephew of Grandma, Dr. Thieu Son Hoang used to lecture at the Communist Nguyen Ai Quoc Institute in the North. He had had articles broadcast on the northern radio waves aimed at the South. After the dismal fall of Da Nang, Dr. Thieu Son Hoang was sent to the city as a member of a delegation consisting of the most notorious cultural figures of the North. The Communist politburo hastily deputed the delegation to Da Nang for its political campaign. Its short-term plan was to reassure the local intellects from fleeing by all means to Saigon.

Other figures among the delegation from the North included Xuan Dieu, Huy Can, and Che Lan Vien. They were famous poets who had joined the Communist world. Their prewar masterpieces were condemned by the North to be sentimental and bourgeois. The authors had also self-censored to be accepted in the proletarian system. On the other hand, their poems were highly appreciated and officially became part of the educational curriculums in the cultural realm of the Republic of Vietnam. The South loved their prewar cultural works and therefore did not pay much attention to their political propensities but continued to hold them in high esteem. The appearance of those prewar poets was a propaganda advantage.

Open public meetings with the delegation and individual figures from the North were held at the Trung Vuong amphitheater on Hung

Vuong Avenue, at various city schools, at common places around town, and in selected clubs and private homes.

The poet Huy Can at the time held the position of Minister for Culture and Information in the North government. In one of the evening meetings at the Trung Vuong City Theater, the organizers knew that the chairperson of the meeting would be Huy Can. The organizers had scheduled a female singer to perform the song "Ngam Ngui." This was one of the inspiring prewar poems by Huy Can. The renowned southern songwriter Pham Duy had arranged the poem into a very heartwarming song. Attentively listening to the song for the first time in his life at the meeting, Huy Can was so touched that, to the onlookers' stunned surprise, he could not hide his deep feelings in front of their inquisitive eyes.

Ms. Hong Cam, the chief editor of the Phu Nu Magazine in Hanoi, was another of Grandma's relatives. She was also a high profile member of the April 1975 northern cultural delegation to Da Nang. A military truck drove her to BaNgoai's home when Grandma had just come back from her late-afternoon food shopping. Grandma did not recognize her until she introduced herself. Grandma did not even know that she had a relative by the name Hong Cam. Grandma was unable to figure out how Dr. Thieu Son Hoang and Ms. Hong Cam knew where she was living. We discerned only over later conversations that northern organizers have done their research. They determined family connections and located Grandma's whereabouts in order to have the driver deliver Dr. Thieu Son Hoang and Ms. Hong Cam to their intended destination. Dr. Thieu Son Hoang, Ms. Hong Cam, and other members of the delegation had not been delivered to any official destination of the new government. It was a calculated move. Coming to their relatives as kin who had been missed after such a long time, the delegation created the feeling within the occupied city that their appearance was simply a result of their personal sympathy for their long-lost families and not by any orchestrated scheme.

Besides the personal pocket of pre-cooked dried rice she carried on her shoulders, Ms. Hong Cam came with a piece of polyester fabric of four square feet or so. It was of the same type of material that Sicovina, the textile manufacturer on the outskirts of Da Nang City, had produced abundantly for the southern market. Ms. Hong Cam donated the piece of fabric to Grandma as her valuable reunion present, saying, "As an editor in chief, I had the privilege to buy this precious item before I left Hanoi, just for you. It costs me half of my yearly fabric ration."

Both Dr. Thieu Son Hoang and Ms. Hong Cam stayed with Grandma. Grandma fed them abundantly. In order for them to attend meetings and shows, I gave each a ride on my Vespa. Both of them stayed until Saigon fell to the Communists. They then left. They did not tell us whether they went back to Hanoi or they proceeded southwards. We thought they must have gotten a new assignment to go further south. During their stay, through conversations we uncovered interesting aspects of the northern state of affairs.

When asked about the rice pockets they had carefully wrapped and brought along, Ms. Hong Cam sidestepped from any answer. Dr. Thieu Son Hoang sincerely revealed its secret:

"In the paper commissioning me, and everyone else, to go south, the government clearly prescribed the rice pocket as vital due to the fact that, as the paper said, the South has no rice to eat."

"That's interesting! We have no rice to eat?" I asked mockingly, holding off my laughter. "Dr. Thieu Son Hoang, you may be right! We don't have that kind of pre-cooked and dried rice. We never had them."

"You're kidding me!" Dr. Thieu Son Hoang sincerely observed.

"Not at all. Not at all!" I pretended a serious response and continued: "We only cook as much rice as we need any time we want to eat. No dried rice, only fresh-cooked for every meal. Hey! But I don't see your inseparable dried rice pocket on your shoulder anymore?"

"It doesn't make sense to keep carrying it along." Dr. Thieu Son Hoang answered with a laugh.

"Why? Weren't you afraid of starving to death because there's no rice in the South?" I jokingly asked.

"You're laughing at me again!" Dr. Thieu Son Hoang said without any sign of being humiliated, while Ms. Hong Cam seemed to swallow any bad feeling about our conversation.

"No, I'm not. Am I a wag? Sorry for having spoken without thinking," I said, since I thought Ms. Hong Cam might feel hurt.

"On the way here I saw rice and packs of dried noodles everywhere, even scattered on the roads." Dr. Thieu Son Hoang said, seeming not to worry about the uneasiness of Ms. Hong Cam. He kept going on: "In Hanoi, you must have a ration card to buy a very limited amount of rice. You must have special privileges to buy a pack of ready-made noodles from the government food store. Here, Grandma treated us with sumptuous banquets way beyond our wish. There's no need of the pocketed dried rice."

I anticipated that the chance of my going back to my teaching career under the new regime was very dim. I was not sure whether Dr. Thieu Son Hoang had ever published anything. When I asked if he could find me some interesting books so I could translate them into Vietnamese and have them published to earn some money for living, Dr. Thieu Son Hoang nodded and said, "That may be a good idea."

After thinking for a moment, Dr. Thieu Son continued, "But it may not be feasible."

"I hope I'm capable," I replied.

"That's not the issue. The issue is that no foreign language book can be found."

"You're well respected by people at the Vietnamese embassies overseas. You could ask them for books. Would you?":

"No one at the embassies has the guts to do that," Dr. Thieu Son explained. "Traveling outside embassies is very limited and strictly monitored. They have to go out in pairs so each one supervises the activities of the other for a subsequent report. No book or magazine can be bought without pre-approval."

I turned to the editor of the Phu Nu Magazine, who looked unhappy about what Dr. Thieu Son had said. "Dear Ms. Hong Cam. How about if I write some things and you help publish them?"

"That can be done," she replied.

"Do you have any practical suggestions or recommendations?" I went on.

"Sure. You have to go through the required steps."

"What are they?" Her reply had piqued my curiosity to learn more.

"First, your article must be brought to your local union for assessment and a vote. If the article is locally accepted, it must be presented next to the central cultural committee. If your article is appraised to be publishable at this level, then it will be forwarded to the government branch of paper resources."

"After going through so many levels of scrutiny, what will be left in the article that is mine?" I felt puzzled upon hearing about the process.

"Don't interrupt me." She went on, "If the annual paper allocation is still available, and your article is of higher priority, they'll publish it."

"If it's published at the end of such a long journey of censorship and budget allocation, it'll lose both the initial content and its timeliness."

"Then your article should be a timeless one," the magazine editor recommended.

"But it's not mine anymore. It's only a product of censorship."

Ms. Hong Cam did not like my point of view. Once she left, she never contacted me or Grandma or anyone else in the family.

Grandma's home was close to the bus and train stations. During the first few months after the fall of Da Nang in March 1975, several other relatives and unknown persons from the North converged to Grandma's home. One of them was a senior lieutenant of the military engineering squad. His name was De Huynh, and he claimed to be another of Grandma's relatives. The engineer told Grandma that he had passed by her home several times during the war. We had no way to verify his assertion. He asked Grandma of the whereabouts of her older brother, Mr. Thua Hoang. Being told that Mr. Thua had gone to the United States as a refugee, the senior lieutenant confidently stated, "He'll soon be enlightened and then he'll want to repatriate."

Some other uninvited visitors were a farm director, Mr. Tuyen Huynh, and his brother. They came after Saigon was seized. The two of them were on their way to acquire the pineapple farm An Ha in a distant suburb of Saigon. These gentlemen were disillusioned party members. They stayed several days with Grandma. The stopover was only long enough for them to go around the city. They wanted to contemplate, as the two of them told us, "the poverty and misery of the South under the exploitation of the Americans and their puppets."

"The propaganda machine has told us so." Mr. Tuyen relayed the message he had been hearing for such a long time. Prior to leaving BaNgoai to go south, Mr. Tuyen advised Grandma, "If any one of you needs some type of paper to go around, see me."

Another unexpected visitor was a retired military division commander. The former Communist general was a native of South

Vietnam. In 1954 he had left his family in the South to regroup to the North after the Geneva Treaty went into effect. I did not know how Grandma came across this division commander or why she brought him home. The gentleman proudly confided, without being asked, "I've retired with good allowances. I was provided with a single home."

"What type of home? It must be a very good one. Isn't it?" I asked, thinking of a mansion the North government might award to a military division commander after he had risked his life for so many years on the battlefield.

"It's a single house."

"A multistory brick home?"

"No. It's a thatched one with woven bamboo walls pasted with mud." The commander proudly gave a detailed description of his residence. "It's a privilege. You know, with such a house, it normally must be shared by two or three different families."

"You've gotten remarried, haven't you?"

"Of course! I own several oxen and a garden. I manage a cooperative farm." With expressive pride, the retired commander got into specific details of his belongings.

"How about your former wife and family?" To my curiosity, the uninvited guest showed some excitement in his response to my inquiry:

"That's why I'm rushing to the South. My ex-wife lives with a son. When I told the son in the South about my home in the North, he said, 'Your home is not comparable even to the kitchen of my mom's house.' He told me his mother has a fleet of buses. I can't believe it—how a southerner, subdued by the US puppets, could be that wealthy. He must be lying to me. That's why I'm so anxious to see the status of my ex-wife."

"So, that's why you hurried south!"

"You know the currencies of the two parts of the country are different. There's nowhere to do an exchange. I was given some currency of the South. Unfortunately, it's only enough for the train ticket to here. Now I'm penniless."

"Sorry to hear that," I commented.

"Your mom was so nice. She did not know who I was but, upon hearing my case and without any hesitation, she invited me for a night's stay. Without her help, I'd have been on the street."

"We'll buy you a train ticket to your destination," I offered.

"That's what your mom told me too. The train fare is a huge amount for us northerners. It's incredible that you, southerners, are so kind and generous."

"It's no big deal."

On his return trip the retired commander stopped by grandma's home to thank her and to tell us that he could not believe his ex-wife was such a wealthy one.

"My son was right. My fortune in the North is nothing compared to the wealth of my ex-wife. Even a minister in the North cannot dress up as elegantly as my son. Everywhere I went in the South, things look so luxurious and comfortable." The retired commander kept praising the friendliness of southerners and the good lives they were leading.

It's possible that word of grandma's hospitality was so widespread that many unknown people kept coming to her home. Among them was a young person who claimed to be an artist. He went south to sculpt and erect a statue of Ho Chi Minh somewhere.

The intercity bus station, which was empty at the time, was about half a mile from grandma's home. An unpaved dusty road connected the bus station to the Da Nang air base. The red dirt road crossed in front of the local Military Medical Center Duy Tan C17.

Restructured from a French military barracks, the well-equipped twelve-hundred-bed Duy Tan C17 medical center was the main military health-care institution of the First Region. Among its many departments, there was one section the center reserved to care for the northern wounded soldiers. A well-paved avenue connected the center to the other side of the city through the air base. Surgeon Hanh Phung and Dr. Luong Pham, the head of the External Medicine Department, were among the renowned physicians working at the center.

During the last days of March 1975, many South Vietnamese combatants had been transferred over to Duy Tan C17 Medical Center from battlefields just days before the fall of Da Nang. Many of the injured were seriously wounded. The volume was great, and many of them had not yet been appropriately taken care of.

I had no information about who in the Da Nang Military Management Committee had taken over the Duy Tan Medical Center. The North was currently preoccupied with the battle to overcome

Saigon. They had not sent fully trained experts to take over the technological arm of the South. Only underprepared technicians for the urgent fighting needs along Ho Chi Minh trail were available. Coming out of the jungle, these low-level specialists took over every sophisticated sector of the technically well-equipped South. Presently, the North did not aim at getting technical. They were only interested in military victory and political issues.

Once the C17 Medical Center was taken over by the winners, surgeon Hanh Phung—who had operated on Nhi Ha—Dr. Luong Pham, Dr. Co Nguyen, Dr. Tai Nguyen, Dr. Ton That Sang and most of the resident physicians were sent to Ky Son concentration camp. It was interesting that the BBC falsely announced that the new victors had appointed Dr. Luong Pham to be mayor of the newly occupied Da Nang City. Dr. Luong Pham had actually killed himself in the brainwashing camp on April 3, 1976.

Resident physicians were subjected to brainwashing. South Vietnamese military patients at Duy Tan Medical Center were all mercilessly evicted from the center without being treated. Describing the tragic situation of the wounded soldiers being expelled from medical treatment in such a lamentable state, military poet Trang Y Ha recorded the following verses:

> *My both legs injured*
> *Got sawn to the knees fractured*
> *The wounds are still festering*
> *Skin is not healing.*
> *On the South's Liberation Day*
> *Carried by my wife as a newborn baby*
> *I sadly left the Military Medical Academy*[13].

Trang Y Ha was fortunate to have his wife still around to carry him away from the occupied hospital. Most of the wounded in the Duy Tan Military Medical Center had served in the First Military Region but their hometowns were far away. None of their relatives were around to help alleviate their miseries. No means of communication were available for them to reach their families in the current chaotic consternation. Charities had been displaced. Half of the Republic was under fierce battles. Their relatives might be desperately running. The wounds of the C17 military patients had not been given first aid; some had no limbs to move. Expelled from the hospital, those poor patients just lay dying along the dusty road under the frying sun.

Once the northern troops actually entered into the heart of Da Nang, every family in the area had to host two northern soldiers. Two of them, clad in yellow uniforms with no name tags, came with their weapons and lived with us, ate with us, and lorded over our family. We did our best to be nice to the two uninvited visitors and to feed them adequately. Being invited to eat with us, neither of them consumed more than two small bowls of rice at each meal. They never touched any of the delicious dishes on the table. The intern soldiers avoided any lengthy conversation with our family members. The two of them were always at each other's side. They showed high curiosity at everything in our home but never directly asked us any question. Asked whether in the North they have what we have, their answer was always a repeated chorus:

"In our North, we have everything!"

"Do you miss your wife or girlfriend?" To this question they jointly replied, "We miss Uncle Ho!"

It was almost fifteen days since the Da Nang doomsday, but the food market had not reopened yet. Meat, poultry, fish, vegetables all disappeared. The local market was but a deserted place full of garbage and flies. Fortunately, we still had plenty of rice in the pantry. Although we had been looted during our failed escape, plenty of fish sauce, shrimp paste, and salted fishes were still available in the remaining containers. Vegetables in the garden were growing fresh in the spring sun to feed us for quite a while.

Living right on the beach had its advantages. During the first few days of occupation, some fishermen started taking the risk of sneakily doing a little fishing near the shore. We were able to purchase some of their tiny catches at an unseasonable dear price. The small trade of fish must be done furtively, especially when the two soldiers were living with us, since consuming meat and fishes under the new regime was condemned as the capitalist way of life.

The presence of the Communist soldiers in the family put us in an awkward situation. Listening to the BBC news to follow up with the unfolding plight of the Republic had to be done surreptitiously.

At night time the soldiers reported back to their command post and went patrolling the area. They only returned to our family at dawn. However, we were well aware that our family was always under a close military watch. Our German shepherd warned us of the soldiers' close patrol with his continuous growls and barks throughout the dreary nighttime.

2. White Christmas

D
ay and night, the news on the BBC and VOA airwaves foretold the inevitable. The Saigon debacle was to come.

Divisions of northern Communist infantries converging from the captured First and Second Military Regions of the Republic were advancing to the III Corps territories. They were on their combative way to the final destination: Saigon, the capital of the Republic. While Phuoc Long, Binh Long, Binh Duong, Long Khanh, Binh Tuy, and Phuoc Tuy fought for their survival against the northern forces, the political platform at the very heart of the Republic went through waves of deplorable vicissitudes.

In the Central Highlands, the Second Corps was completely destroyed. In Quang Tri and the cities of Hue and Da Nang, First Corps soldiers simply melted away without putting up fierce resistance. The devastating defeats suffered by the Army of the Republic of Vietnam (ARVN) prompted the National Assembly of South Vietnam to question President Nguyen Van Thieu's handling of the war, thereby placing him under tremendous pressure to resign.

In a last-ditch effort to save South Vietnam, President Nguyen Van Thieu ordered the 18th Infantry Division to hold Xuan Loc at all costs. Xuan Loc was but a small town of thirty-eight thousand located on National Highway 1 and about forty miles northeast of Saigon.

As the political crisis in Saigon worsened day after day, Liberation Army Commander Tran Van Tra and North Vietnamese 4th Army Corps commander General Van Tien Dung made a combined effort to capture Xuan Loc to open the gateway to Saigon. Over a period of twelve days and nights, both sides displayed feats of courage, leadership, and determination. During the early stages of the battle, the ARVN 18th Infantry Division under General Le Minh Dao beat off numerous attempts by their Communist enemies to overrun the town, forcing North Vietnamese commanders to change their crusade plan.

The fight for Xuan Loc produced one of the epic battles of the Vietnam War. Certainly it was one of the most heroic of the Army of our Republic of Vietnam. On April 9, 1975, Van Tien Dung attacked the ARVN 18th Division with his entire IV North Vietnam Army Corps, consisting of four infantry divisions supported by extremely heavy artillery fire of twenty thousand rounds of missiles and rockets. General Le Minh Dao and his courageous men caused tremendous losses of heavy weapons and human life to the IV North Vietnam Army Corps. The whole Republic looked at the Xuan Loc battle with a fragile hope. Holding out, insurmountable, for twelve long days and nights of ferocious combat, our infamous 18th ARVN Division also lost more than half of its courageous troops and heavy weapons.

Under pressure from all sides, President Nguyen Van Thieu resigned on April 21, 1975. In Xuan Loc, General Le Minh Dao and his six hundred surviving fighters were surrounded by ten thousand North Communist combatants. In the meantime Allies of the Republic displayed no gesture of military support. General Le Minh Dao and his courageous remaining troops were finally overwhelmed by the massive North Vietnamese army. The tiny town of Xuan Loc was overrun by the colossal 4th Army Corps on April 22. The Battle of Xuan Loc was the last powerful battle of the Vietnam War. Unfortunately it was the deciding point of the calamitous plight of our Republic.

One week after being sworn in as Nguyen Van Thieu's successor, the elderly President Tran Van Huong on April 28 had to transfer his volatile presidency to the northern supporter Duong Van Minh. The US ambassador to Saigon, Mr. Graham Martin, asked Tran Van Huong to leave our country for his safety. The seven-day president answered Ambassador Martin by saying, "I know the current situation is very dangerous. Now the ambassador has invited me to leave the country. I thank you. But I have given it some thought, and I have decided definitely to stay in my country. I also know how much suffering and humiliation will pour down on the southerners once the Communists come to Saigon. I was their top leader; I volunteered to stay and share with them a rather painful humiliation and the suffering of a people who have lost their country."

The US embassy in Saigon destroyed its papers and hurriedly called in squads of helicopters to evacuate American personnel. On April 29, 1975, the US Task Force evacuated US personnel and Vietnamese who might suffer as a result of their past service to the allied efforts. From Vung Tau, Hancock launched the first wave of rescue helicopters to Saigon. Operation Frequent Wind was activated. The American radio station regularly began to play Irving Berlin's "White Christmas," the signal for American personnel to move immediately to the evacuation points.

By 5:00 am on the morning of April 30, on the helicopter Lady Ace 09, US Ambassador Graham Martin was flown to the *USS Blue Ridge*. Thousands of evacuees were rescued from the Communist forces closing in.

Only two hours after the last US Marine security force element was extracted from the embassy, Communist tanks, under the flag of National Front for Liberation of South Vietnam, crashed through the gates of the nearby Vietnamese Presidential Palace. General Duong Van Minh broadcast his appeal to South Vietnamese armed forces to stop fighting and lay down their arms. Duong Van Minh surrendered his government to the northern invaders on April 30, 1975.

The capitulation order by Duong Van Minh spurred a torrent of refugees out of Saigon. South Vietnamese Air Force aircraft and helicopters loaded with air crews and escapees made for the naval ships. Nguyen Cao Ky, who had made big announcements that he would fight to the death, was among the first escapees by helicopter to the warships. This aerial exodus was paralleled by an outgoing tide of junks, sampans, and small craft of all types bearing a large number of the fleeing population.

Duong Van Minh's order to surrender marked the beginning of multiple heroic responses.

Major General Nguyen Khoa Nam, a native of our Da Nang City and 4th Corps/4th Tactical Region Commanding General, sitting in his armchair, fully dressed in ceremonial uniform, decorated with all his medals, shot himself at his Can Tho military headquarters around midnight on April 30, 1975, when he was forty-eight years old.

Summoning his staff, his mother, and his wife, Lt. Gen. Le Van Hung, deputy commander of the IV Corps, said, "A commander who cannot protect his country, his position, then should die at his position for his country." Ordering his mother, his wife, and everyone to go home to their families, General Le Van Hung returned to his office and locked the door. The general killed himself with a .45 pistol. It was about 9:00 pm on April 30, 1975.

Brigadier General Le Nguyen Vy, Commanding General of the 5th Infantry Division at Lai Khe, was born in Son Tay province in North Vietnam. After receiving Duong Van Minh's order to surrender, at 11:00 am April 30, 1975, General Le Nguyen Vy committed suicide by pistol at the 5th Division headquarters in Lai Khe rather than surrender to the enemy.

Brigadier General Tran Van Hai was a native of Can Tho and commander of the RVN 7th Infantry Division at the Dong Tam Base. At midnight on April 30, 1975, the General killed himself with a cup of lethal drugs at Division Headquarters, Dong Tam Army Base, in the city of Dinh Tuong of My Tho province.

Many others—officers, soldiers, and civilians all over the South—killed themselves instead of surrendering to the northern Communists.

At about 2:00 pm on April 30, 1975, hours after Duong Van Minh surrendered to the Communists, people nearby heard several pistol reports from his home. After hesitating—in fear for their own safety—his neighbors got into his home in Quy Nhon to find Major Dang Si Vinh, his wife, and his seven children each lying on a single mattress, all dead, each killed by a single .45 caliber bullet, lying in pools of blood that had gushed from the horrible holes at their temples.

In a note he had left, Major Dang Si Vinh wrote

> *Dear neighbors. Forgive us. Because our family would not live under the Communist regime, we have to end our lives in this way that might bother you.*

Also in Quy Nhon, Colonels Nguyen Huu Thong and Le Cau, 22nd Infantry Division, killed themselves in April 1975. Navy Major Le Anh Tuan, Air force Major Nguyen Gia Tap, Major Ma Thanh

Lien and his wife, all killed themselves rather than surrender to the Communists.

Twelve monks and nuns immolated themselves by fire at their Duoc Su pagoda in Phung Hiep, Can Tho, on November 2, 1975.

In an article reprinted by the *New York Review of Books* in 1977,[14] Father Andre Gelinas, a Jesuit priest, said that as many as twenty thousand Vietnamese had committed suicide since the Communists took over the South.

Saigon was a total debacle, as My Le and I had predicted. The whole Republic of Vietnam of ours was lost to the northern Communists. Singing the triumphant chorus "As if Uncle Ho Were here On the Great Victory Day," the Communist victors started a new page of history.

As expected, the first page was a red one.

As Southeast Asian Affairs reporter Seth Mydans wrote in the April 24, 2000, issue of the *New York Times,* in South Vietnam perhaps sixty-five thousand were executed by their self-proclaimed liberators.

Colonel Ho Ngoc Can was the chief of Chuong Thien Province. On April 30, 1975, he refused to surrender to the enemy. Along with his troops, the colonel fought with all his might, holding the provincial headquarters until 11:00 pm on May 1. In the last minutes, he ordered his soldiers to leave the headquarters for their safety. The colonel heard about the suicide of his IV Corps commanders. As a devoted Catholic he could not kill himself. When his forces were out of ammunition, he fell into the hands of the Communist force. Brought to the execution field, the colonel asked his captors not to blindfold him and to let him salute the RVN colors with his uniform on, and the colonel haughtily stood looking at his executioners. Colonel Ho Ngoc Can and Major Trinh Tan Tiep were publicly executed by the Communist captors at the Can Tho Stadium on August 14, 1975.

Dang Van Kien, a national police sheriff in Quang Ngai Province, was forced into a well with eleven other political prisoners. The liberators then killed them with a grenade explosion.

Master Sergeant Dang Xuan Hoan, a national policeman in Phu Huu Detention Camp in Binh Duong Province, was taken into the woods by camp guards and executed on May 15, 1975.

Mr. Huynh Chin, of the popular Forces 49th Platoon, was executed in Phu Cat Prison with six fellow detainees on May 1, 1975.

Nguyen Cong Hoan, the person who in 1963 has poured gasoline on the Most Venerable Thich Quang Duc and ignited fire to immolate the monk alive, in 1976 became a delegate of the Communist National Assembly. He disclosed that three hundred persons were executed by liberators in his hometown Phu Yen after 1975.

The honeymoon days Da Nang had diffidently enjoyed during the month of April 1975 prior to the Saigon debacle had come to an end. Former military and civil personnel were ordered to register at multiple designated stations of the Military Management Committee (MMC).

I reported to my teaching institution. Educator Trinh The, the headmaster of the school, had been put in T.154 jail in Tien Phuoc. A newly self-proclaimed principal took the responsibility of gathering the registrations of the teaching body. Teacher records were in turn submitted to the MMC. A new label, *puppet*, was then used to designate personnel and citizens of the former regime. I was demoted to simply a puppet among millions of fellow puppets.

My Le reluctantly reported to the former First Region Public Health Center on Hung Vuong Boulevard. Dr. Truong Dinh Tri, head of the center, had escaped overseas. The newly self-established center head was a short female physician. Presiding over the registration station of the Health Center, the physician could hardly write My-Le's name in her illegible handwriting.

The new administrators of the Health Center were not able to familiarize themselves with the lab procedures and equipment. The situation put My Le and her fellow lab technicians of the old regime under intense pressure. Those who had come out of the jungle and established themselves as the public health administration were hardly able to read and write. Doctors' stethoscopes were around their necks. They held the rights of control and the power of life and death. Unfortunately, however, health laboratory methodologies and terminology were unknown to them.

First, My Le and her liberated puppet fellows had to guide the newcomers how to read and write Vietnamese sentences fluently in a very short time. My Le and her friends had never trained to be language teachers, who might have handled the task more easily and effectively. A much harder step for the reluctant technical puppets was to familiarize the newcomers with complicated laboratory technical terms. Fresh out of the jungle, they were highly skilled in combat techniques but had little educational background. Most of the existing terminology was in English, which was completely unknown to the jungle fighters. Lab procedures were also entirely unfamiliar to them. To achieve these professional training goals, a regular student must spend at least a year in school to learn basic language skills, at least another six months to learn a foreign language such as English, and more than two full years of technical formation. Three to four full years are needed for a student to obtain the health-care associate degree. After only about two short months, the liberators at the Da Nang Public Health Center surprised My Le and everyone by proclaiming themselves graduated.

In the meantime, there was at least one daily political training session the puppet technicians had to attend. In one of such sessions, the newcomers stated a theory that startled their listeners:

"Each and every person living in the former South Vietnam was a criminal against the revolutionary regime."

"We were technical people working for the health of others. How can we be criminals?" one of the puppet attendees at the lab sternly argued.

"You puppets! As you revived a sick or wounded southerner, you made him into a healthy combatant against the revolutionary regime. That's your crime!"

The stated criminal charge was a pre-established policy. It was reiterated by different liberators in multiple circumstances to every class of listeners at every individual and public brainwashing session.

Ironically, after proclaiming themselves graduated from the lab preliminaries, the newly graduated personnel required the existing puppet technicians to take lab tests to be certified. If not certified, the puppet personnel must leave the organization; that was the rule. The order was such an unreasonable requirement.

"How can you, freshly graduated people, examine and certify the technicians who just taught you?" the leading puppet lab physician objected.

Realizing the absurdity of the directive, the test mandate got cancelled. However, other tactics were maneuvered to purposely eliminate the targeted puppets from the system.

Several months later, My Le was demoted to become a cook for the health center. Other puppet laboratory technicians were sent to clean the city roads and collect garbage.

At home, besides BaNoi, My Le had a live-in maid to help with kitchen chores. Cooking was not her strong point. To cope with her new culinary assignment at work, in the very early morning My Le biked to the beach to purchase the lab's daily fish ration. She then hurried to the early market to buy food to prepare meals for the center. The lab's kitchen had seldom been used before. The lab had no food-storage facility. The kitchen was not well equipped for meal preparation for a big collective, either. An experienced lab technician, My Le had to use her own initiative to find ways to tackle the difficult culinary tasks with minimally available equipment and no extra help.

Unable to sustain such a humiliation and the unprofessional cooking job, My Le befriended Dr. Luyen Phan, a physician from the North who had taken over the regional Malaria Eradication Center on Le Loi Avenue about a mile from the Public Health Center. The physician came to Da Nang with a little boy who was of the same age as Nhi Ha. His wife was at that time attending a medical college in the Soviet Union. Dr. Luyen was one of the few open-minded experts who appreciated the technicality of a specialist. Dr. Luyen willingly submitted a request to transfer My Le to the malaria eradication lab. Before 1975, the center was a well-equipped private clinic owned and managed by Dr. Luong Pham, a resident physician at the Duy Tan Military Medical Center. The liberators sent Dr. Luong Pham to Tien Lanh brainwashing camp, where he killed himself. The clinic was confiscated and turned into the Malaria Eradication Center.

Liberated life was, unfortunately, not that rosy for my poor My Le.

In wintertime, My Le and her female coworkers had to climb up to the remote mountainous area of Dai Lanh in Quang Nam Province to engage in the implementation of the "increasing production policy." Winter in mountainous central Vietnam is the most extreme cold season, especially during the days of constant drizzle. Cold wintertime was the beginning of the season for transplanting young rice seedlings into the muddy fields. Far away from family and city life, and in the skin-cutting cold, My Le and her coworkers rolled their sleeves up to their armpits and their pants to their crotches and waded into the fields of muddy knee-deep water that swarmed with blood-sucking leeches. The lab technicians stood in a line, bending over the whole day to hand-plant rice seedlings into the cold mud.

During wartime in those remote mountainous areas, such as My Son and Dai Lanh, the uncultivated fields were planted with mines and unexploded missiles, rockets, and bombs. The war ended in April 1975. In 1977 six people were killed in mine-clearing operations around My Son. Grazing cows were sometimes blown up. After peasants and domestic animals had lost their lives in those dangerous fields, most people stayed away from such regions.

To realize the government policy of Increasing Production, civil service personnel were sent to work in those fields regardless of the imminent deadly danger. Fortunately, poor My Le did not ignite any such deadly hidden explosives while she labored.

A month or so later, when the rice plants were waist-high, My Le and her team had to go back and steep themselves in the rice field to weed out unwanted grass. Having been cut by the sharp rice leaves, My Le dreamed of having protective gloves and hip-high boots for the work. Her team had to get to the rice field at the end of the crop season for harvesting.

It was prearranged by the Malaria management that during their rice field assignments, My Le and one of her female coworkers stayed with Mrs. Tuan, a poor resident of the sparse hamlet. It was a leaky one-room thatched cottage of about three hundred square feet. Mrs. Tuan lived in the isolated hut by herself, with only a skinny old dog. She was not the kind of talkative person to reveal her family status. Her husband, if she had one, might have joined the jungle fighters and gotten killed. Her cottage stood on the hillside, surrounded with some slender banana plants. The plants looked meager, as if there were a permanent water shortage. Stunted plants and poor, rotten bamboo walls could not shield the exposed hut from winter's icy air currents. Next to the dirty cooking spot on the ground, a narrow creaking bamboo bed was reserved for My Le and her female coworker. Mrs. Tuan lay on a very low bare bed made from two rough, narrow, and poorly assembled boards. No blankets were available. Mrs. Tuan curled herself up in a raincoat made of palm leaves. Rolling themselves in nylon raincoats, My Le and her coworker, reshuffling over and over, could not doze themselves into deep sleep. It was impossible to keep the biting cold of that rocky hillside from making its way into their shivery bodies.

In the hot and humid summer time, My Le and her coworkers were sent several miles higher into dense wilderness to work at gravelly soil sites. Their assignment was to hoe away weeds and dig up the barren ground for cassava planting. The humid area was infested with snails, leeches, and mosquitoes, and the ground was hardened under the boiling sun. Even in early morning, workers were drenched in sweat. There was not enough water even to drink. Washing was a luxury. The nearest springs with some running water in the scorching summer were miles away.

This was how My Le and her coworkers took part in the lab center's labor plan to realize the government policy of Increasing Production. That was Good Labor. "Good Labor converts gravel and stones to rice," as the slogan said.

The majority of employees at the Malaria Eradication Center were freshly arrived from Hanoi. Their technical skills were questionable. Most of them assumed supervisory or secretarial positions. It was unbelievable for them to see a southern puppet lab technician dissecting a female Anopheles mosquito for anatomical study. Brought from their northern world, their professed motto for life was as follows:

"Increase personal revenue, reduce expenditure, actively walk off with goods, and proceed to stealing."

On a national level, the new regime prioritized party membership and manual labor over competently qualified specialists and public health care. Individually, public servants were thinking not of responsible service but of stealing. Worrying about this policy and the current social mood, My Le was apprehensive for the future of the country. The degradation of morality and of social services became a constant weight on her mind. In the meantime, the majority of population could not be concerned about their future prospects. Their persistent obsession was nothing but to get a piece of food each day and to have something to cover their naked bodies.

Temporarily, as a government employee, My Le enjoyed a few priorities that unemployed and nongovernmental workers might be envious of. She was provided with a ration card for cloth. With the card she was eligible to purchase from ten centimeters to a total of five meters of clothing material a year from the government store at a subsidized price. Five meters of material per year for our family of three adults and three kids. How could everyone be clothed decently? Five meters were hardly enough to clothe the three children to go to school. Nothing would be left to cover the three adults. We might have to go to work or to the market naked.

1978 Cloth ration card

Describing the ironic situation, the masses sang a folk song:

There were shirts but no pants.
Uncle Ho wishes happiness to his inhabitants.
But how can?

Speaking on the restricted condition of textiles and the resulting national clothing deprivation, Mr. Nguyen Co Thach, the then Foreign Minister of the Socialist Republic of Vietnam, did not hesitate to confess to reporter Jose Van der Sman, "As you see, the suit I'm wearing, the special suit I put on to welcome you, is not mine. I am the only foreign minister in the world who has to borrow clothing from the government."[15]

Mr. Minister! You have the government to borrow clothes from, for a business trip abroad. But for an ordinary housewife to leave her home, where can she rent a piece of cloth to cover her impudent nakedness?

Each month the food ration card allotted My Le a kilogram of meat and fifteen kilograms of rice. Food sold by ration card at government stores was actually a combination of rice, dried manioc, and barley.

And the folk song mocked:

Living with Ho Chi Minh
An inch of nail must be registered.
For a gourd you must wait in a queue,
Potatoes needed? Show food stamp as your cue.
Barleycorn instead of rice for food,
Students without books and forms.
Independence and Freedom, where're they from?
Curdle yourself! Happiness will come.

Trading rice on the free market was forbidden by law. Manned checkpoints were set up everywhere, especially along main roads. If caught in rice trading, traders were detained, their merchandise seized, and their household ration cards confiscated. Hungry lives became lives of deeper poverty and miserable hardship. But no one could survive without relying on the black market, even at the risk of paying a very dear price of money and personal safety.

Before 1975, the agricultural countryside of the Republic of Vietnam, mostly in the northern provinces, produced nearly enough food for local inhabitants. Arable land in this region is rather small in area and not very fertile, which limits the production. Sometimes the harvest could not be reaped as a result of flooding and other natural disasters. Local Communist insurgents had been known to preempt the fields and confiscate the harvest from farmers. Commercial hoarders may have created artificial scarcity for their dishonest profits. However, rice had never been as scarce as it was now. Before, food prices might have been up and down. The government and aid agencies might have had to provide extra help, especially when the region was struck by natural disasters. Nonetheless, we had never before eaten barley or manioc to survive.

Covering four million fertile hectares of southern farmland, the Mekong River Delta was, on the other hand, a huge granary. On July 7, 1959, Moyar reported in the *New York Times* that in South Vietnam, "rice production went from 2.6 million tons in 1954 to 5 million tons in 1959."

Fifteen years later, in 1974, our South Vietnam produced 16 million tons of rice a year. The total output was more than enough for 20 million of its inhabitants. On average, there were 800 kilograms of rice a year or 4 pounds a day for each southerner while only 6 cups or 2 pounds per head a day were needed. The extra 8 million tons might be exported, sold on the black market, or mysteriously supplied to the jungle fighters by underground traders and Communist supporters. Meanwhile, the Northern propaganda machine cajoled their people that the South did not have rice to eat. Northern officials going South each had to carry along a small bag of cooked dried rice to eat. Northern people was told to bite a grain in halves for southern hunger relief.

Communist writer Duong Thu Huong, author of *Paradise of the Blind*, spent years of the war in the jungle, seven of which were in the two-mile Vinh Moc tunnel in the Vinh Linh District of Quang Tri, the most heavily bombarded region. Her mission was to "sing louder than the bombs" and to give theatrical performances for the North Vietnamese troops, to tend to the wounded, bury the dead, and accompany the soldiers. She was one of three survivors out of the forty Communist Youth Brigade volunteers she led during the Vietnam War. Joyfully following the victorious North Vietnamese Army as it rushed to occupy Saigon on the morning of April 30, 1975, the cultural warrior who had given many years of enthusiast service for the war, instead of loudly singing the triumphal chorus "As if Uncle Ho Were here On the Great Victory Day," choked up with tears and exclaimed, "Heavens! we have been systematically hoodwinked," when she witnessed for the first time the naked truth about the South.

Thirteen years after the 1975 liberation, in 1988 a household monthly rice ration was reduced to 15 kilograms, which was equivalent to a quarter pound of mixed food per day per household member.

After the 1975 liberation, food and rice disappeared mysteriously. It was suspected that under the new regime, poverty and food shortages were the result not of production deficiency but of standards established under a premeditated policy to subdue the whole population. The Nazis had done as much. Stalin applied the same policy on his Soviets.

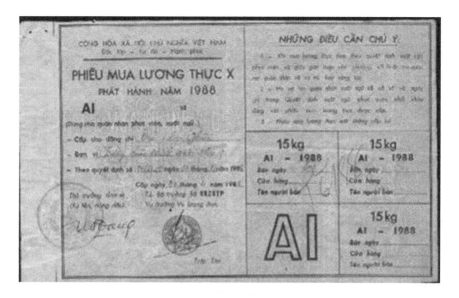

1988 15 kilogram food ration card

The hellish Vietnam War had ended. Destruction had ceased. Productive land had expanded. The labor force had increased. Then food output must be proliferating abundantly compared to wartime. This was, however, not the actual situation. Convoys of trucks and long railway trains transporting mounds of bagged rice were seen going north every day. In the meantime, people were starving for rice. There was public speculation that the Vietnamese Communists were paying their debts to the Red China with rice. Moreover, by putting people in a state of starvation, the policy forced our whole country into total dependence on government food supplies. We all became like Pavlov's dogs, pre-conditioned to respond only in a pre-established manner to the stimuli of the boss.

Thus we were conditioned to lead this new type of life. The southern population was liberated from cheese, milk, and the debris of false social prosperity of the capitalist way of life. So said the liberators.

3. Lofty mountains

I challenge if any one of you can tell
The number of plants in a rice field,
The number of turns a river follows,
The number of layers of flying clouds?

My Quang Tri birthplace was in the tropics. Summer was so incredibly hot. The whole region was damp with high humidity. Candles on the family altar melt and bent down under the daily heat. Additionally, the so-called "south wind" blowing from Laos was rumbling day and night as an endless storm. Fires inflamed areas every day. Rivers became infiltrated with saltwater from the ocean. In my early years at home, my sensitive baby body was covered with an itchy rash. With a handmade paper fan, my mom cooled me down and lulled me to sleep night after night with inspiring lullabies. Through numerous long nights by a flickering oil lamp, with tender affection, mom evoked in my sleepy childhood mind an intense desire to learn the wonders of nature.

Each time I looked up at the roaming clouds high above on a beautiful afternoon, I could not help asking myself over and over the same questions the folk song had induced in my soul:

How many years did the moon grow
That it is said to be old?
How many years ago were the mountains born
That their youthful appearances still adorn?

A lullaby such as this one is only a Vietnamese word game. Nevertheless, the lullaby and the previously mentioned folk song being sung over and over generated in my thoughts many questions about the surrounding environment. Songs like these ones became a permanent obsession. The majestic Long Mountain Ridge lends an awesome power to the horizon west of my birthplace home. Looking up to the awe-inspiring Long Mountain I could not help daydreaming. I was lost in thoughts of being such a person who could build mountains up and create blue rivers and crystal-clear streams.

My years in middle school taught me that two thirds of my Vietnam was covered with primeval forests and unexplored mountains. From my home, in the evening breeze, I was able to gaze with fascination at the setting sun gradually going down behind the western ridge. I have dreamed the dream of Nguyen Cong Tru (1778-1858), who wrote

> *My will is to cut down mountains and fill up rivers,*
> *To make myself a hero known to the furthest borders.*

At night on the dark slopes of the majestic peaks, woodcutters lighted the darkness with ghostly flickering flames. The wild scenes had a charismatic attraction that kept haunting my childhood reveries. I visualized that someday I would explore the wonders of the lofty undulating ridge standing constantly dark purple behind the cloud curtain. The Long Mountain rose as a great wall alongside the western flank of my country. I should make myself into the type of person whom the poet had mentioned in his epic poem.

Unfortunately, I had not had the chance to carry out the dream I cherished so much in my younger years. Neither had many of my countrymen, especially during wartime. It was only when the war was over and we, the southerner puppets, were liberated that we started venturing unwillingly into those forests filled with toxic waters and tropical diseases.

The jungles of my dream were now opened to many of us, not as a place to explore wonders at will but to confine us for brainwashing and forced labour.

The news from the liberators was that former civil and military personnel of the defeated puppet government were to gather at

---

certain locations with food and personal belongings. It was for a three-to-ten-day training, they advertised. How nice it sounded! Only ten days at most. It was understandable, reasonable, and necessary to be retrained so that we would be able to adjust smoothly to a new life. We had no complaint about it. Ten days or a little bit longer in an introductory class was totally comprehensible.

On May 4, 1975, the Da Nang Military Management Committee announced

"At 8:00am sharp this morning, all former regime officers must gather at 2 Dong Da Street to hear about the situation of the country."

Another notorious MMC designated location was at the provincial Buddhist Phap Lam temple at 123 Ong Ich Khiem Boulevard under La Thanh Ty's control.

It was officially announced. Transported with delight, everyone gathered. It was nothing. Only ten days at most! Everyone gathered, noisily laughing with radiant faces and nothing on hand. A short lecture took place. The remaining time was for entering names and some details of personal records on a long roster. By day's end, all who had shown up had been silently transported on enclosed military trucks to the Vinh Dien prison twenty miles away.

As Seth Mydans reported on Southeast Asian Affairs for the *New York Times*, some four hundred thousand military personnel, civil employees, religious notables, and blacklisted members around the South showed up for the promised three-to-ten-day training. They were kept, grouped into different classes, and imprisoned, not for three days, nor for three months, as the liberators duped the whole South. They were interned for an indefinite number of years, in diverse concentration camps deeply hidden in remote mountainous areas for forced labour, brainwashing, and inhuman torture. Many never got the chance to return.

To the camps' interns, to their relatives at home, and to the whole liberated South, North Communist cadres explained that reeducation was an Act of Clemency. This was described in a policy statement:

"South Vietnamese are guilty of betrayal and therefore owe a blood debt. Your crimes deserve the death penalty. But the revolution, out of clemency, has permitted you to be reeducated."

In Ky Son brainwashing camp, the instructor told Dr. Tu, a former physician at the Duy Tan Military Medical Centre, the same statement that was told to My Le and her laboratory coworkers:

"Your crime is so great. You treated the wounded puppet soldiers so they could fight against the people."

Prior to the 1975 liberation day, the whole world anticipated a bloodbath in the South. Before April 30, 1975, the Communist general secretary Do Muoi along with some central party comrades designed a bloodbath program. Military and civil servants of the Republic of Vietnam, marines, army rangers, personnel of the village commune, rural development cadres, police, intelligence agents, parachutists, Phoenix[16] officials, division chiefs, regiment chiefs, battalion commanders—each of these groups was referred to by a specific code in the bloodbath scheme. Different types of death penalty should be imposed on those coded groups.

The proposed bloodbath scheme was so much criticized and condemned by the worldwide community that General Secretary Do Muoi and his government were not able to carry it out as they had planned. Only the concentration camp was implemented, where blacklisted prisoners were put to death individually and silently.

Mr. Tran Dinh Quan, teacher, songwriter, and folksinger, and teachers Truong Van Hau and Le Quang Mai from Da nang's Phan Chu Trinh public high school were rounded up for brainwashing at concentration camp An Diem in Thuong Duc District. So did two educators from the neighbouring Nguyen Cong Tru High, Mr. Trinh Huy and his brother Trinh The. Mr. Trinh The was the school principal. He died of torture in his solitary confinement cell.

His Excellency Nguyen Van Thuan, Catholic auxiliary bishop of Saigon, was captured on August 15, 1975. His father was my godfather. Pushed down to the storage cellar of the military ship Hai Phong along with fifteen hundred other prisoners, the bishop was transported to the rigid concentration camp in the remote Fansipan range. The bishop spent thirteen years in jail, nine of them in solitary confinement at Vinh Quang prison. Ho Huu Tuong, a Trostkist and renowned Vietnamese philosopher was a schoolfellow of French philosopher Jean Paul Sartre and writer Albert Camus. The seventy-year old vice president of Van Hanh University was brainwashed first at Phan Dang Luu jail and then at Z30C of Ham Tan camp until he died in June 1980.

Among my relatives, I could name some of them who were brainwashed in different concentration camps for years. Uncle Buu Doan, my dad's younger brother was jailed for having been a uniformed policeman. He died shortly after being released. My first cousin, Mr. Du Duong, was brainwashed for a shorter time. Unfortunately, he also passed away after his jail term. Another of my cousins, Mr. Dieu Ngo who was an ordnance captain, was released from his miserable dark days of torture after going through several labor camps. He became disabled and died at a very young age.

Several of My Le's relatives had long reeducation terms. Mr. Ly Tuong, My Le's first cousin, was former State Representative. Mr. Ly Tuong went through most of the most rigid prisons in the far North where he helped many inmates to stand strong during their endless years in penitentiaries. Captain Si Duong, My Le's cousin, was a former military attaché to the First Corps commander. I do not remember specifically where or for how long the captain was jailed. Mr. Ngo, our brother-in-law, was drafted when he was a high school teacher in Saigon. After going through multiple brainwashing prisons in the South, he was released to become a retail baker selling his bread to earn a living at the school where he taught prior to Black April 1975.

We should add to the list the following acquaintances of ours. Major Anh Kiet, one of our best friends. He stayed in Tien Sha Harbor until the last minute to be in charge of the refugee evacuation maneuver. His brainwashing time was first at Ky Son camp and later at Tien Lanh. One of our villagers, Mr. Giai Bui a former senator, was also jailed in the Tien Lanh camp. His wife died in poverty during his jail term. Mr. Thai and Mr. Phong Nguyen lived very close to us in our small hamlet. Mr. Phong had been the village head before 1975. Mr. Thai had joined the resistance movement against French colonization and later left the Communist alliance to return to city life. Mr. Phong was released, while Mr. Thai died in prison. Several other villagers, distant relatives and childhood friends of My Le, such as Captains Hieu, Chinh, and Hoang; Major Truc; and so on, were brainwashed in Tien Lanh camp.

That is to name those who were our loving relatives or whom we have worked with and had close contact. The majority of brainwashed puppets were sent to the remote prisons up in the year-round coldest mountains far away in the North.

The Heaven Gate prison on Fansipan in the province of Ha Giang on the border with China was the most famous brainwashing camp, where many of our miserable southerner puppets spent years. Many of them left their remains in the deserted wilderness there. Among the well-known prisoners from Heaven Gate was the Buddhist Venerable Tue Ninh from Thanh Hoa. The famous monk was tortured to his death. In the April 29, 1985, International News Conference sponsored by the Commission on Human Rights at the Freedom House in New York, one of the former prisoners of Heaven Gate, Mr. Doan Nghiem Minh, related one of the terrifying tortures at Heaven Gate. The wardens heated up a handmade iron hat and put it on the head of whomever they wanted to inflict severe pain. Other techniques are described in Dennis Rockstroh's *The Hidden Horror of Vietnam's Camps*:

> The torture techniques included: ripping out fingernails with pliers, whipping with live electric wires, hanging inmates from the ceiling and beating them, forcing prisoners to drink water and then jumping on their bloated stomachs, an arm tied over shoulder and behind the prisoner's back, and 'mental torture' of being forced to bow while being insulted. [17]

Another notorious concentration camp was the Correction Camp Xuan Phuoc A-20 in Phu Yen Province. Political prisoners from the South who had been sentenced to death were kept and tortured mostly in A-20. Among the big names I know of that were held in this renowned A-20 camp were

> Phan Duc Trong, notorious Cao Dai clergyman
> Dinh Van Kip, Cao Dai clergyman
> Nguyen Van Thanh, Hoa Hao Church dignitary
> Thich Thien Minh, Venerable Buddhist monk, a native of Trieu Phong District, Quang Tri. He died in captivity in October 1978
> Thich Phuoc Vien, Venerable Buddhist
> Dinh Binh Dinh, Catholic Priest
> Nguyen Quang Minh, Catholic priest who died in captivity
> Duy Lam Nguyen Kim Tuan, writer

Vu Anh, journalist
Hoang Kim Quy, tycoon, died in captivity.

Reverend Nguyen Van Vang was an eloquent Redemptorist preacher. When I was an eighth grader, it was my delight that the thin reverend came to our area. Enchanted by his eloquence, people in the city, Christians or not, were pouring in to listen to his fascinating three-night homilies. There was no auditorium big enough to hold so many excited listeners. The local school set up an illuminated platform in the immense school yard. The oratorical platform looked out to the Nhat Le River. Whispering willows fenced the meeting yard. The voluminous audience was so silently following his sermons that the willows' whistling was picked up by the microphone and mixed with his softly spoken words.

Reverend Vang was captured on December 2, 1976, from St. Vincent Church, together with his brother, who also was a priest. They were convicted of revolution against the South liberation. His brother, Reverend Nguyen Van Hieu, was executed by firing squad. Reverend Vang was sentenced to life in prison. He was sent to A-20 correction camp and shackled in confinement cell number six next to Buddhist journalist Vu Anh in cell number five. As journalist Vu Anh reported later, the food was but a few slices of dried cassava in a small cup. The guard poured into the cup a heavy salty brine purposely to create a deadly thirst in preparation for further torture.

Both of the priest's legs were shackled to an iron bar that was threaded through the cell's wall and secured with an outside lock. During the daytime, both his wrists also were shackled. He sat in a curved position almost naked until his death ten years after his captivity.

4. Spider web

Quang Tri, my hometown, had belonged originally to the O District of the ancient Champa kingdom. In 1306 Jaya Simhavarman III (1288-1307) offered this part of his northern kingdom to the Vietnamese king as a dowry to marry Vietnamese princess Huyen Tran. Since 1802 the former Champa region got renamed Quang Tri. However, Quang Tri officially became a province only in 1832 under Emperor Minh Mang. Champa traces are still scattered around the countryside of my village. My Quang Tri is only a thin stretch of stunted land sandwiched between the Long Mountain Ridge on the west side and the Pacific Ocean on the east. My Quang Tri fellows, especially people living in the countryside, worked laboriously year round to barely survive in the severe climate. Difficult living conditions formed a mysterious bond that closely joined us to the locality and to each other.

The love of an adventurous life might have driven my family ancestors to leave Red River Delta in the North to venture into the newly acquired region from the Champa kingdom. It was probably under some audacious aspiration that later on my father left his stable land-survey career to imperil his life in clearing the wilderness for farming. My big brother might have inherited the intrepid traits from our forefathers. After leaving his Chieu An organization in the imperial city of Hue, my brother also moved his family to the hazardous and not-fully explored Central Highland to work and die. Our family members were so attached to the native land, dense with mountains and forests, on the verge of the raging Pacific Ocean.

Lofty mountains! Who has earthed you up so high?
Fathom rivers! Who has dug you down that deep?

Lullabies such as those verses, which were my mom's favourites, were full of unanswered questions regarding the wild territory of the country. Mom planted those questions in my young heart to arouse my desire to learn and pioneer endlessly. Unconsciously, she might have been urging me to continue the adventure-filled tradition of our forefathers.

Discovering the wonders of the Long Mountain Range was my lifelong dream. However, My Le was the first female in the family who, prompted by unwanted circumstances, actually took the risk of venturing into the mysterious, desolate woods and jungles.

In my war-torn country, many of My Le's longtime girlhood friends had their dolorous share of the postwar sorrows. Their husbands and relatives were either military officers or personnel of the former Republic society. After being liberated, they were sent for brainwashing in various concentration camps. Ky Son was the main jail camp for most prisoners of the former First Military Region of the Republic.

Hidden in the mountainous rainforest of Bong Mieu in Tam Ky District of Quang Nam Province, the prison camp Ky Son was next to the Vang stream. The camp had four jails numbered 1, 2, 3, and 4. Jail number 1 was for southern military officers ranking from major to colonel.

Back in the 1960s when I was the Culture Committee councillor of my parish, I got one of my friends, Mr. Minh Ho, to teach at the parochial middle school Nhat Le. Later on, Mr. Minh Ho joined the armed forces, became a major, and was established as the deputy commissioner at the Military District I Court of the Republic. Maj. Minh Ho was the youngest of the four brothers, An, Nghinh, Quy, and Minh. Mr. An was My Le's former English teacher. While Maj. Minh Ho was the commissioner of the Military District Court, his three brothers defected to the jungles to join the Communist front against the Republic. One brother—Mr. Nghinh, if I remember correctly—was caught and brought to the Military District I Court where his younger brother was the deputy commissioner. Mr. Nghinh was put in jail. In the Communist 1968 Tet Offensive he was rescued from jail and went back to the jungle.

After Da Nang fell to the Communists in 1975, Maj. Minh Ho's brothers came back to the city. Mr. Ho Nghinh became a member of the Fifth Central Party Committee. The three Communist brothers played deciding roles in the Da Nang Military Management Committee, which sent Maj. Minh Ho to jail 1 of the Ky Son prison camp.

Other prisoners I knew in jail number 1 were Col. Le Dinh Ai and Lt. Col. Nguyen Van To, deputy mayor of Hue. Maj. Truc and Maj. Lac, My Le's distant cousins, were also imprisoned there. Maj. Truc had been my elementary school teacher before he was drafted. Surgeon Hanh Phung, who had operated on our son Nhi Ha, and medical doctors Luong Pham, Co Nguyen, and Tai Nguyen from Duy Tan Military Medical Center, were in jail number 4.

Captain Hieu, former head of the Tien Phuoc District and a native of our village, was detained in jail 2. Captain Chin, another Ky Son prisoner, was my classmate when we were attending the Mateo Phuong School in Dong Hoi before 1954. He got married to Ms. Quynh, one of My Le's friends. These military officers and their wives were mostly from our area. My Le shared many girlish experiences with these best childhood friends of hers.

"Dear sister! I haven't seen you buying so much of the junk stuff before." Spotting the wife of Captain Hieu buying excessive bunches of lemon grass and pork meat at the local market one afternoon, My Le curiously greeted the lady with the question. Among friends, young Vietnamese ladies cordially address each other as "sister" and young men as "brother."

"You know. This weekend I'm going to Ky Son to see Hieu," the lady disclosed. "I'll make him food he can use for a while."

"When do you go?" My Le asked. "Let me know. I may join you."

"That's interesting! You want to go to Ky Son camp? To see whom?" With a wondering look at My Le, the lady paused then half-heartedly continued, "If you decide to come along, we'll meet early this coming Friday morning, around five a.m. Some other ladies will be at the intercity bus station as well. We'll take the early market bus to Tam Ky."

"Thanks for the information."

"Hey! You look so frail! Can you climb the trail to the camp?"

"No big deal!"

"You have to wear tennis shoes or something similar to climb the sloping trail. It must be an hour-long walk. But why do you want to come?"

"I just want to come. Your husband's my childhood friend."

My Le prepared a dried mixture of ground meat, shrimp paste, and lemon grass and stuffed them in Guizgos containers. Knowing that hard-labor residents of the camp were very much in need of sugar, My Le brought along packages of sweet candies and dried ripe bananas. To help the men fight against malaria in the mountainous environment, where the fever was prevalent, My Le hid malaria drugs in tiny packs. She knew which drug was the best. The packs would be secretly handed over, one by one, to the detainee to avoid being confiscated by the camp guards. My Le had been on malaria eradicating trips several times. She had enough experience to put on a neat working outfit appropriate for the strenuous expedition.

Reaching the bus station in dapper garb and with a bulky bag that Friday morning, My Le surprised the group of wives visiting the Ky Son camp. Some threw an inquiring look at her. Others murmured behind her back. However, no one said anything directly to her. The ladies knew well that I was not in the camp being brainwashed. Uncle Su was also at home. My Le's other brothers were in Saigon. None of her direct relatives was in Ky Son forest. The visiting ladies might have gossiped about My Le's intention to join them as they constantly wondered whom she was going to see at the camp. Would it be a secret guy? Or a boyfriend? Who would be the man she risked getting into hardship and political difficulties to see? Those were the unanswered questions that haunted the minds of the visiting ladies.

Hours of suffering on the multi-stop market bus finally ended. The group of visiting ladies had travelled only sixty miles from Da Nang on National Highway1. Several extra miles on dusty local roads must be covered. The visiting ladies hired motorbike rides to the first checkpoint at the foot of the hill. It would have taken several more long hours if there had been no ride available and they had the gut to walk. From the checkpoint the visitors climbed the hilly trail to the main gate of the camp on the verge of the abandoned gold mine Bong Mieu. Every visiting wife showed her identity and visiting permit to the gatekeeper. They were then shown to the waiting shed.

Each detainee was allowed only a short meeting with a relative in the presence of a prison guard. Important messages were exchanged in clever cues only understood by the two involved persons. Scattered in the conversations, the detainees kept saying out loud, the learning is good, the labor is good. While hearing that, My Le and the other female visitors could not hold back their tears as they looked upon the emaciated physique of their loved ones. Mountains and forests of the lovely country, once the immense golden source of an ever-developing fatherland, had been turned by the long, destructive war into a hellish detention imprisoning the victors' brothers indefinitely.

There were attempted escapes by some detainees. Most of them were killed in the run. Others were caught and brought back, brutally beaten, and locked up in confined cells, or silently executed in the dense jungles. Very few escapes were successful. Having been the head of the Tien Phuoc District before 1975, Lt. Col. Le Dinh Ai knew well the terrain of Ky Son. He and Pilot Captain Nguyen Van Loc were among a very few prisoners who successfully escaped Ky Son camp in November 1976.

During their labor excursions out of the camp, detainees Tran Lam and Captain Nguyen Van Hung contacted the Fulro, a group of ethnic highland people fighting against the Vietnamese Communists. Together with the Fulro leaders, they worked out a tentative plot to take over the camp.

Because of the Fulro connection and the frequent escape attempts, Ky Son inmates were later transferred to Tien Lanh labor camp, much deeper in the dense jungle. Camp Tien Lanh, which stood near the Tranh River thirty-five miles from Tam Ky, had much tighter security.

Prisoners in Tien Lanh concentration camp could not forget one of the detainees, the heroic engineer Tran Quang Tran. Mr. Tran laboriously collected, bit by bit, damaged pieces of electronic components and batteries he found in the jungle on his labor trips. With singular engineering skills he made them into disguised bottles of working electronic communication devices. Mr. Tran surreptitiously distributed them among fellows at different jailhouses. Engineer Tran telecommunicated with trusted prisoner-fellows, assigning specific tasks to leaders of the different groups of detainees in an audacious plot. He mapped out a multi-step conspiracy to first take over the Tien Lanh camp and seize its sources of weapons to establish a resistant zone, next to liberate the district of Tien Phuoc from the Communists, and finally to recapture the whole of Da Nang City.

The plot was revealed by a traitor. Leader Tran was captured together with more than a hundred conspirators. Tran was sentenced to death by the military court established right in Tien Lanh camp and executed on June 19.

Tien Lanh camp was therefore strictly guarded. It was a much longer journey from Da Nang to Tien Lanh camp. To Tam Ky Township, visitors had to travel some seventy miles on a dirty multi-stop market bus. After following the local road 616 on hired motorcycles to Tien Phuoc District, they had to climb uphill for hours, going through not one but several strict checking points. Due to the rudimentary means of transportation, the journey took a whole day. Visitors had to stay overnight before seeing their relatives the next morning.

Visitors had to hurry back before being caught in the dark jungle of the next nightfall. Daylight is very short in such mountainous sites. On hazy days, clouds came down and caught in the dense treetops like a lid, blocking out the light and creating a chilly atmosphere that mixed with the everlasting damp stone-cold air of the area.

My Le could not take leave from work and was unable to summon enough physical strength to spend the whole day climbing the sloping trail to visit the new concentration camp.

On the following wives' visits to Tien Lanh reeducation camp, one of the wives, not seeing My Le within their company, voiced her surprise:

"Hey, My Le does not join us to see her boyfriend anymore!"

"Boyfriend? Who's hers?" asked another of the ladies in the group.

"If it's not her boyfriend, then who else did she visit? Her husband and her brother are both home. It must be her boyfriend. The guy seems to be a Navy major. Their hidden relationship must be very deeply involved," some other lady matter-of-factly stated.

"Are you daydreaming?" a more mature lady asked. "How do you know they are having an affair?"

"His personal driver drove My Le to the major's spider web several times. Ha-ha! What was it for? What were they doing there? A gal and a guy in a den? Hey. You guys tell me!"

"You're fabricating the affair, aren't you?" the quietest lady in the group asked with a doubt-filled voice.

"Let me tell you this. It must be because of something very interesting that the major's legal wife left him," the storyteller told the group. "As for the womanizing major, he chose to stay back when he could have left on a navy ship any time he wanted."

"I don't understand," somebody said.

"Nothing's difficult to understand. Love is blind. He stayed behind to be with his mistress. Ha ha! He ended up in jail. Poor him. And his mistress didn't want to come to see him anymore!" The lady laughed.

"If they're so involved, why didn't My Le join our group to pay her boyfriend a visit today?" argued the unconvinced lady. "Because of the treacherous trail the girl has to travel," the story teller responded.

"When you're in love, it doesn't matter if you climb three or four mountains, wade through seven or eight rivers, or cross nine or ten passes to come to each other, as the folklore says."

"Then, maybe because of her husband's jealousy," the story teller concluded.

The gossip continued during several trips. Fully occupied with the interesting love affair, which they recounted over and over, each time with some added details, the ladies did not pay attention to the physical suffering they endured on the treacherous trail to the brainwashing camp.

The love story was leaking to the villagers. People stared at My Le when they saw her on the street. Staying behind, My Le vaguely suspected her lady friends might think of goofy things to explain why My Le would endure hardship to pay visits to the mysterious camp detainee. The gossip was fully recounted to My Le by one of her friends several weeks after she stopped joining the visiting group of ladies.

It was also a Friday afternoon. After work My Le went downtown. Her lab office was in walking distance to the nearby downtown; however, My Le did not frequently go there. Before Black 1975, we often went to mass at the diocesan cathedral and ate favourite dishes afterwards at various bistros. We might shop for specially designed clothes for our children. The liberation cut those luxuries off.

One of My Le's coworkers at the lab lived on Dong Khanh Avenue next to the Han Market. The young lady had been working for the lab before 1975. She was looking for a chance to escape overseas. Being capped by the liberators with the same type of puppet hats, having the same aspirations, the girl and My Le befriended each other easily. My Le accompanied the girl on her way home as far as to the Han Market.

Coming across one of the ladies from the group of camp-visiting wives, My Le thought of the erratic gossip about her. Leaving her coworker, she went to confront the lady. My Le burst into laughing to greet her:

"How silly you guys are!"

"Hey! What are you talking about?" My Le's strange greeting had caught the lady by surprise.

"Don't pretend innocence! Tell me. What did you guys find about my affair with my boyfriend in the camp?" My Le mockingly asked.

"Is he really your boyfriend? Didn't your husband know your affair?"

"My husband? Sure. He did."

"Did he get mad at you? Didn't he?"

"Do you believe it?"

"Who is he?" the lady asked with a smile.

"Do you know Maj. Anh Kiet?"

"That's the guy you've seen at the camp? Tell me your secret. It must be very interesting. Who is he? I'm curious."

"It's him." My Le could not help laughing at the crestfallen lady. After a minute, My Le took time to explain. "He's President Thieu's nephew-in-law."

"Oh! No wonder you traded your husband for him."

"You silly! Who told you I traded?"

"Didn't you?"

"No!"

"They told me his driver drove you to his den. What did you do with your honey there? How evocative it is! I knew. That's why his wife left him to the Communists and ran away. Didn't she?"

"What do you mean, evocative? Damn your imagination! My friend told me of all the crap you guys made up. The major's driver never drove me anywhere."

"Don't tell me your honey drove you by himself. Did he?"

"What a crock! His driver picked up the major's children and ours from school and drove to his residence at the end of the day."

"And you came to him pretended to bring your kids home?"

"Stop your silly imagination! My husband picked up our kids when he was done with his classes."

"Really?"

"During the last days of Da Nang, the major organized the evacuation of refugees to the South. He bound my son's wound when my son got hit by rocket that night at Tien Sha."

"Your son got hit?"

"We almost got killed by missiles."

"Where's his wife? Did she leave him for you?"

"His wife brought their children to Saigon and then sent them to Taiwan. Who told you she left him for me?"

"Then why did you come to him?"

"You silly! When we met the major at Tien Sha on the last day of Da Nang, his wife phoned to ask him to let her come back to Da Nang with him. She managed the Vietnam Airline office in Da Nang. But where was the plane to transport her back to the city? And he couldn't let her back in such a situation. He stayed on duty to the very last minute even after all commanding generals left the area."

"Poor guy! Didn't you two ever get involved? Tell me."

"No! You crack me up! He's not my boyfriend. He and his wife are our family's close friends," My Le said with sadness in her eyes, while her friend looked at her contemplatively.

"You've befriended President Thieu's relatives?"

"Don't say that. We didn't butter up."

"Sorry. I didn't mean it."

"The major has no relatives in Da Nang. As best friends, we have to help him as much as we can. Now the camp has moved. I'm so sorry for not being able to venture into the remote jungles to see him. He did ask me for some items he needed for hard labor, and it's broken my heart for not having helped him."

When the Port Authority changed hands in April 1975, Maj. Anh Kiet reported to the Da Nang Military Management Committee. The puppet major was sent to Ky Son reeducation camp and later to Tien Lanh. He was jailed in prison number 1. One midnight at the beginning of July 1976, Maj. Anh Kiet and Lt. Col. Nguyen Van To were led out of the camp into the jungle by the prison guard Truong. The two of them were to be executed that night. For some reason that nobody knows, a commanding officer of the camp came to bring both of them back. They were spared.

The major's wife and children left Vietnam to join her father, who was the Vietnamese ambassador in Taipei, China, before the fall of Saigon. The major's only relative left in Vietnam was his frail eighty-year-old father living in Saigon.

Unable to help the poor major anymore, all we could do was to pray that he and all brainwashed inmates could enjoy early release before being permanently liberated from this world by hard labor, malnourishment, diseases, and both mental and physical tortures.

Only several months after the fall of Saigon, the major's old father got a visitation permit from the government to come to Da Nang on his way to the labor camp. The poor old father assumed, he told us, that there must be some type of mutual agreement between the major and his wife. The father wanted to know whether the major kept the agreement and therefore decided to stay on his job of evacuating the refugees to the very last days of Da Nang.

The frail father left us to summon his last strength and climb up the perilous trail. We saw him off in the hope Maj. Anh Kiet was still alive to see his dad. We hoped the sad old gentleman had reached the remote concentration camp to pay a visit to his imprisoned son. However, My Le and I have not heard from the major or his old father ever since.

5. People's tribunal

Saigon fell to the Communists at the end of April 1975, a month after the debacle of Da Nang. The two soldiers living with us left without a word. Their presence had brought us some experience and insights into the dark side of the Communist machine. Strictly controlled, mutually supervised, blindly shut off from the outside world, prejudiced by propaganda creed, malnourished but armed with advanced weapons, similar to half-blindfolded horses, the Communist fighters had but the forward one-way aisle on which to advance. Consequently, they were able to achieve victory over the mighty open-minded world.

After many extremely inflammatory months of crisis, life gradually regained some degree of normality. We started feeling the freshness of the soon-coming fall. The politically boiling days subsided as the hot summer gave way to the mellow rays of the glittering sun. Autumn was the time for young boys and girls to come back to school. Several school buildings in the city had been simply closed or turned into offices or public housing for the enjoyment of the winners. Teachers who had run away and now returned were either permanently dismissed or temporarily reestablished before being definitely substituted.

Young children anxiously looked forward to the coming mid-autumnal festivities. Bewildered by recent innumerable horrors, parents were not in the mood to spend money to celebrate the younger generation's festival. For this special festivity, paper lanterns had been handmade for the enjoyment of the children. However, multicolor lanterns were not available anymore. Songs praising the moon, and the legendary couple Chi Hang and Chu Cuoi at the mythical banyan on the moon, those melodies and similar juvenile songs were considered sexual remnants to be banned.

Everyday-life necessities were hard to find in the markets. The city look somber as the beauties in colorful dresses could not be seen in the streets. Life appeared stagnant since cars no longer cluttered the roads. On the radio and public loud speakers, sentimental melodies were substituted with continuous high-pitched singing voices or shrill murderous shouts. Some shops half opened for sporadic trade while many family items were seen displayed along the roads for sale.

Trapped behind, I persuaded myself that I should accept the actual situation. In the hope of ameliorating the lives of the younger generation, I decided it would be better for me to contribute the modest share of my limited abilities to the common building of the new society than to inactively wait and see or to pessimistically lodge endless complaints.

Combining the parish choir with local band-loving youth, I organized an evening talent show on an open stage temporarily set up at the beach under the starry sky. Not intended for the celebration of a victory we never wanted, the show was but a token of our good faith in the new situation. It was our attempt to alleviate, after such tragic days, the stifling atmosphere that was burdening everyone's hearts and minds. Some less-politically revolutionary songs were included in the unpresumptuous theatrical performance. The audience was not as big as expected. The mass appreciated the show with cold applause. They were anxiously thinking of the past that was lost and the uncertain future to come. The local police authorities, who preapproved the show and its contents, appraised it unfavorably. They rated the general tone to have sounded too religious, rather than revolutionary. The show was considered inappropriate in the existing political climate.

Following an order from the Military Management Committee, I reported to the Nguyen Cong Tru High School on Le Thanh Tong Street. The principal of the school had been sent to a concentration camp together with his brother. A junior-high teacher had silently quit his teaching job several years ago. He disappeared into the jungle to join the Front of People Liberation of the South. Together with the advancing Communist troops, he came back to the city and set himself up to be the head of the high school.

I could no longer see the faces of most of my brilliant students. The joking girls had vanished away to the bygone. Brainy students might have gotten lost in the chaos of evacuation. They could have been mistaken for disguised military personnel and therefore been killed. They might have been judged by their student appearances as children of high-ranking puppets and been exterminated during the rebellion. Else they were probably far away in an overseas refugee camp. They might be mentally looking back to the occupied city, to the friends they left behind and dearly missed. Those students who showed up to class looked distracted and did not seem to focus their attention on anything. Pitifully, in their poor young age, they had lost their innocent looks and unconsciously put on worry-filled stares.

We were a month into the new school year but could not get any information about the new curriculum. All the self-installed headmaster did was to tell every educator what to delete from the curriculum or to criticize their dress style as either useless luxury or a bourgeois expression of personal status.

South Vietnam had a twelve-year educational system while North Vietnam had a ten-year structure. How to reconcile the gap, nobody knew. Curriculum subjects were also different. Obviously, being considered politically capitalist topics, subjects such as logic, psychology, ethics, and citizen education were totally eliminated from the curriculum. Former history books were carefully discarded. While everyone was stumbling, I continued to be in charge of Vietnamese Literature.

Classes were thin. Nobody knew yet if there would be graduation test sessions at the end of the school year. Students were troubled about their educational future. Educators were worried about their employment status. Would they be validated to be on the payroll? The government was focusing its efforts on purging and brainwashing. The academic atmosphere was more worry-filled than educational.

For me the teaching was uneventful until I was summoned to see a Culture Protection policeman in one of the school's empty classrooms.

The policeman did not introduce himself. Dressed in the yellow police uniform, he did not have any name tag on his outfit. Later on I found out he was a deputy chief captain working under the district police chief, Maj. Dinh. The captain started the unexpected interview saying, "You have a lovely beach home enclosed with a barbed-wire fence. The oleander in full bloom looks so beautiful."

Knowing that this type of interview opening was to indirectly inform me that the police were holding detailed information about me, I politely responded, "Thanks for the compliments and for having a close look at my living conditions. But you aren't here for such compliments, are you? I'm anxious to know the purpose of the interview. Please don't beat around the bush but get into the details."

The police captain went straight into his recitations, leading to his accusation. "You do not drink. You neither smoke nor gamble. Neither do you have any friends. We know that you're an international spy put in place for the after-war strategy. We need your confession." He sat up straight to utter his solemn condemnation from a threatening posture.

"Sir, I'm by no means a spy." Staying calm and speaking without hesitation, I told the police captain some details of my service life. "To fulfill my required military services, I chose to become a police cadet for two years. My records at the old police archives did not fill up a single page, and you may already have it in your own hands. You know well of my private and public life. Some of my students who know me well got involved in revolutionary actions and were put in jail. They are free now. They may let you know who I am. That's all I can say. That's my real identification. My own life is evidence of the truth of my declaration. Verifying my statement lies in your own hands."

Being directly investigated by a top-ranking police officer, I realized my case was serious and receiving special attention. Dismissed afterwards, as I anticipated, from my teaching position, I became jobless and fell into the designated category to be sent to the New Economic Zone (NEZ).

According to my assessment, it was possible I would not be sent there. NEZs were mountainous regions lying along the strategic borders of Vietnam, Laos, Cambodia, and China. Small groups of uncoordinated former South Vietnamese military forces were consolidating against the Communists along the borders. Being characterized as a spy, I could not be sent to those strategic zones. Concentration camp must be the other possible option they had for me.

When asked "If the Communists come, what will happen?" by a student, I answered that "for my generation, each of us may get a terminal shot or may have to spend our last days in concentration camps." The Communist liberators had definitely come. They had proved my statement to the inquiring student not to be fully valid.

Not all southerners perished as I had wrongly generalized. The bloodbath was not as widespread as I had speculated. In their article "Vietnam 1975-1982: The Cruel Peace," Desbarats and Jackson[18] recorded only some 65,000 of my generation who were executed by the self-proclaimed liberators, far fewer than I had foretold. Some high-profile victims I know have been named in previous paragraphs. The fact was that only a small number of my generation was killed, while I was spared.

Neither were all of my generation put in concentration camps as I had forecast. In their "The Black Book of Communism," Courtois and his collaborators estimated the number of Vietnamese people who were put into reeducation camps as between 500,000 and 1 million out of a population of 20 million. From a 1985 statement by the Communist Vietnamese Foreign Minister Nguyen Co Thach, 2.5 million people went through reeducation.[19] The officially published ratio was only 12.5 percent of the southern population. It was not 100 percent as I had subjectively speculated without basing my judgment on scientific probability. According to published research in the United States and Europe, some 250,000 perished in the brutal reeducation camps.

I was shortsighted. My answer to the student's inquiry did not cover every possible liberation measure. One such action I had mistakenly left out was the infamous People's Court.

A people's court was not a new invention. Two thousand years ago, according to the New Testament, Jesus was put under test by a Jewish people's court set up by the Pharisees. A lady was brought in front of the gathered crowd. The Pharisees accused her of prostitution and sentenced her to be stoned to death. The accusers asked Jesus for a final decision while the stone-throwing mob was waiting. That was the typical process of a people's tribunal. Jesus Himself was also the victim of the people's court when the mob falsely accused Him of urging people not to pay tax, of working to overthrow the Roman colonization. They shouted the death sentence: crucify him! Crucify him! And they went ahead and killed Him.

In a people's court the accused has no legal protection and no rights to appeal. The tribunal is composed of people who have no legal experience and no impartiality but the perverted will to kill. No evidence is brought out. The court attendants have no knowledge of the accused wrongdoings. They are goaded by some unknown accusers to deliver a kill verdict not based on any provable crime but simply by the political intention of the accusers that the court attendants should side with them. Otherwise, the attendants will be considered criminals who have sided with the accused and must also be killed.

After the liberation day of April 1975, people's courts were set up in virtually all southern Vietnamese cities. The objectives and procedures of the Communist People's Court were simply to kill blacklisted people and to spread the reign of terror over the localities. Charges were intentionally political and flimsy such as that the accused was wicked, evil, antirevolutionary, a spy agent, an underground activist. The tribunal was composed of people new to the area, and there was no evidence but fuzzy accusations. The penalty for those vague offenses was meted out not by any judge according to any law but by some of the stuffed-up elements from the prodded mob who simply shouted out the penalty: Kill him! Kill him! The summoned attendants were to repeat the "Kill him! Kill him!" chorus to show that they were backing the unknown accusers.

When I answered the question of one of my students, I was shortsighted not to have thought that someday I would be brought to the ill-famed people's court.

Local police summoned residents of the three hamlets in my neighborhood to the beach at night. The beach was lying calm while the court attendants gathered only several hundred yards from my beach home. The beach was chosen because there was no other place large enough to accommodate the residents of three hamlets. It was a night at the end of a lunar month. There was no moonlight. The weather at the end of a lunar month was normally overcast if not rainy. On such a cloudy night, the mob was only able to see a number of indistinguishable silhouettes. They could not clearly recognize any individual. The accusers would be shrouded in anonymity.

On that ominous night, the gathered audience formed a half-circular ring facing some unknown figures sitting on a bench. Uniformed policemen were around. The only court subject that night, I was put in front of the bench of unknown people and facing the ring of audience. There was no table, no bill of indictment, no clerk to record anything.

There was a banner. In the dim light the banner was hard to read. If I did not misread, the banner displayed Ho Chi Minh's slogan: "Nothing's more precious than Independence and Freedom."

After a long whistle from a local uniformed policeman, a creepy silence fell. Waves lapping against the sandy seashore sounded louder about a hundred yards away. The breeze turned chilly. My name was announced. My heart skipped a beat. My trembling hands sweated in the cold. The whole site turned appallingly dark to me. Thing happened so unpredictably that I could not stand firm on my trembling legs. Somewhere in the crowd, My Le might have had difficulty choking down her anguish.

An unknown woman accuser spoke up in a northern pitch accusing me for about more than five minutes of antirevolutionary crimes. I could not clearly recognize her accusations partly because of her northern parlance and mainly because I was hysterical with terror. Dreadful documentary pictures of people's courts by the Soviet photographer Dmitri Baltermants revived in my mind. Past experience told me that nobody being brought to the Communist people's court could ever survive.

Another woman cut into the lengthy accusation of the first by shouting out, also in a northern tone, "Down with the imperial spy! Death to the imperial spy!"

Not being well worked up, the mob of spectators did not repeat the chorus as expected. The "Kill him!" refrain was not sung by the crowd as in other people's court sessions. These ordinary honest people, who might not really know who I was or what I had done, did not blindly put themselves in a position against me simply because an unknown accuser vaguely charged me with crimes without citing any credible evidence. I felt a little bit relieved when the death sentence was not uttered by the assemblage. There was no court decision. No further accusation. Unknown people on the bench anxiously moved back and forth in a panicked way due to the unpredicted happening. The trial became unexpectedly bland and insipid. Dead time lasted. The bored crowd started disbanding; first a few scattered people and then big groups left the scene. Neither the organizers nor anyone else paid any attention to me standing there dumbfounded.

Meticulously set up, the people's court session held against me experienced an obvious failure due to the negative reaction of the goodwilled mass. Living in a legalistic world, our southerners were not ready for the lawless setting and the process of the Communist people's tribunal. People gathered as neutral spectators. Their inherent impartiality had not been extinguished by threats and coercions to docilely obey the inhuman management of the new rulers. Having been occupied for just a short time, our southerners had not been turned into doctrinaires who blindly listened to whatever the propaganda machine was saying. They would not play the perfect ass and flirt with the regime by choking the inner voice asking them to behave conscientiously. Our beloved fellow residents had saved me this time by staying silent.

The new regime had not yet had enough time to turn southerners into inhuman beings who would bring members of their own family to the people's court, who would accuse their parents or siblings of meaningless crimes and get them killed, such as in the infamous case of the family of Mr. Nguyen Khac Vien.

Director of the Foreign Languages Publishing House, author of the "History of Vietnam," the most notorious writer and campaigner of the North, Dr. Nguyen Khac Vien was the son of Mr. Nguyen Khac Niem, the then rector of the National Academy. The latter was also the father of Ms. Nguyen Phuong Thao. During the bloody Land Reform in the North, Ms. Phuong Thao personally brought her father to the people's tribunal, denounced him, accused him of fabricated crimes, and brought about the death of her upright father in 1953. The poor man was brutally killed simply because he was a typical figure representing the class of Intellects, one of the four condemned classes under the Communist reign. The Intellects, the Wealthy, Landowners, and Local Notables were the four social divisions to be wiped out of the Communist socialist world.

Nationwide and citywide, I simply was nothing but an ordinary teacher. Among the educated residents of the locality, as far as I knew, besides a pulmonary physician who had relocated, only Mr. C. Nguyen and I were college graduates. Mr. Nguyen, who was the younger brother of My Le's sister-in-law, had been sent to the brainwashing camp. I was the only typical intellect left in the area and should be executed to set up a model of the Communist anti-intellectual revolution.

I knew that the measure carried out on me, although it had failed so far, would not end there. There would be brainwashing classes where local residents would be coached to react favorably to the accusers of the people's court.

Apprehending the next disastrous outcome, My Le and both grandmas pushed me hard to run away. They could not stand the situation. I would be killed in the next people's court if I chose to stay.

Everywhere in our police-dominated country, household members had been individually counted in the household registers. Police at every locality checked every household daily. Illegal residents would be easily detected and caught. Households with illegal residents would be punished. There was no safe refuge I could go to. Moreover, if I disappeared from my household without permission, my family's household register would be confiscated. All ration cards would be seized. My family members would become illegal residents and would be held responsible for my absence. To run away, the whole family must go together. And the safe refuge could only be found overseas. I thought about it over and over, but there was no solution available on hand. Moreover, leaving our poor fatherland and our miserable country fellows was but a heartbreaking option in a situation of ultimate despair.

I felt mentally exhausted waiting for my next tribunal, which I anticipated in the very near future. How could I maintain my spirit without being terribly agitated to think that I would be brutally executed in the very near future? That was what the people's court was for. At nighttime, the growling sound of the ocean waves did not lull me into a peaceful sleep but woke me out of haunting nightmares. I was obsessed with the endless echoes of the crowd's screaming a death sentence for me. The court organizers could prod any of our family's previous live-in maids to stand against me as was done in many other court sessions. A live-in maid could accuse me of fabricated crimes. During the 1953-1956 campaign against landlords in the North, many servants had been stage-managed to effectively accuse their former employers of having plundered, battered, or even raped them, or of any other worst criminal actions the management of the people's court could imagine, to put the defendants to death.

Usually, the victims of people's courts were not mercifully killed by a firing squad. Pushed into a hole, they were buried up to the neck and left to a slow death by suffocation. Or in the countryside somebody would drive a laboring instrument such as a ploughshare back and forth over the victim to slowly cut his head. In my locality, there was no ploughshare. I was thinking of being buried to the neck or drowned in the nearby ocean. My sleeping time was haunted with such nightmarish cruel executions that I was about to go through. The entire family was in a state of terrible alarm and depression.

Almost a month later, when the moon was but a dark spot on the gloomy sky, the second local people's tribunal was summoned, also at the chilly beach. The crowd grew bigger than before. Residents of the two non-Christian hamlets were mobilized to attend, to outnumber my villagers. People were intimidated into not staying home. During previous brainwashing sessions, people had heard about me. Somehow they became interested to know what would happen to me. They had not been familiarized as to what the people's court was.

The same scene unfolded as it had in the previous court session. The same banner was up there. With mixed apprehension and curiosity, people of all walks of life formed a half circle about four or five yards away from me. In the dim light I could not discern who was in the circle or on the presiding bench.

As a female accuser started the charge, the crowd fell into total silence. Was the accuser a new one or the same person as in the previous court session? Nobody knew but the court organizers. All I could say was that she must come from the North. Her northern accent betrayed her. The unknown woman flung her arms and took some steps forward. After a lengthy accusation, she pointed at me and shouted to her highest pitch, "You're a puppet teacher. You poisoned young generations with anti-Marxist-Leninist philosophy. Down with the anti-Marxist puppet teacher!" The accuser paused for the mass reaction.

There was some indiscernible puerile babble. Disappointed that no precisely favorable response was heard, the lady then voiced some other accusations that my confused mind could not fully recognize. After taking a short break to breathe, the lady shouted louder: "Everyone listen! At schools he spied against the revolts of revolutionary students. He's an informer. He's a police dog running after revolutionary teachers. Death to the police dog!"

The woman stopped short again. She seemed to be waiting for the crowd to echo her call for the death penalty. They reacted with indistinct murmuring. Several minutes of no activity passed, which was not acceptable in a people's court.

A frail silhouette of a young man stepped out of the crowd. My heart skipped a beat. The crowd became irritated as the youth started speaking.

"Being a former student, I participated in a student oratory contest several years ago. Mr. Tri was a contest judge. A certain contestant delivered a very revolutionary speech with very majestic eloquence. His address stirred up a dynamically hot response from the audience. The contest judges deemed the speech politically inappropriate."

"Down with antirevolutionary thugs!" The woman accuser interrupted the student's assertion with her angry shout. Nobody responded. A minute passed. The student continued his discourse, saying, "Mr. Tri was one of the judges."

"Down with him! Down with him!" The previous lady accuser stood out of the throng, waved her both hands, goaded up the crowd again with her loudest call. I heard a couple of weak responses from the mob. A couple of persons from the presiding bench rose up from their sitting positions, raised their fists to the air to stir up the crowd with their repeated "Down with him" echo. I heard some more weak replies from the crowd. Various people from the crowd gathered around the student. Raising his right hand up in the air, he loudly announced, "Mr. Tri was the only one of the jury who argued. 'This is an oratory contest. Is the contestant's speech the most eloquent? If it is, and I think it is, we should give the contestant the gold medal. We don't judge the political implication here but the rhetoric of the speech.' The judges bent to Mr. Tri's argument. That revolutionary student then got the contest award."

The student stopped short without giving any conclusion related to my status. The assembly understood what his story meant to me. There were whispers in the ranks of people. The disclosure of the frail student had a counterproductive action on the court atmosphere. The student disappeared; probably he was aware of the ill consequence that might happen to him since he had spoken in my defense. The mob became somehow irritated.

Then a lady with a heavy Quang Nam accent stood out from the crowd. Her simply-clad stout body looked imposing against the dusky skyline. She might have been in her sixties. Everyone turned toward her with irritated expectation. Some members on the presiding bench shuffled excitedly.

"Mr. Tri lives close by my home. Twice a day he is back and forth from schools. I know him well. He stopped by my shop very often to buy noodles for his family. He's not a spy. He's a friendly and kind person to everyone in my neighborhood."

Several voices echoed the lady's statement:

"A good person! Good person! Good person!"

Thanks to God. The crowds from one end to the other clapped their hands tumultuously to back the stout lady. The boisterous applause drowned out the quelling whistles of the police. The previous lady-accuser disappeared. She might be afraid of the unfavorable mass reaction against her. Individually and then massively, people broke the ring and flocked with glee to where I was standing. Some of them hugged me and jumped up excitedly. The police failed to drive people away. The remainder of the crowd started dispersing one after the other in the darkness of the night. Unable to keep people in order, uniformed police and the presiding members finally retreated unhappily from the scene, neither imposing any decision nor paying any attention to me, their intended victim.

I was among the last persons heading home. I could not believe I could get out of the trial alive. Deep inside, my heart rate had not yet returned to normal. A chilly sensation was still crawling up and down my back. My cold hands sweated. By my side, My Le was crying at the unbelievable happy ending. Others were wondering out loud about who the female accuser was. Looking back one more time to the fateful beach, which was now deserted and calm, I silently said a thanksgiving prayer to the heavenly Lord. The kind fellowship of the unknown people who voluntarily defended me touched me so deeply.

During the people's court I was disturbed to follow all the details as they unfolded. The oratory contest mentioned by the unknown youth had been organized for several years by the local school district administration under the sponsorship of the Rotary Club. It was probably due to the heated political issues that later on the school district eliminated the yearly contest. As for the student who got the gold medal that year, I could remember the event but had an unclear memory of who he was. I did not remember the details of his speech and did not know whether he got into any political trouble afterwards.

Thanks to the student's eloquent speech, for which I spoke in his favor, and thanks to the unknown youth and the stout lady who spoke up in my defense, I was effectively acquitted from the inevitable death penalty of the People's Court.

On my way home I was thinking of the allegation of my accusers. I did not, could not, and never wanted to spy on my fellow teachers. I had known the various political trends of some of my students. Some of them had even challenged me. Through the local news, I had been aware of multiple students being arrested, but I did not know them by name. Most of the arrested students were from either Phan Thanh Gian High or Bo De High. I did not have the privilege to teach at these high schools or know the students well. Their names might have appeared in local newspapers. I might have seen their names but could not remember any. I was teaching at five other senior high schools in the city. The number of classes I taught was more than fifteen. The number of students in those classes was more than seven hundred each school year. I could only recognize a few faces and names. If some of the students were missing from the classrooms, it was impossible for me to recognize their absence. Moreover, the schools where I taught were less politically active. From the Communist perspective, the students attending these schools could be characterized as neutral or somehow antirevolutionary. They did not join antigovernment demonstrations and hunger strikes. In short, I did not remember any specific imprisoned student.

There were rumors that several renowned teachers were Communist sympathizers. However, no one laid hands on them.

Two notorious teachers in Da Nang City, whom I knew, were jailed because of their pronounced antigovernment activities. Mr. Vinh Linh was one of the two. Living on Nguyen Thi Giang Street and teaching mathematics at several high schools, Mr. Vinh Linh was the speaker for the leftist lady Mrs. Phan Chu Trinh. He was captured and sent to the Thanh Binh Center of Strategist Interrogation after he had gone into the jungle to associate himself with the Communists. Personally, I was well aware of his political view and activities but did not have any information about his position in the antigovernment activities. Other teachers in the area did know his leftist venture as well. Mr. Vinh Linh was a prominent figure in the area. His leftist involvements were obvious to the government security agencies and to the public. He participated in several public antigovernment demonstrations.

Mr. Vinh Linh and I were close friends. He was my mentor on my first days in Da Nang. I chose him to be the godfather of my first son. Before he got deeply involved in leftist activities, his fellow teachers and I used to spend weekend nights at his residence on the second floor of his sister's spacious two-story building. His father and his sister occupied the first floor.

I did not share his political views but had a very close relationship with him and his relatives. We respected each other. Mr. Vinh Linh never attempted to talk other teachers into joining his political side. He subscribed to the French periodical "Planet" and maybe because of the periodical's political point of view he was considered pro-French and anti-American. At some time he intended to join the religious congregation of Little Brothers of Charles de Foucauld in Africa. When he was kept at the Thanh Binh Center of Strategist Interrogation, his friends, fellow teachers, and I did help him by bringing food and cigarettes. He had a frail body but was a very heavy smoker.

Once Da Nang fell to the Communists, Mr. Vinh Linh was sung as a hero. He became a typical figure mainly because he was a Catholic, an intellectual, a prominent teacher, a revolutionary figure, and a political prisoner. He became the chairman of the local group of Ho Chi Minh Communist Youths and a delegate at the National Congress.

I had no personal knowledge of the other educator, but his case was well known in the Da Nang political circles. Mr. Xuan Nguyen was a teacher at Phan Thanh Gian High. He was a declared Communist. The head of the secret police department at Da Nang police headquarters took him into custody. It was rumored that Mr. Xuan offered his own daughter to the head of the department. In return, the latter released Mr. Xuan from jail. Central Police Headquarters in Saigon subsequently sent a special delegation to remove the head of the secret police branch from his post and bring him to Saigon for disciplinary action.

Most city dwellers were aware of the antigovernmental activities of the two above-mentioned teachers, of their supporters and their arrests. The unknown lady who accused me in the people's court session could not cite the name of any student being disciplined as a result of my own activities. Vague accusations did not enchant the southern listeners. If she knew the names of the two well-known teachers mentioned above, the lady accuser might have avoided naming them in her accusation to avoid the possible reverse effect. Her vague accusation did not impress our impartial audience. I doubted if the sturdy ingenuous lady who dared to stand up for me in the people's tribunal had any knowledge of these two teachers or of my relationship with them.

Nobody knew who the advocating youth was. He might not be one of my former students. He stated he was one of the oratory contestants. Students from tens of local high schools, public and private, competed in each yearly contest. I remembered the case the youth brought up but could not recall the name of the eloquent student.

My Le found out easily that the advocate lady of mine was Mrs. Muoi, a local vermicelli maker. She lived two houses away from grandma's home. Grandma, My Le, myself, and sometimes my little daughter bought fresh vermicelli from her home shop almost every morning to feed ourselves.

The unknown youth, Mrs. Muoi, and the backing crowd saved me from the death verdict of the people's tribunal. Thanks to God and thanks to our good neighbors. After two failed sessions, the people's court was not held any more in my area. I was acquitted, but I knew my misery would not end there.

6. Lessons to learn

Before being established as an independent administrative entity directly under the former central government of the Republic, Da Nang City was part of the Quang Nam Province. Surrounded by such districts of Quang Nam Province as Hoa Vang, Hoa Khanh, and Dien Ban, the late autonomously established City of Da Nang consisted of three districts of its own. First District covered the downtown along the right bank of the Han River. Second District stretched northward alongside the Bay as far as the junction of National Highway One. The less developed Third District lay from the left bank of the Han River to the eastern beach. Famous Da Nang resorts such as Marble Mountain, Tien Sha Harbor, and My Khe Beach all lie along the eastern periphery of what was once the Third District.

Though I had lived in Tam Toa in the Second District for more than ten years, I had not taken time to explore the many surrounding districts of the Quang Nam Province. I did have a memorable visit to the ancient town of Hoi An. That was where my love life with My Le blossomed to fruition. I had paid pilgrimage to Tra Kieu where St. Mary was believed to have appeared during the persecution of the Catholic faithful in the nineteenth century.

My Le and I had climbed several times up the Marble Mountain where giant statues of Buddha were set in splendid stalactite grottos hundreds of meters above sea level. However, I had not ventured far in rural sectors of Quang Nam Province. My Le might have had more experiences of the province than I did. Thankfully, the Communist liberators had provided me with the time and opportunity to know some deserted parts of remote countryside within the province.

As I had suspected, within about a week after my second session of people's court had failed, I was summoned to attend the out-of-city reeducational sessions.

Spotted with several newly built wooden sheds surrounding a wide open meeting ground in the center, the brainwashing camp I attended was established in a wasteland on a remote hillside in Hoa Vang District. The lonely sheds were the only structures that could be seen in the immense barren hilly field. No sign of any residences or villages for miles around. There were no big trees. The wasteland was fertile enough to have living big trees; why none were around was a mystery.

The brainwashing sheds were large enough to house thousands of interns at a time. It was an open camp. There was no encircling fence, but grayish indigo plants as far as the horizon. If anyone was wandering around the indigo hills he would be well exposed. The low-growing indigo plants could not hide any moving human or animal. It was springtime. The pink indigo blossoms released a subtle aroma in the breezy air in the early sunlight. The rural landscape looked so calm and peaceful under the bluish firmament.

Foreign visitors might mistake the camp for a retreat sanctuary. It was but a brainwashing center where I was among its interns. When I was hauled to the camp, there were plenty of detainees who might have arrived weeks or months ahead of me. I did not know what My Le had put in the small bag she insisted I carry along. Of course, neither My Le nor any other wife of a brainwashed puppet could pack enough basic necessities for her beloved one for years of use in reeducation camp. The first question in my mind upon reaching the camp was of the length of the concentration term. Our liberators had previously told the whole country that the training class was but a three-to-ten-day session. It ended up being an indefinite jail term for many. I kept my faint hope for a short-term training. However, I had prepared my mind for a long stretch in penitentiary or even a lifetime term away from my family and the rest of the world.

We new interns had no way to know the number of guards and reeducators in the camp. No uniform personnel. We only recognized a couple of the camp brainwashers based on their normal appearances or on the one-to-one working sessions. The attendees of the open camp were not required to wear prison uniform either. Everyone was in his or her daily outfit. And so were the camp personnel. That was the way for the concentration-camp personnel to mingle with the detainees without being easily detected.

The first thing the reeducation interns had to do over and over every single morning from the first day at camp was to rewrite their confessions. By being rewritten repeatedly the submitted confessions of an individual could be compared against each other to reveal to the investigators any inconsistencies. From some negligently erratic discrepancies, the investigator could debunk critical details that the detainee had tried but failed to cunningly hide. The investigator could accordingly go an extra length into exploitation to apply severe sanctions.

Besides a long list of names of direct and distant relatives, their addresses and professions, each detainee was requested to write down the name of person or persons who knew or witnessed whatever the detainee was confessing, as well as the time and location an event happened.

After the written confession of the day was submitted, targeted detainees were to work individually with a camp officer on his or her newly submitted confession. Interrogators focused on some details that the interrogators wanted the detainees to expand on and provide more details. Questions were also directed so the person under investigation might accuse or reveal something about one or more blacklisted detainees from whom the interrogators wanted to extract information. To safeguard themselves in the hope of being released sooner, some detainees accused other detainees of factual or fabricated antirevolutionary crimes. The accused detainees were taken from the open camp to an outcast one. The accuser might or might not be freed as expected. Camp management might keep those who stabbed their co-inhabitants in the back as useful tools for further detection of the ill intentions of other camp interns.

Around noontime, some blacklisted individuals were called to have their written confessions read on the loudspeakers in front of the assembled detainees at the open meeting ground under the burning sun. Mingled in the audience, camp personnel posing as camp detainees stopped the reading every now and then to shout slogans such as "Down with puppet regime!" and "Down with antirevolutionary puppets!" The listeners had to shout in their loudest voice "Down! Down! Down!"

in response to the exhortations. Seeing what had been happening, I anticipated that I could be called someday to read my confession to the public. It was better to be prepared in advance for such a possibility.

Among the reeducation interns were all types of society members: teachers, writers, singers, students, physicians, technicians, parish council members, religious leaders, low-ranking southern military and police personnel, old government employees, social workers, business owners, street vendors, local notables, retirees, people who had joined the Viet Minh movement in the '50s and then defected, refugees who had fled North Vietnam in 1954, former workers for the French colonization, members of political parties in South Vietnam, and blacklisted people, to name some of the long list of categories.

It was a sunny spring day one week into the reeducation term. What I had anticipated actually happened.

A platform about the height of a standing person was set up in front of the open meeting ground. I was called up to the platform and given my own personal confession to read in front of the whole camp assembly. With foresight, I had composed my confession the way that it might be more beneficial to me and somehow interesting to the audience. Besides long insignificant details of my teaching career and my service time at the local police headquarters, I intentionally focused my confessions on two main topics.

The first focal point was the pride of being a Vietnamese. I clearly described two incidents I had experienced. During my first year at the University of Hue, I studied English literature in a class taught by an American professor by the name of Izzo. He might have been in his late forties, and he had a slim but athletic built. I did not know which state in the US he came from. Dr. Izzo and his wife drove six hundred miles every weekend from Hue to swim at the southern Vung Tau resort. Being so proud of our famous Perfume River, we young students of the newly established Republic of Vietnam once asked Dr. Izzo:

"Why do you have to drive a thousand kilometers to Vung Tau to swim? Is it that you don't like our Perfume River?"

Instead of giving a verbal response, Dr. Izzo covered his nose with a mocking attitude. His sarcasm hurt our pride so much that the experience was never out of my mind. Later on, whenever I recalled the unpleasant memory of Mr. Izzo's response, I could not help thinking of the Perfume River as an open public toilet visited by the residents of the citadel of Hue early every morning. That was the shameful image the people of the imperial citadel had created of its famous Perfume River in the perception of foreigners.

Another incident had left an inerasable imprint in my memory. In the 1960s, the song "Borders on a Rainy Afternoon," composed by Nguyen Van Dong, was a big hit. It once was sung by artist Tran on a Canadian radio station. When asked by the Canadian newsman, "Mr. Tran, could you please disclose your nationality?" the singer sidestepped.

"I am a Montagnard," Tran responded.

It was shameful that, instead of proudly professing to the whole world that he was a Vietnamese performer, he sidestepped to state incorrectly that he was an ethnic minority from the highland. The singer's answer maimed the pride of his Vietnamese fans.

The second focal point was a daring confession. As I mentioned previously, when I was asked by one of my students, "If the Communists come, what will happen?" I clearly stated that "for my generation, we may get each a terminal shot or be put in reeducation camp; for your generation, you may be soldiers on the Laotian or Cambodian front lines for the United Indochina Plan."

When publicly reasserting this professed conviction on the brainwashing podium, I was thinking that my opinion must have been reported to the Communist police prior to my brainwashing session. Publicly reiterating this political view while being actually reeducated, in my calculation, had multiple purposes: to confess my previous antirevolutionary point of view, affirm the truth of my statement, and establish the authenticity of my confession.

The audience stayed mostly silent as they listened to my confession. I could not guess the intention of the camp faculty in letting me read my declaration to the audience. However, I could see the audience was amazed at my audacity.

Part of the brainwashing activities was manual labor. Camp interns were puppets who, in the past, earned their living not by their own labor but by exploiting the labor of others. Our liberators said so. Now the revolutionary catchword was that "Labor is Glory."

When I came to the camp, some previous group of detainees had tilled the soil in an area half an hour's walk from the camp. Cassava had been planted in elevated rows and was about to germinate. Some shoots had emerged, a couple of fresh green leaves among wild grass. Our group was assigned the tasks of weeding and filling the rows with more dust to help the new sprouts develop.

Camp management carried out the same procedure the jungle fighters had followed for years during war time. Once, when a jungle fighter group had a temporary stop on their southward path along the Ho Chi Minh trail, they cleared the rocky piece of wasteland to grow sweet cassava. When the next group of jungle fighters came to the area, they had fresh cassava roots to pull up for a little extra nourishment. Cassava roots were not delicious. However, they were still good to add to the dried food the fighters carried on their long way southwards, months away from their logistical supply. Cassava might keep growing for years without care.

Unfortunately, after taking control of the whole country, economic strategists did not change their production strategy to peacetime policy. Vast areas of the uncultivated fatherland—such as thousands of square miles surrounding the concentration camp—were not, because of their unfavorable soil condition, contributing much in the nationwide plan of food production. Strategists should have been able to develop them into mass plantations of industrial plants such as black pepper, coffee, orange, fruit to be canned, rubber trees or the like, instead of cassava. Grown on tiny pieces of land, cassava did not serve any large-scale postwar purposes. Neither was cassava a primary ingredient of our Vietnamese meals. Most of all, cassava had no significant export revenues in the economic long-term strategy. It would be better to liberate our poor fellow citizens from the antiquated ways of small-scale production into an upscale way of doing business to rebuild the country.

Unfortunately, freshly out of the jungle, our new leadership had no long-term vision into the economic future of the country. Irrational piecemeal measures were implemented. Flower beds along city streets were dug up to plant vegetables. Hogs and pigs were tended even in offices and on the floors of multistory buildings. As they had for years in the North, the leadership urged people in the newly liberated regions to practice those ill-considered activities for 'production increases.'

Our assigned work on the cassava field was not that hard, except there were no tools. But we knew the rule: You should not complain.

The revolutionary motto said, "Our hands are omnipotent." Renovated puppets should know how to carry out this slogan in labor.

Exposure to the spring sun and heat for more than eight hours without refreshing water was a real torment. Using your bare hands to till the gravel soil was really an added torture, especially for city dwellers. It was possible that the camp management did not aim much at the cassava outcome. Their purpose was rather to impose hard labor and suffering onto the camp detainees as a type of punishment. Or was it a lifestyle improvement? Feeling that they were ill-treated, some camp detainees retaliated. They pulled up the sprouting cassavas or replanted them upside down to kill them.

Thank God that my reeducation session was only a short term. I was among the selected number of detainees to be released from the camp. As for those being held back, I did not know about their plights afterwards. In my view, the reeducation session I went through was but a screening mechanism. It was a clever way to weed out big fishes to send to remote and more rigid correction camps. My Le felt so relieved at seeing me back from my brainwashing term, a little bit thinner, dark skinned, hollow eyed, and with some grey hair.

The next Monday morning, I showed up at the local police station. I was the second person waiting on line in front of the office that morning. By the time the office door was opened, another four or five people were lining up behind. We came to show the police our release papers. Everyone was in an excited mood. Well brainwashed, we naively hoped that from now on the puppet hat would be removed from our heads and we would be leading a peaceful life among local residents, starting to contribute our efforts to a new era.

In the narrow, asphyxiating reception room equipped with a rough wooden table and two stools on opposite sides of the table, the head of the police station appeared. One person at a time, we were signaled to step into the room.

On my turn, I went in and started introducing myself.

"I knew who you are." The policeman stopped me short. Without showing me to the stool or asking my identity, he verbally overwhelmed me with disciplinary orders without showing me any written document.

"You're home-arrested."

His abrupt statement startled me. All my hope for a peaceful life was gone.

"You have no citizenship. You'll be under the supervision of Mr. Thai. Every Monday morning you must submit a written confession."

I was stunned, hearing the deluge of penalties. I found a gap in his long orders to insert a question:

"Sir, what is the confession about?"

"You confess what you've done during a week: whom you've met, what you've talked about, what type of labor you've achieved to implement the 'Labor is Glorious' policy."

"Sir! How long will my home-arrest term be?" I asked.

"No specified term. It depends."

"Sir. How come? It depends on what?"

"On your degree of Good Labor and self reeducation," was the police head's cold, equivocal reply.

"Should I see you here every Monday?"

"No. Either Mr. Thai or Mr. Tuong will be available at the village office any time any day to directly deal with you. They'll have a close watch on you."

"Any other information that I need to know?" I asked, while I was thinking of my dark future as an indefinite prisoner in my hometown.

"I've told you. You have no citizenship. You're home-arrested. You cannot vote. You cannot sell your house. Your properties are under state management. Your children are not eligible for either higher education or government jobs." The police head painted a darker future not only for me but even for my children.

"How about if my home-arrest sentence is released and my citizenship regained?"

"You're a puppet. You're antirevolutionary," the police head clearly dictated. "Thanks to the regime's clemency that you're spared from death. Your children can never be eligible for higher education or government jobs."

7. Fish in a bowl

TamToa hamlet in Da Nang City had about two to three hundred families before 1975. Most of the homes were lying along a half mile of the Tran Cao Van Street. Walking at his leisure into the hamlet from downtown, a visitor would first see grandma's home on his right hand side along the bank of a small murmuring stream. On his left the Tam Toa Market stretched to the railway. Continuing his walk along the street with an observant eye, the pedestrian would see narrow lanes stretching parallel from the main street down toward the beach on the right hand side and up to the railway on the left. Small houses, hastily built for refugee settlement since the early days of 1954, lined up on both sides of every lane. The police station was located on the left side of the road, at the other end of the refugee settlement. The local police station took control of both Tam Thuan and Ha Khe wards. Two policemen, Mr. Thai and Mr. Tuong, directly supervised the small Tam Toa section.

Policeman Thai was a young and patronizing speaker who treated everyone, young or old, as a baby. I was put directly under the supervision of Mr. Thai. Policeman Tuong had a more restricted behavior. Supervised by two uniformed policemen, no meaningless activity of mine could escape their scrutiny.

Residents of any village in the newly liberated region were grouped into three main designated classes: elderly, mothers and sisters, and workers. I was banded into the local worker class. At least once every other week, at night, Mr. Thai gathered the residents under his supervised realm to a designated home for a reeducational session. Mr. Thai was about twenty-five-plus years old. His heavy accent told us he was from Quang Nam Province. He might have freshly become a policeman only after the fall of Da Nang. Nobody thought he was a well-trained officer. Beside the learn-by-heart versions of propaganda that we repeatedly heard from loudspeakers and from every other reeducator, in every meeting Mr. Thai always yelled at the gathered people, young and old, over meaningless details.

A lady by the name of Vinh was living in a household at the other end of the two-hundred-yard-long lane leading to our beach home. Since the fall of the Republic, Ms. Vinh had engaged in the retail trade of textile material on the black market. North Vietnam during the war was much underdeveloped. All males and females of labor-force age were drafted and sent to the southern front. Production was puny. Distribution was restricted. Cloth, food, and other household items could be purchased only in controlled yearly rations through government distribution stores. After 1975, merchandise from the South was in very high demand in the North. Commodities from the South earned a high price if they were sold in the northern part of the country. North Vietnam was a perfect black market for retail traders to make money. Ms. Vinh was one of the opportunists who risked venturing to the lucrative northern market.

Once, being away from home for many days in a row, Ms. Vinh missed a group reeducational session held by policeman Thai. Upon returning from the trading trip, Ms. Vinh came to the next nightly meeting. The previous illegal absence of the lady trader became the main topic of the meeting. Mr. Thai loudly and lengthily reprimanded her. The audience grew vexed by Mr. Thai's endless harsh words but did not want to speak up against the fiery policeman.

In the audience was Mr. Kinh, a poor handy worker who lived in poverty with his wife and two little children in a tiny shanty on the rim of the canal. His wife earned some extra money to support her family by putting up a small chair and a trestle table in an open space at a corner of the local market and giving people facials and manicures. Under the rain of insulting words from Mr. Thai, Mr. Kinh stood up from the audience and obtained Mr. Thai's permission to contribute his rebuke:

"Dear Ms. Vinh, I don't know whether your fabric trading was reprovable. However, it's owing to your past absence that today all of us here, many of whom are as old as our venerable parents, are excessively reviled. Ms. Vinh, that's mainly your fault."

On top of weekly brainwashing sessions by Mr. Thai, once in a while local puppet people were gathered at the open space of the market, also at nighttime, so the district police chief, Maj. Dinh, could give the brainwashing lecture. Under the dim light of a lonely yellowish low-voltage bulb, the vast area was immersed in darkness. Male and female, young or old, participants squatted on the ground. The lengthy exhortations praising Communism blended with the murmur of water flowing in a nearby stream and lulled the listeners into drowsiness. Reiterating an endless laudation of the invincible revolution, the lecturer kept paying tribute to the super-leadership of the peak intellectuals of the party who had defeated French and American neo-colonialism. Listeners were startled when the major suddenly raised his voice to declare, "Puppets! Listen! The educational goal of our regime is to teach your children to hate you."

Pausing for his audience's attention, the major loudly announced, "I repeat: we teach your children to hate you! They'll point at you to say, 'It's because of you, puppet people. It's because you served the antirevolutionary regime that we, your children, are not eligible for higher education, for government employment. Because of you that we cannot be good grandchildren of Uncle Ho. Because of you that we cannot be first-class citizens. Parents, we hate you!'"

Unwilling to entrust little Ky Nam to the party that would teach him to hate his parents, My Le brought Ky Nam to the home of the St. Vincent de Paul Sisters next to the parish church for his first steps in reading and writing. He was too young and innocent to recognize the hardship of the new life. The Sisters were not allowed to teach at the former parochial school, which had been nationalized. Hired to give private guidance, the Sisters assigned Ky Nam just a few alphabets to write a day. However, Ky Nam was more playful than studious learning, and by the end of each session Ky Nam often had not finished the assignment. The Sisters kept him from going home as long as he has not finished the assigned letters. After her school day, Ky Nam's big sister Huong Giang came to accompany him home. Huong Giang could not wait for him to complete his assigned task. She sneaked in to write the remainder of alphabets so Ky Nam was able to hand it in to the Sisters and go home. Later on, little Ky Nam attended a tutoring class led by a young beauty, Ms. Hien, at a secluded evacuated home in our hamlet. In Vietnamese the word Hien rhymes with Tien, which means *money*. In his childish innocence, Ky Nam kiddingly greeted the lovely girl-tutor any time he saw her around by singing a verse he had made up that, translated, said *Ms. Hien steals money*. The meek young lady responded with a cordial gesture and a glad acceptance.

Nhi Ha, six years old at the time, was attending first grade at the local grammar school. Though too young to understand it, he seemed to be somehow sensitive to the ominous political atmosphere and to the hardship everyone went through. He displayed a quiet behavior most of the time. Having a very nice voice, he was a lead singer in the church's young children's choir. Because of the fall of Da Nang City and the closing of Sacred Heart Elementary school, Nhi Ha had to give up the piano lessons he loved much and performed so artistically.

After the Sacred Heart School was not allowed to run, our nine-year-old Huong Giang attended fourth grade at the nearby Dao Duy Tu Elementary. The school was less than two miles from our home. On her way to school, besides school books and pen, she carried along a broom. At the end of the school day she joined her classmates in sweeping the school yard and the main road in front of the school. It was socialist labor for youngest generation.

Once Huong Giang got home after the school day, I accompanied her on her daily trip around all corners of the hamlet. She was searching for and collecting waste plastic bags to contribute to the mandatory recycle project at school the next day. My little girl had to go as far as to the next village, to the beach, to the local market ground, along the railway, even to the graveyard. With a special handmade tool she raked the sandy ground or mounds of waste to get several pieces. Many kids from her school and from neighboring villages had to do the same thing. As a result, even with my help there was not much discarded synthetic material available for her to collect to meet the set quota. It hurt me deeply to see tears running down her cheeks when she thought of the biting words of the chief student of her class, and the bad grade plus the insulting words from the homeroom teacher for having failed the class in the project contest. Witty and bombastic in debate, Huong Giang excelled academically. Young but having a high sense of collective responsibility, she worked hard educationally and companionably to bring her class to a high pride in its competitive social activities.

On a sunny day of March 1977, the school management sent people to fetch me up to the school. I was shown to the office of the school principal, where the principal, his deputy (who was the party secretary of the school), and a female teacher (whom I did not know) were assembled. The principal, with a resentful look, told me, "Your daughter was such an arrogant pupil."

"Dear sirs and madam, I think she is an intelligent student. Can you tell me what happened?" I said.

"Your daughter denied the teacher's teaching," the principal replied.

"Did she fail any assignment?"

"No." The principal showed his impatience by jumping briskly into details: "When the teacher lectured that human ancestors were primates, your daughter contradicted the teacher, saying, 'Monkeys were only your own forefathers, not mine. Mine were Adam and Eve.' You'd better take her home to reeducate her."

"To my knowledge, I think students can express their opinions. It's up to the teacher to prove which statement is the solid reality."

The party secretary of the school, who so far had not commented, solemnly told me, "Due to her obstinate behavior, your daughter won't be given the title of an 'Uncle Ho's Good Child.' You should know how bad it is not to be an Uncle Ho's Good Child."

"I know, Sir."

My Le and I knew the personality of our little daughter. She was not yet a teenager; however, she viewed things in an intellectual way. She had inherited the directness of her mom's character, which made her stand up without hesitation against whatever she thought incorrect. We could not blame her for such frankness and integrity. She was encouraged to behave honestly and intrepidly. She might not be able to estimate the consequences of her audacious actions. It would not be good for us to teach her to sidestep from the truth or subdue herself to the lies for fear of the possible detrimental consequences.

And she did the same again. I was called up to see the school's management about a month later.

"Sirs, what was the matter with my daughter?"

"When the teacher read from the history book, do you know what your daughter did?"

"I'm sorry, I don't know."

"The history book recorded a total of 4,181 airplanes of American invaders being shot down by the revolutionary forces. Among them there were 68 B-52s. Your daughter argued that all but one were only paper planes!"

"She's wrong, dead wrong, to say that just one single plane has been shot down," I said.

"She's a student and she didn't listen to the teacher and the history. What else can she be?"

"She's too young to do research to confirm what she thought to be right or wrong about the number the teacher said. She just expressed what she spontaneously thought of. The teacher had better provide her with convincing solid proofs."

"What do you mean by solid proof? Whatever was written in the book is the proof."

"Sir, I didn't mean the teacher has to provide evidence to prove every one of the 4,181 cases. Just give details of two or more cases of downed planes to show my daughter's statement was dead wrong."

"You're not here to argue. Your daughter won't be allowed to be in the rank of Red Scarf Young Children. You should educate your stubborn child." The party head dictated the punitive measure.

Right after the 1964 USS *Maddox* incident in the Gulf of Tonkin, Lt. (jg) Everett Alvarez was ordered to attack Hon Gai. His A-4C Skyhawk was the first American airplane shot down in North Vietnam. Lt. Cdr. John S. McCain and Col. Bill Spark were other well-known pilots shot down in North Vietnam in 1967. I knew a B-52G bomber was shot down on December 27, 1972, in Bac Ninh. But it was not true that 68 B-52 Stratofortress bombers had been downed. We, the residents of Da Nang City, knew that another damaged B-52 had landed at our Da Nang Air Base for repair prior to going back to Utapao Airfield in Thailand.

Those distinctive occurrences were kind of milestones in the Vietnam War. Most of us were well aware of these historic events. A history teacher should know them. It would not be hard for an educator with an open mind and a wish to straighten the erroneous thinking of his pupil to refer to such prominent facts, at least to show the pupil there was more than one plane downed. Reporting to the school party leaders for punitive action only put an extra emphasis on the questionable figures cited in the history book.

I did not know the exact number, but I was well aware that more than a single US warplane had been shot down in North Vietnam during the Vietnam War. However, it was but an obvious exaggeration to say the number of downed planes was 4,181, as it has been written in the history books. The official number of 4,181 US downed airplanes, recorded in the Communist Vietnamese documents (and since distributed online), was simply a boast. The Vietnamese Communist sources also exaggerated the number of downed B-52 bombers. Some of their sources said 68, others bragged of up to 88. According to American statistics, 10 out of 30 damaged B-52 bombers were actually downed in combat missions over North Vietnam. The total count of fixed-wing aircraft and helicopters damaged in the whole Vietnam War, not just in North Vietnam, might amount to a number in the neighborhood of the mentioned figures. By one estimate, 1,400 US warplanes were shot down in North Vietnam between 1965 and 1968.[20]

During wartime, shooting each other to death is, unfortunately, a traumatic action that warring sides have to take. Using exaggerated propaganda to win people's minds during wartime is an understandable and inevitable tactic. However, once peace is restored, killing each other is a crime. Using chimerical brags to write the history and educational materials is synonymous with a disrespect of truth and human intelligence, if not an ethical crime.

My daughter could not know the exact number of downed airplanes but knew quite well that the statistics recorded in the Communist history books were an intended falsification and a willful disregard of history and human intelligence.

The propagandists of the system did not hesitate to rant against reality with their bogus heroic stories to deceive credulous minds. Some of the made-up stories were unintelligent to the point they were even against basic laws of physics. One Communist writer—Mr. Tu Anh Tran Bach Dang, if I remember correctly—has written that on the night of December 28, 1972, Communist pilot Vu Xuan Thieu of the Lam Son crew hid his MiG-21 jet fighter in the clouds on high of the Thanh Hoa sky waiting for the coming of the US flying corps of B-52 bombers. When he spotted a B-52, pilot Thieu fired two missiles but only caused light damage. He then exited his hiding place and hurled his MiG-21 into the B-52 to destroy both his own plane and the Stratofortress. Could a MiG hold itself hidden motionlessly in a piece of cloud to wait?

Huong Giang was strongly against the distortion of physical and historical facts and the counterfeit claims, especially in the realm of education, that she had stood up. In my own view, I felt so depressed that the younger generation was being coached with lies over truth.

In Vietnamese Communist society, in order to advance up the social ladder, the first step was to become one of Uncle Ho's Good Grandchildren, a status marked with a red neckerchief. The next step was to become a member of Ho Chi Minh Communist Youth Union, and finally a Communist Party member.

Being the offspring of a puppet father, my children were not eligible to receive higher education, to hold government jobs, to advance into social positions. We knew that. Reeducation taught us so. Furthermore, none of my family members wanted to be a Communist Party member either. As a result, being stripped of the title of a Grandchild of Uncle Ho and becoming ineligible to wear a red neckerchief did not mean anything to me or my children at all. It might make my daughter stand out from the crowd and have an undeniably negative effect on her future in the Communist environment.

After the fall of our Republic of Vietnam into the Communists' grip, I had muttered silently in my heart to accept the hopeless situation and to carry out my possible contributions for the best for my poor fellow countrymen and women and my children's generation. Now reeducation taught me and my fellow puppets there was no future for our offspring in the new society. The future of our young generation was sealed off from opportunities of higher advancement. My Le was demoted from her technical profession to an unwanted job as a cook, and suffered with ill-treatment and hard labor. A puppet, I was indefinitely stripped of citizenship, home-arrested, and put under strict supervision by the local police. Our family members were among the puppets. The total impasse fueled a reluctant compulsion in our fellow countrymen to look for a new path for the future of their families.

At the end of the school year my daughter was academically rated the first of her class, but she was stripped of the school award.

8. Household

More than a year had passed since our city residents gave themselves up to the liberators. The mental wound somehow abated. After initial horrors, people resigned themselves to their fates. Everyone did their best to adjust their chances to live on in the new situation.

The natural world did not change, however. Spring came, followed by summer. Fall arrived, and the cold days of winter succeeded afterwards. The four seasons kept going on their normal cycles. Time is a sedative. Initial terrified feelings turned progressively to subdued attitudes. Family members gradually got used to the absence of their beloved relatives. Younger generations familiarized themselves with leading a deprived lifestyle. Schoolchildren deserted from classrooms to venture in labor, to survive. Former home owners had a dejected stance when they passed by their old homes, which were now occupied by strangers. Weekly brainwashing sessions turned out to be routines. Everyone knew by heart the same repeated brainwashing lessons given over such a long time. Liberation, independence, freedom, reeducation, brainwashing, probation—all those new words in everyday jargon sounded more and more as if they were interchangeable synonyms. Military marching rhythms blaring daily from loudspeakers at street corners stopped bothering villagers.

Bells in temples and churches were not allowed to ring. It was to prevent people from being woken up early. That was to avoid detrimental effects on the residents' strength for their daily labors.

Life went on its way. The majority of people, totally absorbed in daily survival chores, no longer paid much attention to the changes in political platform and social livelihood. What people cared most about was what to eat that day and how to survive in the existing difficult circumstances. The term "future" disappeared from everyday vocabulary.

Liberated and brainwashed, puppet-southerners must be restructured to fit into the new life. Under the former reign of the defeated Republic of Vietnam, each of us southerners held an identification card. Everyone under the roof of a home was considered a family. After our southern families were liberated, the affectionate term *family* unfortunately disappeared from the language of the new society and from official documents. No more family. We were simply a group of people living under the same roof, or a *Household*.

Individually, each legal resident under the new society had to have a People's Proof Document ID card (PPD ID). Holding such a PPD card proved that the holder was a licensed human being. Denied a PPD ID, the poor individual was deprived of every human right. He or she became an illegal living creature.

To legitimize its existence, every household in our new society was required to apply for a Household Register (HR). There were three types of households: single member households, multiple member households, and business households. Only a person holding a PPD ID could be approved to be included in a household register and deemed eligible to stay in the area. Households having legal registers were provided with food ration cards. Only those with PPD ID cards were eligible for civil rights. Without a PPD card, a person was eligible neither for any ration card nor for any civil right.

Once the HR was issued, any member of the household who wanted to temporarily leave the home and stay in the residence of a relative or another household for any reason, even for a single night at a nearby site, the member had to obtain a written Temporary Absence Permit, or TAP, from the police. At the destination, the individual had to show his or her TAP and register at the local police station. Anyone found at another household without the TAP would be held at the police station for investigation and disciplinary action. The head of the household who sheltered a person who had no written TAP would also be disciplined.

Application for the HR must be submitted for approval by the police. While inspecting my HR application for approval, the policeman in charge looked at me with a questioning posture. Pointing to the names in the HR list, he asked, "Who are these strange names?"

"Huong Giang is my daughter. Nhi Ha and Ky Nam are my sons."

"Your children?" the policeman asked in an unsatisfied tone as he held up the HR.

"Yes. They are."

"Your children cannot be named that way!"

"Sir. What's the problem?" I asked, surprised by his statement.

"A female must have *Thi* as a middle name. *Van* must be the male middle name. Not anything else."

"I don't understand."

"Your daughter cannot be named Huong Giang. It must be *Thi* Giang. Your sons must be *Van* Ha, *Van* Nam. Understand?"

"But Uncle Ho's name is Ho *Chi* Minh, not Ho *Van* Minh."

Startled at my remark, the policeman answered with sophistry: "Uncle Ho is an exceptional person; he and only he can be named differently."

"How about Maj. Gen. Vo *Nguyen* Giap? He doesn't have *Van* in the middle," I persisted.

The policeman sternly uttered his ultimatum: "Either you change your children names as I've told you or your household registration is not granted. That's the rule."

There was no publicly stated regulation about how a person could be named. Whatever the police ordered was the law. That law might or might not be enforced anywhere else. It was particularly enforced here, maybe only by the involved policeman. Either I obeyed his order or I would be found guilty of resisting the order of the police. No one could help me out. There was no judicial power to protect me. The police dictated the rule; the police implemented what they dictated; and the police judged the execution of the rule and arbitrarily imposed whichever penalty they wished to bring to bear.

Not every household unit that applied was granted the register. Families listed in the four categories that had to go to the NEZ were categorically denied household registers. Without being listed in an HR, a person became an illegal resident. No Proof of People ID card was issued to an unauthorized person. Hence, no ration card given.

No citizenship approved. No civil rights. No schooling allowed for the children of an illegal puppet. The unlicensed inhabitant must be out of the household, out of his or her home if (s)he owns one. It did not matter whether the home was built or owned by the person who was denied a household register. Multiple reasons, many of them arbitrary, accounted for a household register being denied. People made illegal occupants by that measure were rounded up by security forces and transported to the NEZs. Allen Dawson, in his book, *55 Days: The Fall of Saigon*, reported that the government removed one million people from Saigon and set a target to expel another five hundred thousand.

Saigon, Nha Trang, Da Nang, and most of our southern metropolitan areas were then miserably flooded with such illegal residents. Either these unfortunate people ran away from their own homes to avoid being coerced to the NEZ, or they had fled the famine, diseases, and deadly conditions of those infamous New Economic Zones. Filthy slum huts sprang up along squalid alleys in the cities. Pot-bellied and wrinkle-skinned children were wandering and grubbing street garbage. Police hauled these ill-fated people onto their trucks and transported them back to the NEZ. A short time later, those ill-starred people reappeared at different poor locations in the same or other cities.

In the administrative system of the former Republic of Vietnam, each city, including the City of Da Nang, consisted of several districts. Each district had tens of neighborhoods. The neighborhoods were officially named *quarters* or *wards*. Each quarter/ward had an administrative office with a paid nominated head. Some quarters had a deputy head, some did not.

During the first years after April 1975, local administrative systems had not been changed significantly. The zoning and zone names might or might not have drastically changed. My family had been living in the former Tam Toa Ward. A new ward was formed after 1975 and named Tam Thuan. The new ward combined two former wards, Tam Toa and Thuan Thanh, into a single administrative unit. Mr. Phong, the former head of the ward, was sent to concentration camp for brainwashing. Mr. Thuy held the temporary position during the transition time. Mr. Kiem, renouncing his Catholic practices and assuming the unfriendly traits of a party cadre, was permanently installed as the new head with Mr. Dan his deputy.

Trying to overcome unwanted difficulties, My Le miserably held on to her paid health-care position. Despite discriminatory treatment, being reemployed in the new system was considered lucky. The employee was deemed a state official, not a puppet. He or she was eligible for a government salary and periodic special ration privileges. My Le tried with much mortification to keep the job. In the meantime, characterized as a puppet, I was dismissed from my teaching career, home-arrested, and left unemployed.

9. Cooperative

Another winter was over.

We had experienced some bad hurricanes. Typhoons and inundations were nothing new to our tropical region. The Vietnamese central stretch of narrow land we lived on was the most hit by seasonal disasters each year. We had long learned how to survive these episodes of inclement weather.

The atmospheric conditions of this winter were harsher than usual. For several days the lane leading to our beach home was flooded. Ocean water was up to our knees, around our garden. Our wooden home was swinging and shaking as the violent gusty winds roared through the surrounding willows. Massive waves rose and chased each other like wild elephants in a rumbling race. Luckily, our shaking home withstood the gales. No significant physical damage occurred. It took me days to do the aftermath cleanup. While we were isolated by the stormy weather, we had a couple of happy days without seeing the police around.

As a new spring came along with fresh, glorious sunny days, I had to find a way to earn some meager remuneration and to have something to put in my required weekly confession. The home-arrested puppet had to show the police that he was dutifully carrying out the government's Good Labor policy. Everyone was talking about cooperatives, the socialist mode of doing business. Several cooperatives were formed in my area.

After some hesitation, I followed what would be a turning point of my life; I chose to join the newly formed Rattan Weaving Cooperative. Most of the cooperative members, about ten of them, were the elders in the hamlet. The so-called cooperative did not meet any criteria as actually implemented in socialist collectivization norms. It was only a loose group of people who worked individually in the same profession to produce goods under a pseudo trademark. There were no bylaws regulating the activities of the group, no restricted membership, no management and supervision. Members were free to join and to leave the working group. The group was labeled a cooperative so it could sound socialist rather than capitalist.

I had no experience at all in handling rattan weaving and related chores. Simply relying on my handy skills, I first built the rattan weaving wooden frame, drilled lines of holes along four sides of the frame for mounting rattan strings, bought a sharp chisel and related equipment, purchased rattan, and started being a working co-op member. I learned by trial and error how to split a rattan into several strings, smooth them into good shapes, string them along the length of the wooden frame, and then knit the horizontal strings into weaved products.

The first empirical steps of the self-teaching process were hard. The sharp rattan strings and the chisel kept cutting into my fingers. It took me time to learn how to hold the knife the correct way to evenly smooth the rattan into equal strings without cutting them short. I did the job in my home, alone. No training was available. Table and chairs were removed so the materials and the wooden frame could occupy our breakfast area. The whole day I either squatted on the ground to split and smooth the rattan strings or curved my back around the frame to weave the products. The strings had to be woven taut. There was no product inspection. No co-op management. No work-point[21] voted and granted by management as in the real socialist labor model. It took me quite a while to finish a single product. I either sold my output to any clients I happened to find or submitted them together with the other members' products to the cooperative for wholesale. It was time-consuming to complete a ten feet by four feet piece of woven rattan mat. Not enough such pieces of mat were completed in a week to worry about how to get them sold. Hand-woven rattan mats could be made into multiple household items such as screens, chairs, baskets, hammocks, and so on. As I grew more skilled in the technique of smoothing and stringing rattan into woven products and our home became piled up with material garbage and waste, rattan became scarce and the market gradually declined. Our rattan cooperative step by step advanced to death's door and then died silently.

New types of cooperatives cropped up all around.

Motorized vehicles disappeared from the market and the roads. Gas was restricted and could be purchased only by ration card, which was available only to designated individuals. Riding a motorized vehicle was expensive because of the high price of gas. Moreover, it was held to be bourgeois in our new society. Bicycles became the affordable main mode of daily transportation.

In December 1976 the Vietnamese Fourth National Party Congress adopted the Second Five-Year Plan for the period 1976-1980 and defined its plan of building a socialist economy. With its limited government budget for 1976, amounting to US$2.5 billion, and prospective investments amounting to US$7.5 billion for the period between 1976 and 1980, the Vietnamese leaders claimed that the country could bypass the capitalist industrialization stage necessary to prepare for communism. The 1976-1980 Five-Year Plan set ambitious goals for the average annual growth rates for industry, agriculture, and national income. However, the plan set its sights on practically modest targets. The plan projected that each household at the end of the Five-Year Plan would have a bicycle and a thermos. Sensing the favorable direction given by the second Five-Year Plan, bicycle frame manufacturing cooperatives mushroomed everywhere in the South in response to anticipated high demands.

The former teacher who had failed in his rattan-weaving career now fearlessly jumped onto the promising new labor bandwagon. In the rattan cooperative, with a big, sharp chisel I had split and smoothed the rattan strings. Now, with a file, I learned how to bend myself over a rusted bicycle frame eight hours a day to smooth it into a shining shape.

This was a hard and unhealthy field of work. After laboring on the bicycle frames for a while, the rust and corrosion turned my fingernails into such a dirty, colorful, and rough shape. The rust and corrosion also turned a silent worker into a noisy fellow. His intermittent coughs could be heard at work, at home, and everywhere. One of my fellow teachers, Mr. Luong Hien Nguyen, former philosophy teacher at Phan Chu Trinh Public High, after being dismissed by the new government in 1975, joined another bicycle frame filing cooperative at a nearby ward. He died as a result of inhaling toxic dust from the corroded bicycle frames. I was afflicted with a severe cough, while my back and my arm muscles ached as well.

In the very early morning, before reporting to the bicycle frame cooperative, I got bags of bread from the nearby baker to deliver to various destinations on the outskirts of my beloved city. With a big sack full of hot French breads tied onto the back of the bike seat, I rode as far as Phuoc Tuong on National Highway 1 to deliver to a military barrack before dawn. In the fresh cool air of early dawn, the warmth from the bag of bread made the lone bike rider on the deserted road feel a little bit less chilly and dull.

On the seven-mile journey home, the hungry cyclist stopped by the intercity bus station and squatted next to a lady peddler to buy a squeeze of her cooked sticky rice. The first rays of a new day had not yet shown themselves on the eastern horizon. I sat on a nearby low stool in a corner of the station's yard, among a mixed group of people of all strata of society and devoured in a rush the sticky rice with some salty roasted sesame. As the sunlight started radiating and the bus station became noisier, I got choked up at the thought of my family's situation. I thought of My Le and our little children. Usually My Le went to work without eating the first meal of the day. Grandma might feed the kids each with a thrifty noodle cup before they started a new school day. My frugal breakfast done, I hastily reported to the bicycle frame cooperative. If I came late, the limited amount of frames might have been already assigned to other co-op members. Nothing would be left for me to work on that day.

Those hard labors filled up my weekly confessions. I submitted them to the police to show I had been a Good-Labor worker during the week. Hard work gradually chewed up time and health; however, it could not earn me enough money to support my family.

"Darling, I know you try to show the police you're laboring well," My Le murmured into my ear in the darkness one night. "Do you hear our dog's growling all night long?"

"Honey, I know," I confided. "The police are shadowing our home at night. Keep your voice down."

"We were in fish sauce processing before. I think we should start doing it again to earn a living," My Le suggested. "Give up your bicycle frame work. It's not healthy at all."

"I was thinking a lot about it. But we have several disadvantages I think it's hard for us to overcome," I replied to her proposition.

"Honey, are you worrying about money?" she asked.

"We've lost so much. Our bank deposits were wiped out because of the liberation. Group investment members ran away without paying us their shares. Uncle De Hoang fled overseas without returning to us the money we lent to him for his profitable investment. Looters hauled away most of our fish products and our family's valuable equipment. Our accumulated assets for many years dissipated in a couple of eventful days. Honey, you and I want to restart the profitable fish-related business. But it cannot be possible with only our bare hands. That's one of the big obstacles."

"I may have a solution," My Le surprised me by saying. "We could sell some of our remaining belongings. And I'll talk Mrs. Chau into redeeming the diamond she gave me as security for cash."

"You may ask Mrs. Chau. But don't have high hopes about it. Diamonds have lost their value lately, since everyone is trying to sell them to survive. Mrs. Chau may not want it back. As for selling our belongings, you know our scooter cannot be used. No gas available. If I ride it, the police will condemn me for leading a bourgeois existence against my home-arrest status. But we cannot sell it on the market either. The police won't allow us to sell valuable items. They've said our property was under state management. And there's another obstacle."

"What's that?" My Le asked. "I don't want to hear negative opinions."

"Honey, you have to consider this." I could not help looking into potential risks and letting her know. "To buy fishes, I would have to come to the beach to deal directly with fishermen. That would make the police think we were looking for a means of running away."

"But we have to do something." My Le was running out of patience. "You cannot let the rust eat up your fingers day after day. I don't want you to die of inhaling poisonous iron dust like your friend Luong Hien."

Thinking hard about the plan My Le suggested, I ventured into finding some way to implement her fish-processing suggestion. To have a legal cover, first I joined hands in founding the Seafood Processing Company Thanh Ha under the direction of a high ranking Communist Party member. The company was in the twin wards Thanh Khe and Ha

Khe. I did not contribute any share but my management skills and my fish-processing expertise. I served the company as a paid management employee.

Initially, I tested the waters with great care and fear. As an employee of the Thanh Ha Company, I assumed the responsibility of purchasing fishes at the Thanh Khe Seafood Buying Station (SFBS) where the fishing boats had their catches classified and weighed for proportional fuel rations. After a while, I realized that neither the police nor anyone else was taking any notice of my frequent contact with fishermen at the beach.

Realizing the favorable situation, I went around the hamlet, talked to people in the village who were actually running or were interested in fish-processing businesses, and invited them to meet at my home on the weekend. Mrs. Le, Ms. Vinh, Mr. Thanh and his wife, and several other villagers responded to my invitation.

"Dear friends, if the police come, please tell them we are getting together to form a co-op. I've mentioned to policeman Thai the purpose of tonight's get-together. I'll try to keep the meeting as short as possible," I began by reassuring them. Nobody said anything. I got into the focus of the gathering.

"Our family was in the fish sauce business for a long time. And so were most of you. We want to come back to the business. However, under the new Communist regime, individual ventures are condemned as the capitalist way of life. Individuals engaging in the same type of business activities must be working in a cooperative."

Seeing I had the attention of the attendees, I continued my opening speech: "In our village, there is a rattan cooperative, a bamboo-blind cooperative, a bicycle-frame-filing cooperative, and a bronze-casting cooperative. Now I suggest we'd better group ourselves into a local fish-processing cooperative."

"Does that mean we have to contribute capital and become shareholders?" Mr. Thanh, who was one of the dismissed teachers, posed the question.

"This is a cooperative, not a corporation."

"What's the difference?" Mr. Thanh asked.

I took the opportunity to explain to the whole gathering as I answered Mr. Thanh's question. "For the time being, everyone in a cooperative simply works on his or her own. Each individual may produce a greater or smaller amount of goods and may earn more or less from his or her product, independently. Cooperative members do not invest shares into a co-op as shareholders do in a corporation."

"Then what is the cooperative for?" another attendee asked, and I spelled out some more specific aspects of a co-op:

"Individuals cooperate with each other in sharing their expertise, in finding consumer markets, in privately lending capital, in reporting the outcome to the local business association. So, the local government has records of achievement to periodically report to the upper levels of government. Working in a cooperative is the way to prove a person is legitimately laboring to earn a living the socialist manner. Cooperative is the type of business this socialist government highly recommends."

My Le added her recommendation: "That's the government policy, and as far as it does not greatly interfere with our business, we'd better follow the policy."

With my imprecise presentation, the attendees might not get a full comprehension of the issue. There was no published guidance about cooperatives. The actual practice was elusive even in the thirty-year-old North Vietnamese Communist world. If the attendees kept asking me for specific details of the co-op organization, its management, powers, and limitations, I might not satisfy their inquiries with documented criteria as needed. The attendees got into heated debate. Some protested. Many defended the idea of forming a co-op. Fortunately no one asked for written co-op bylaws. The atmosphere of the discussion was getting very excited.

Calming people down, I said, "It seems to me that a cooperative should be formed. Before we come to the final decision, members of the fish-processing cooperative should be aware of the following details."

"Are those details going to be put in writing?" Mr. Thanh's wife interrupted.

"It's better that we submit some written paper about the cooperative, specifying its name, its scope, a list of its members, and the name of a cooperative representative," I said. "As far as I can, I'll try to make the paper simply an informal one that does not bind myself or any member to any specific commitment or financial liability. Is that fair enough?"

"Let's choose a name for the co-op," My Le said. Realizing that Mr. Thanh's wife had indirectly mentioned the thorny issue of co-op bylaws, My-Le tried to steer the discussion in another direction by stirring up everyone's mind with the suggestion that the group find a logo name.

"Does the name the 'Fish Processing Cooperative of Tam Thuan' sound good?" I caught the chance to advance my suggestion.

"How about 'Tam Thuan Seafood Cooperative' instead?" Mr. Thanh said.

"No. You should know that Seafood Cooperative has a much wider scope, which is not ours," I replied. "For example, we don't sail to the ocean to catch fish. We won't trade every kind of sea products, live, salted, or canned. We won't do farm-raising of fish. We won't perform every service a seafood company may do. For long term, we may in future. For the time being we'll do only the two jobs we're currently doing: fish sauce processing and shrimp paste processing. In short, it's a fish-processing business, not overall seafood business per se."

"Then let's go with the name 'Tam Thuan Fish Processing Co-op,'" recommended Mrs. Le, who lived on the same lane that led to our home.

"I vote for that," Mr. Thanh volunteered, and then added, "If there are no other suggestions, we should vote for that. Please raise your hand if you agree." Mr. Thanh counted the hands and declared, "We have an absolute majority to name our organization 'Tam Thuan Fish Processing Co-op.'"

I conveyed some more features of the new co-op. "Nominally, it's a cooperative with ten members or so. Practically, each individual works separately at his or her private shop using his or her own resources. Each one is responsible for the source of material, the quality of products, the consumption of the final commodities, and the management of his or her own profits."

Seeing a lady's hand raised, I asked, "Ms. Vinh, what's your question?"

"It seems to me you're a member of the Thanh Ha Seafood Products Company, aren't you?"

"Sister! Thanks for your question." Knowing the lingering obsession in some attendees' minds that might not be favorable to my position, I elucidated: "Let me take this occasion to clarify the issue. Thanh Ha Seafood Products was a company. Shareholders contributed capital to form the company. The company management consists of paid experts who may or may not be shareholders. Shareholders may or may not directly work in the company. Company profits are periodically distributed proportionally to the number of contributed shares."

"Are you a shareholder?" the same lady asked.

"No. I contributed no share to the company. I am but one of the company founders. I drafted the charter for the new company and its internal regulations. I contribute my fish-processing expertise. I am but a paid employee in the company's management team."

"Is there any conflict of interest by being a worker for a seafood company and a member of another fish-processing co-op?" somebody said, getting into deeper particulars.

"In Thanh Ha Company I'm a paid employee. I have officially worked for the company since I stopped working in rattan and bicycle frame cooperatives."

"A full-time job?" Somebody asked.

"It's an hourly paid position. You know, there's work when there are fishes. They won't pay me for sitting idle every day. I'm free to work a second job in my own time. There's no conflict of interest. The company is well aware of the fish-processing business of my family. Furthermore, we're well protected. Thanh Ha focuses its products on Classes II and III of seafood. My own business and our Tam Thuan co-op process mainly Class IV fishes."

"Why don't we make our cooperative into a company?"

"Brother Thanh! That's my dream!"

"Can you give us some details of your dream, which I am dreaming too? Please," Mr. Thanh insisted.

"That is beyond the scope of today's discussion. Let's chat later, among friends. OK? Anyone who's not interested may leave."

"Please. It may be interesting," some attendee insisted.

"I've been thinking deeply about a real seafood company in which we own our fishing fleet to catch selected types of fishes. I want to have our own farms to raise appropriate types of seafood for sustaining the business. I'm dreaming of having our own manufacturing plants for mass production. Our company would sign contracts to supply large quantities regularly to domestic and overseas customers. The company may have branches at multiple locations for specific operations. That's what I'm dreaming of. Doesn't that sound great?"

"That sounds wonderful," Mr. Thanh said. "Why haven't you carried it out?"

"My political status won't let me handle big projects for now. My property is under state management. Furthermore, if we build our own fishing fleet now, they'll say we plan to escape the country. Investing huge amounts of capital in big businesses at this time, when the state is constantly campaigning to destroy the bourgeois, would be similar to inserting our own heads into the capitalists' noose for strangulation. Does anyone of you want to venture into such situation?"

"Then how was Thanh Ha Seafood Company not seen as a capitalist venture?" Mr. Thanh kept luring me into further explanations.

"Brother Thanh! If I'm not mistaken, you're one of the Thanh Ha Company's shareholders, aren't you? You don't know its background, do you?"

"Don't know what? What do I have to know?"

"The main founder of the company, Mr. Nguyen Van Ba, is one of the high-ranking Communist Party members from the North. He is the umbrella covering the company. He has higher and bigger umbrellas to support his venture as well. Local government and party members back his endeavor. The head of local government and the party secretary are honorably sitting on the company's board of directors. Mr. Nguyen Van Ba invests no money. He was granted multiple shares as the president of the company. His main contribution was his seniority as a party member."

"Do you have any other information you want us to know?" Mr. Thanh queried.

"All of you are now members of our co-op. If anyone wants to stay out of the co-op, please say so. I would like to take this occasion to inform you of some political aspects of the business. These are not critical but interesting to know."

"What are these?"

"Brother Thanh, be patient. A company with shareholders and paid employees is the business model of capitalism. It's not socialist. Cooperation is the business policy of the Communist mode. Strictly speaking, in a co-op, members own everything. However, in reality everything—capital, labor, means of production, end products—must be governed by the co-op management."

"What does that mean?"

"That's the triple policy of People own, the Party leads, and the Government manages."

"Clarify please."

"OK. It's not easy to have a precise clarification. Let's take the example of a farming co-op. Specifically speaking, a member of the farming co-op owns the pond in his backyard; he owns and feeds the pigs he raises and the oxen in his cow-house. However, in order to sell the pigs or kill them for food, the member has to get the approval of the co-op management."

"Why?"

"Because the member owns but the co-op manages. A co-op member cannot salvage the duckweed in his backyard pond to sell without permission from the co-op management. Members work under the leadership of the cooperative board. The board gives members labor points and distributes necessities accordingly. Each member gets food and everything else based on the points he or she earned. That's how the member owns and the co-op manages. That's the socialist norm. All individual business styles must be wiped out to establish the collectivization."

"It's confusing," piped up an attendee who so far had stayed completely silent.

"Let's take this analogy. You spend your money to buy a car. You're the owner. However, the ownership certificate won't allow you to drive the car. Only a licensed driver can drive. The party is the sole licensed driver for the owner. The driver must drive according to the direction of the house manager. The Government is the exclusive manager of the owner. Does that make sense?"

"It sounds scary. Is it how our co-op will work?" Mr. Thanh voiced his concern, while the attendees sat in an uneasy silence.

"In the current context of ambiguities, the way our fish-processing co-op works does not strictly fall into the perfect socialist model. And nor do all the existing local cooperatives. There are no published regulations for co-op business plans in our liberated regions. They talked about cooperatives. Cooperatives have been formed everywhere, but I can say they're fake ones. Existing cooperations do not perfectly follow any socialist model. And neither does ours."

"Do you think, once the grip on the South becomes much tighter, the way the co-op is working will be changed?"

"I couldn't say yes or no definitely. Let's look at the real world. Cooperatives in the North brought negative results. Farmers killed their cattle and domestic animals. The harvest level declined badly. Co-op members gave up, deserted, or left the co-op to work individually. You all should know that I do not advocate going against the socialist way of doing business. We should just try to earn our living in a way the state does not prohibit."

"That doesn't sound good for long-term business." Ms. Suong, Mrs. Le's young daughter, who so far had followed all the discussion silently, expressed her concern.

"Young lady! You are looking toward the future. That's good. You and the younger generation should be aware of some social factors which may change the future direction of the socialist world."

"What are those factors? Could you give us some insights?" Ms. Suong went on, posing an interesting question.

"Let's look back a little bit in order to predict future trends. During the days the North was struggling to conquer our South, agricultural cooperatives in the North degraded so badly. The level of rice production declined miserably. Mr. Hoang Kim Ngoc, the then famous party secretary of the Vinh Phuc Province, fought hard for the liberation of his area farmers from the dogmatic theory of collectivization, to grant them the so-called 'household contract' model, which was a loosened mode of agricultural cooperatives. While avoiding being seen as private business, this type of venture was in fact a real individual model of production under the label of cooperation. Mr. Kim Ngoc was disciplined by the dogmatic central thinkers. Vinh Phuc Province was then integrated into Phu Tho province to become the new Vinh Phu. However, the Resolution of Mr. Kim Ngoc's provincial Committee brought wealth and prosperity to farmers. The production exceeded the target. Cooperatives from other provinces followed Mr. Kim Ngoc's lead, and the Central Party Committee quietly accepted the fact, though it was against their socialist principles. Mr. Le Thanh Nghi, chairman of the National Planning Commission, had to admit the impossibility of applying the economic laws of socialism. Cooperative somehow became nominal, and this is what we are now dealing with.

"Sorry for the long lecture," I continued, while the audience looked somehow lost. "The tension between theory and actual production is rather complex. The younger generation will have more opportunity to make improvements. For our older generation, we will be safe in doing what our Tam Thuan Cooperative is going to do."

Thus the Tam Thuan Fish Processing Co-op came into existence. The cooperative existed only on paper. In real life, nobody in the cooperative ever knew anything about the business of other members. Some of the co-op members did not get involved in fish processing at all. Co-op membership was but a kind of label to show that a member was working legally to earn his or her living. In practice, the free market was our everyday life. For my family, the Tam Thuan Fish Processing Co-op was a convenient front behind which we could run our business without getting into any trouble with the economic police.

Fish sauce processing used to be BaNgoai's expertise. My Le and I got involved in the business as a left-hand activity before the fall of our Republic. We lost so much fish sauce and shrimp paste during our failed attempt to evacuate our family from the besieged Da Nang City. To raise enough funds for restarting the business, My Le and I had to sell some of our belongings.

Before the fall of the Republic of Vietnam, Mrs. Chau, a resident of our hamlet and a close friend of My Le's younger sister, had invested in some type of national bond. Later on, Mrs. Chau pawned her bond certificate and a diamond with My Le in exchange for cash. After the fall of our Republic in 1975, bond certificates issued previously were but pieces of waste paper that had no face value under the new government.

My Le and I were in need of cash to restart our fish-processing business. My Le repeatedly asked Mrs. Chau to compensate her for the lost value of her bond certificate and to take back her diamond in return for cash. After the fall of Saigon in 1975, when everyone sold everything for survival, the price of diamonds deteriorated so much. Mrs. Chau categorically refused either to pay any money for the loss of her bond value or to redeem her pawned diamond. Desperate, My Le sold the pawned diamond on the black market to raise some funds.

After the 1975 fall of the South, people had lost their trust in the new monetary bank notes because of the uncertainty that resulted from repeated money exchanges and devaluations. Consequently everyone, poor or rich, invested in precious metals and diamonds. Not long after My Le had sold the diamond on the black market, the price of precious metals and diamonds increased with dizzying speed. Knowing that My Le was in the disadvantageous situation of being the wife of a home-arrested puppet husband, Mrs. Chau sued My Le for predatory lending. Mr. Kiem, head of Tam Thuan Ward, summoned My Le for a hearing at the local ward office.

At the hearing, Mr. Kiem did not let My Le present her case. Based simply on Mrs. Chau's one-sided charges, Mr. Kiem imposed a monetary penalty and punitive action on My Le for not returning the diamond to its owner.

Upon hearing the imposed penalty, Mr. Dan, the deputy head, intervened.

"Mr. Kiem, I suspect something was not clearly explained in the accusation. We must hear the case from both sides. Let me handle the case." Mr. Dan argued with Mr. Kiem, took over the case, and said to My Le, "Tell me your story, please."

"Sir. More than a year ago, with the intercession of my sister, Mrs. Chau pawned her bond certificate and a small diamond to borrow a sum of VN$50,000 from me. She promised that when the bond matured in May 1975, I would cash it and Mrs. Chau would compensate the shortfall in cash by redeeming her diamond. But when that time came, her bond certificate was not recognized by the bank anymore. And I lost money."

"Did you ever ask Mrs. Chau to redeem her diamond or to pay you? Or did Mrs. Chau pay you any interest?" Mr. Dan continued.

"Sir. No interest was ever paid." My Le went on to describe the situation to the deputy chief. "I asked Mrs. Chau to redeem her diamond several times. She didn't. My family desperately needed some money to survive. Mrs. Chau neither compensated the lost of the bond, nor agreed to redeem her small diamond, nor paid any interest at all. Nothing. The length of the lending term had long passed. I have lost money because of her invalidated bond certificate. I had to sell the diamond to have some money for living. Yet I'm still suffering a big loss because the price I got for her small diamond was not high enough."

"Mrs. Chau, you've heard Mrs. My Le's narrative. Do you have any argument against her statements?" the deputy chief asked. He waited for any response from Mrs. Chau and repeated his question again without getting any reply from the plaintiff.

"You didn't answer my question," he continued. "That means Mrs. My Le's statements are just and true. Your accusation is false."

He paused for the accuser's reaction, then resumed his statement upon hearing no word from Mrs. Chau:

"You cannot and will not claim anything from Mrs. My Le. I may fine you for perjury. If you behave responsibly, you should compensate Mrs. My Le for her loss. Go home."

10. New life

H*ow impossible it was*
For us to range over
The immensity of a vast ocean,
The fathomless depth of a river
And the sinister heart of the other.

Our Vietnamese ancestors often wondered about how to understand the hearts and minds of other people. Our forefathers thought it might be even more difficult to understand the obscurity of human hearts than to measure the profundity of the ocean. They expressed their surmise in those rustic verses. They then conjectured that long coexistence with a partner would reveal his true personality. They summarized their wisdom with an analogy in the following ode:

Staying up sleepless
Makes the restless night so long.
His hidden nature will expose best
When the guest stays over long.

We southerners had long heard of who the Communists were. We actually got to the whole truth only when we had lived long enough in the Communist world.

After the traumatic experience of 1975, we southerners learned the hard way to adjust our lives to somehow become accustomed to the new physical and mental difficulties.

During the first few months after our Republic fell, southerners were suffering tragically because of the hubris of the so-called 'thirtieth revolutionaries.' The latter were yesterday's scum of society who now, dressed up in yellow uniforms and eared hats, posed as revolutionary fighters or Liberation Army combatants. They went around every locality to impose intimidation and havoc on people. They got their 'thirtieth revolutionaries' label since they made themselves revolutionaries only on the last day of the Republic, the infamous Black April thirtieth.

Lacking enough police force to dip their hands down to every corner of the newly conquered social infrastructure, the new government turned a blind eye to the abuses of these thirtieth revolutionaries. The victors temporarily controlled the newly seized territory by the horrors the late-date rabble spread to every soul.

Once the northern conquerors had gained a full grip on the South, they implacably dissolved their political tool, the National Liberation Front of South Vietnam (NLF). Leaders of the NLF such as chairman Nguyen Huu Tho and armed forces general commander Tran Van Tra were uncompromisingly dethroned. Those thirtieth revolutionaries were then adamantly wiped out. Their reign was replaced by that of the Communist police.

Now the power grip was tight. The majority of antirevolutionary puppet people were rounded up in concentration camps. Communist cadres had full and direct control, down to the lowest levels of the southern society. It was time for the Communists to achieve different phases of the Anti-Comprador Bourgeoisie Campaign (ACBC) to fully subdue the liberated southerners.

It is understandable that any new owner of a second-hand home has no other choice than to remodel the home he takes over, one way or the other, to his preference and comfort. The issue lays in whether the aesthetic capabilities of the new owner ameliorate or degrade the quality of the establishment he took over.

In 1954, after the Vietnamese Communists took over North Vietnam, replacing the French colonists, the North's new owners hurriedly implemented the infamous Land Reform Campaign to restructure their freshly acquired society. Not only were land, rice fields, properties, homes, and even the lives of farmers adamantly taken away; innumerable innocent people, even those who had significantly contributed to the Communist cause, were eliminated via the so-called

People's Courts. Hundreds of thousands of lives were lost, as officially recognized in the History of the Vietnamese Economy[22]. Land Reform could not, however, be realized in the more industrialized South Vietnam. Another plan, the ACBC, was to be widely developed throughout the entire newly liberated domain.

Months of continuous convoys of 4V trucks were heading northward. The name 4V stood for four mocking Vietnamese words, "Vao Vo Vet Ve," which means "Go South to Scavenge and Bring to the North." Deep in their hearts, southerners felt a bitter sorrow to see the northward-going convoys stacked up with television sets, shortwave radios, refrigerators, gas burners, electric fans, furniture, motorcycles, shoes, coffee filters, building materials, and garments—everything designated by the liberators as the "scum of fake luxury." Common folk used the 4V word to express their mental suffering caused by their loss of property and to satirize the overt scavenging actions.

When the convoys stopped their 4V transportation, the first phase of the ACBC, the Asset Inventory, actually began.

Targeted individual owners of businesses and private households were instructed to complete a written declaration of inventoried assets. It did not matter whether the asset was big or small; used, unused or freshly arrived; valuable or not. Owners were ordered to submit their itemized declarations to the local Inventory Committee.

After each owner submitted the declaration, all members of the blacklisted family or business entity were rounded up into a closed room, usually right inside the selected household or business, by Liberation Economic Police, who then carried out a thorough search of the whole home or business establishment.

Searchers opened up walls, dug up floors, overturned bricks and ceramic tiles, uprooted landscaping plants and turned over containers, unearthed gardens to hunt for hidden precious and valuable items. Anything found, valuable or not, that was not on the submitted list was confiscated as a token of the owner's ill intention to hide. Found items were taken as incontrovertible criminal evidence to justify the immediate and permanent expulsion of the whole group, bare-handed, from their own home or business.

There went the opinion that for some blacklisted entities, the searchers unearthed items that had been buried not by the owners but by the searchers themselves to serve as reason to take over the owners' property.

What if nothing was hidden and found? It did not matter. If an entity had been blacklisted and targeted, the so-designated "capitalist" owner and his family were sent out of the establishment for the simple reason that it would be the best place for the state to set up its business. In that way the property was nationalized.

There was no compensation. Owners of nationalized property should feel lucky for not having been jailed. The notorious Da Nang Jewellery owner was one such person expelled from his home completely empty-handed. Tycoon Hoang Kim Quy did not benefit from this type of indulgence. He died in the A-20 concentration camp.

Some owners, knowing that their property would be taken over one way or the other, signed a paper expressing their willingness to give it away to the liberators. Evicted families might be given an empty, wasted home outside the urban area. Normally they were sent to the New Economic Zone. Most driven-out families ran away to live illegally somewhere far away from their original home cities. They might bribe some authority to change their real identities to live under a new cover until they found way to escape to freedom.

Within a week or so from the first day of the ACBC campaign, new owners' faces appeared at many luxurious confiscated homes and businesses. The accents, outfits, and manners of these new owners could not conceal their northern identities. They displayed beaming faces similar to those of poor kids who, for the first time in their whole lives, received a luxurious gift they could never have dreamed of.

Less than a hundred yards from grandma's home on the right hand side of Tran Cao Van Street there stood a pharmacy store. After the asset inventory campaign, the owner of the store was removed. A dark, skinny fellow came from nowhere to take over the store and turn it into his private home. One late afternoon, to the stunned surprise of the passersby, the new owner, clad in new flower-design pyjamas, stood on the open road beyond the doorstep of the old pharmacy and looked in the direction of the local market. It was rush hour. People working downtown and people returning from food shopping were bustling home. With his left hand on his hip in a proud posture, the skinny fellow raised his right hand high to the sky and repeatedly and in a very proud and loud northern voice called out to his young son who was running around somewhere:

"Where're you, son? Come home! Come home right away! We have fried fish tonight to celebrate!"

For most northerners, fried fish was a delicious feast they had not had for many years. For the jungle fighters, fried fish was only possible in their dreams. Considered to be a rare treasure, a fried fish dish was announced publicly to the passersby when the fellow pretended to call his son home for dinner.

11. Money entering poor homes

L ike the wind blowing through an empty hut,
So is the money entering a poor tattered shanty.

Thus goes the Vietnamese folk song. Some of our southerners were poor. However, considered as a bloc, southerners were not money-deprived but had led comfortable lives. To equalize the standards of living between North and South, new rulers were conducting the next phases of the ACBC, which included several instances of currency exchange.

Prior to the Communist takeover in 1975, a chicken cost less than five *dongs* (VN$) in the South. To enjoy a steamy cup of noodles, we paid the vendor three dongs. In Da Nang City, twelfth-grade students each paid VN$400 (US$15 in 1975) a month to attend a private high school. A teal of gold (1.5 ounces) was selling at less than VN$3,000, or US$100 at the time.

Unifying the monetary system for a country is a necessary measure and should be done. The liberators were carrying out that measure in several consecutive phases. The general public considered that the measures were implemented with hidden economic and political intentions. Speculation was that the premeditated plans were designed mainly to strip the wealth from southerners. Nevertheless, the plans could neither improve the life of the North nor impoverish the South.

On September 2, 1975, five months after the debacle of Saigon, the new rulers started the first currency exchange.

Every southern household was allowed to exchange without any limit all the former southern money of the household into "liberation dong" at the rate 500 former southern dongs to one liberation dong. To somehow disguise part of their big fortunes, wealthy southerners distributed their money among their money-short relatives. The relatives then performed the exchange, returning the new liberation dongs to the owners to get bounty commission.

The September 1975 currency exchange startled the Communist regime. The new dominators could not believe that even a poor southern family had that much money after they had been made five hundred times poorer. The rulers realized that the wealth of the southerners at that exchange rate was still much higher than they had expected.

On April 25, 1978, the Communist vice prime minister Do Muoi signed the decree numbered 78CP. The decree was kept secret until its release on May 3, 1978. Under the guise of a "Reform of Industry and Commerce" campaign, the decree was widely known as the Bourgeois Attack. Mandating a new currency reevaluation, decree 78CP set the following criteria for the money exchange.

In North Vietnam, one old dong would be exchanged for one new Vietnamese dong (VN$1.0). In South Vietnam, one old liberation dong earned a new VN$0.8. To cut away big currency fortunes from southerners and make them equal with northerners, the 78CP decree stipulated a maximum amount a household could exchange based on different categories.

The specified maximum for urban areas was:
Up to VN$100 for a single-member household.
Up to VN$200 for a two-member household.
An additional VN$50 per member could be added for households having more than two members. However, for a multiple-member household the maximum was set at VN$500.

In the countryside, the maximum was much lower:
Up to VN$100 for a two-member household.
An additional VN$30 per member for households having more than two members. However, the maximum a household could exchange was set at VN$300.

For the cash fund balance of units such as army or economic organizations, if the State Bank had not specified a stock level for the unit, the exchange returned no more than new VN$1000. If the unit did not open an account at the Bank, the allowed maximum was new VN$500.

Any amount of money of a household or unit over the prescribed maximum, if it could be proved to have been earned by self labor, should be submitted to the national bank, else the extra became garbage.

On the early hours of May 3, 1978, the whole country was put under martial curfew. Uniformed police patrolled every corner of the South. Nobody could guess what was happening. At daybreak, the news of a new currency exchange was officially announced. Nobody was allowed to leave the locality until the military curfew was lifted. This measure was to prevent southern owners from contacting poorer relatives and dispersing the owners' money among them for exchange as had happened before. However, this prohibition was unnecessary because the great majority of southern households each owned much more money than the imposed VN$500/ VN$300 maximum amount.

A household must show its household register to participate in the money exchange. No household register, no money. Illegal people living on the streets went bare-handed. Once a household had performed its money exchange, the household register would be stamped and signed and could not be reused in the same money-exchange session.

On May 2, 1978, the afternoon prior to the curfew day for money exchange, My Le and I luckily had emptied our purse to buy, by blessed good chance, tens of metric tons of sea salt from the government depot, at a reduced price, for our fish sauce processing business. We had no idea of the upcoming money exchange. Hundreds of 100kg bags of sea salt were piled as high as the roof of Grandma's shed. To pay for the salt purchase, we spent almost all our family's available money and Grandma's as well. Our two families' combined amount of money left for the next day's exchange was less than VN$200, way below the set maximum amount for an urban household.

Not many households were in such a lucky situation as ours. On average, the fortune of every southern family had been cut more than two thirds after the May 1978 money exchange. Yesterday's billionaires and millionaires of the South, after a dark single day, had been magically made into poor owners of VN$100 like any other destitute. Everyone was thus enjoying social equality. In cities, some wealthy people emptied big bags of old bank notes from their balconies down to the roads underneath. Bags of old money were seen floating on rivers. Many wealthy people around the South committed suicide after they became as poor as any other penniless wretch overnight.

However, it was not a satisfactory outcome for the dominators from the North. Southerners must be liberated further.

Later on, after we had left the country, a new currency exchange was again planned and executed. Details of the new plan were kept highly secret as had been done in 1978. The process steps and the exchange quota were also very much similar. The September 1985 currency exchange was decreed 02/HDBT-TD and entitled the "Price Reform Campaign." The campaign was led by Mr. To Huu, the Chairman of the Council of Ministers.

The maximum amount of money that could be exchanged as set by the 02/HDBT-TD decree also depended on the class of the owner.

Each multi-member household was eligible to change up to 2,000 new currencies. Up to 1500 new coins could be exchanged by each single-member household.

Each licensed industrial and commercial business unit was permitted to change up to 5,000 new currencies.

Ten old (1978) VN dollars were now exchanged for one new VN dollar.

The 1985 exchange campaign was said to aim at erasing the bimodal price system and removing the coupon mode. In reality it had disastrous effects on everyday life and on the country's business and industry.

Each industrial and business entity was allowed by the 02/HDBT-TD decree to have up to VN$5,000 at most. With such a limited amount of capital, responsible economic strategists could not figure out how the country could do real business on a national level and within the international market. Without enough liquid assets, most enterprises closed out their businesses, went bankrupt, or got nationalized. The whole country was put into wait mode for the unavoidable debacle of the whole system. Some optimists looked for a brighter side: once the proletarian cadres had collected more money than enough for themselves, they would become the new class of capitalists and reinvest their excesses into a possible economic reform to create a pseudo-socialist market economy.

The immediate outcome of the 1985 exchange campaign was deplorable. Consumer demand decreased because buying capability was restricted by the limited amount of household money. Owners of households and enterprises were robbed of the money that they had accumulated through perseverance and hard labor. Investment capabilities were demolished. Merchandise prices rose ten times higher. Inflation became uncontrollable. People exchanged goods rather than pay cash. Others relied on US dollars or gold leaves in trading. People lost their trust in the government's management of the monetary system.

Penniless.

However, southerners were still sitting on immensely valuable natural resources. They were well experienced in building up wealth, too. Immense farmlands stretched to the horizon along the Mekong River banks. Vast fertile lands covering Central Highland had not been taken away from landowners. Factories lined southern urban roads. All kinds of merchandise were still piled up in the stores of southern owners. The transport fleets were under private southern hands. Sophisticated technology could be handled with much skill only by southerner technicians. Bank notes had been stolen through multiple money exchanges but precious metals and diamonds had not left most wealthy hands after the Asset Inventory.

Policy makers had to find other measures to take over these bountiful resources.

During the war, average southern families built up some fortunes of their own. As mentioned previously, in its second five-year plan after 1975 the Vietnamese politburo could only set the targets to simply equip each household with a bicycle and a thermos. Meanwhile, average southerners had well equipped their homes with advanced apparatus such as TV sets, radios, refrigerators, electric fans, gas ranges, motorcycles, jewellery, and other expensive household furnishings. Advanced equipment and furnishings were also seen in many homes in the countryside. We might see porcelain or ceramic wares and rare wine bottles displayed in buffets behind an expensive living room set in many southern homes. Besides their luxurious domiciles, many pleasure-loving urbanites were equipped with extras such as sculptural furniture, cars, boats, water sleds, and the like.

When ration card mode went into effect, food trading was strictly prohibited. Puppet southerners were rounded up for long-term brainwashing. Left behind, the female of a household had to shoulder the responsibility of a family breadwinner. She was used to being a good, capable homemaker but was an unskilled business handler. Now, pushed into an extreme situation, the female head of a household had no choice other than to take the risk of venturing into trading banned goods, for the survival of her family. Multiple arrests and confiscations turned those miserable feminine bread suppliers into desperate decision makers. They had to sell their home equipment and furnishings, one piece at a time, and finally the house itself. Rice and food became scarce on the market; sale of private property was the last resource to feed hungry children and to have the minimum expenses for periodic visitations to beloved ones in faraway concentration camps.

Before she got married to Captain Chin, Ms. Quynh, who was living less than a quarter of a mile from Grandma's home, was the only daughter of a local middle-class family. Every night a family maid brought a basin of water to the bed for Ms. Quynh to wash her feet. After the 1975 liberation, Captain Chin was brainwashed indefinitely in Tien Lanh concentration camp. Mrs. Quynh, in her extreme circumstances, cautiously ventured into forbidden rice trading to keep her three very young children from dying of hunger. She had to find some extra food supplies for her periodic visitations to her captain prisoner. Once, when their mother was arrested and unable to come home at the end of the day, Mrs. Quynh's three little children fell to ground, cried bitterly, and then fell to sleep unfed in the wide-open home. After selling everything she could find, Mrs. Quynh divided the home into two parts and rented one out.

Southern resources left the grip of southerners via multiple avenues: 4V convoy, money exchanges, ration cards, brainwashing in concentration camps, impoverishment policy, household inventory, Bourgeois Attack, Price Reform, Reform of Industry and Commerce, etc. However, southern resources were still abundant. To transfer such resources and wealth-developing equipment to the hands of liberators, another plan was devised.

12. New E Zones

It was almost dark. The winter sun rolled up it rays early and went to bed ahead of time leaving a cold shimmering light at the end of a gloomy day. My Le and I were at the point of closing all our daytime activities. Electricity was out. Night lamps were on, lighting up the warmth of a gathered family. We shut our doors and were ready to enjoy dinner with our children in the hope of going undisturbed into a peaceful night.

I went out to lock the front gate at the entrance of our beach home.

"You have to come up to my home now!" BaNgoai told me as I reached the gate.

"It's late, Mom. If there's anything, why don't we wait until tomorrow?"

"Have you had dinner yet? Both you and My Le come up right away after you have dinner."

BaNgoai did not enter our home. Some stars poked the cloudy sky to hesitantly shed their faint lights down. A sea breeze was coolly blowing. Without any further explanation, Grandma turned to walk away in a hurry. In the twilight, BaNgoai was but a disappearing silhouette. It was alarming. Something must be very urgent.

Any day when I did not report to work at Thanh Ha Company I was at Grandma's home, from early morning until late evening busy with seafood-processing chores. That was one way to avoid policeman Thai coming to my home. I only worked around my home garden every now and then. BaNgoai had no need to come to our beach home for anything, anytime.

Early that evening, after work, My Le had stopped by Grandma's home. None of us heard or saw anything unusual from Grandma. I tidied up the seafood processing area and left Grandma's home to accompany My Le on her way to our beach home about an hour earlier. We were ready for dinner when I went out to lock the front gate. And Grandma came. The alley looked darker as the neighborhood had only scattered oil lamps burning. I sensed the abnormal urgency. It must be something quite important that Grandma did not want to disclose. Or she might not want to be seen around. When I brought Grandma's imperative request to My Le's attention to see if she had any suggestions, My Le was taken aback as well.

Both My Le and I ate dinner in a hurry. Overcoming the cold darkness, we showed up as soon as possible at Grandma's home. Our children were highly alarmed at both of us abnormally leaving the home at such a late time of night. It was suspicious to the police when I, a home-arrested person, was seen travelling around in the darkness of night. At the steps up to the threshold of Grandma's home, we could vaguely see Grandma, Ms. Thien Huong, and her mother in the dim living room. The three ladies sat silently under the yellowish flickering light of an oil lamp. The electricity was out so often these days, and it happened this very night. The road in front of Grandma's home was dark. The living room tenebrous. Everyone in the living room was of a sinister appearance. Their quivering shadows on the surrounding walls were wiggling as if underworld spirits were dancing around.

A lovely girl, Ms. Thien Huong was in her early twenties when Da Nang was taken. Grandma had chosen Ms. Thien Huong to be the godmother when my first-born daughter, Huong Giang, received her confirmation. Thien Huong had been living with her mom at the local Thong Nhat military housing center. I was not quite sure, but it seemed to me that Thien Huong's father was an infantry major. Then Da Nang was liberated. Her father was put in reeducation camp for brainwashing. The victors liberated Thien Huong and her family out of their housing center. Seeing their helpless situation, Grandma brought Thien Huong and her mother, Mrs. Kim, home. They were housed in the empty shed attached to Grandma's house on the bank of a tiny babbling canal.

Ms. Thien Huong had just graduated from high school when Da Nang was lost to the Communists. She used to be a nice and funny girl with a smile always on her lips and radiant eyes in her lovely face. Now she looked very subdued by the unwanted situation. As for her mother, we always saw her with tears. Every day she returned home quite late from odd sustentative activities to provide her desolate family with the daily minimum necessities.

"Dear brother and sister, I've told Grandma I've signed up for the NEZ." My Le and I had not yet made ourselves comfortable in the chairs when Mrs. Kim perturbed us with her unexpected disclosure.

"You both should find words to explain to her. I've run out of things to say," Grandma told us seriously, and then retreated from the living room.

Recently, Ms. Thien Huong, her mother, and village residents, me included, had been repeatedly summoned to consecutive night meetings. Liberators were campaigning to have city dwellers signed up to move to New Economic Zones or NEZs. After being under ceaseless mental pressure for weeks, after sleepless nights, Mrs. Kim made known to Grandma her deplorable decision.

Upon hearing the heartbreaking disclosure from the lady, Grandma had rushed to our home insisting we come up, without informing us of their plights. Grandma had brought the two ladies home when they were kicked out of their military housing center. Every one of us well realized the difficult circumstances Mrs. Kim and her family were in. We had been so afraid that Mrs. Kim might make a mistake. And now whatever we were apprehensive of had actually happened. Grandma, My Le, and I attempted to undo what the lady had done.

"You actually have signed the agreement for the NEZ, haven't you?" I did not know where to begin with the conversation but simply asked such a nonsense question.

"We've told you we did," the lady responded.

"I'm very sorry to hear that. Could you tell us the reason why you have done so?"

Mrs. Kim seemed to be searching into the past and kept silent for a little while. So I repeated my question, saying, "This is a life and death decision. You have to let us know why you came up with such a terrible decision so we may be able to find a better solution for you."

"I've thought more than twice. I've gone through sleepless nights because of it. You know, in the 1960s the Republic of Vietnam also established many prosperous zones, the so-called agrovilles. I wish my husband hadn't been in military service at that time. In that case we might have gotten a piece of land in those regions to set up our own farm."

"I see what you've said. But you should know that to establish those agrovilles our Republic government first found fertile zones, prepared the land, built roads, and established public health posts." I enumerated the works that had been done prior to welcoming the comers to the agrovilles so the two ladies could see the differences between the agrovilles and the NEZs.

"You know. Whoever came to settle in the agrovilles were first quartered in temporary tents while they were building their own permanent homes using provided materials. When they moved into their new home they'd built, the temporary tents would be in turn occupied by the next group of people. Once settled down, they were given an acre or so of well-prepared land and provided seeds to start their farming. If they were capable, they were welcomed to expand their farmland later. At the same time they were provided food until their first harvest came. They were lent funds to build their new lives. Sister, do we have anything like that for the New Economic Zones you are applying for?"

"I see," was Mrs. Kim's short answer after my long enumeration. Hesitating for a couple of seconds, she then continued in tears, "But by volunteering to join the NEZ, I hope my daughter's dad can be released sooner from his penal servitude."

"Sister, don't believe in what they've said. Most families like ours, each has at least a family member in concentration camp. I have attended those meetings as you and many others have. I've listened to what the campaign staffs have said. You should know the NEZ is simply how they want to kick southerners out of their homes into deserted arid regions."

The lady seemed to be thinking hard about what I had disclosed. She did not say anything. The oil lamp shed such a faint light that I could not see the reaction on her emaciated face.

My Le made an additional attack: "We didn't sign up. None of the other families signed up. May be one or two of them did. But why did you? Why didn't you consult Grandma and us?"

The poor lady broke her silence. "Sister, the liberators gave their assurance. By answering to the call to the NEZ, the family is speeding up the release of their family member from reeducation camp."

The last pedicab made its homebound trip on the road in front of Grandma's home. The squeaking noise of its grease-deficient old wheels was sounding as evocatively along the road as the grinding noise of the trolleys lowering the casket into a grave.

"You and Thien Huong go back to your room and think it over. I cannot stay any longer. It's late. Too late. The patrolling police may come any time. If they see us gathering here late in the night, they may hold me for questioning. I have to go home. We'll see you tomorrow."

I went through a sleepless night painfully reflecting on the plight of young Thien Huong and her desperate mother. Their case haunted our minds throughout the next day. This poor mother, her daughter, and innumerable others of our southerners were tense and anxious for the fate of their imprisoned relatives; at the same time they were put under heavy mental pressure, their civil rights deprived, their existence rendered illegal, their economic and human conditions besieged. They were pushed to the wall until they resigned themselves to the fate of chance.

My Le and I got our dinner early and came to Grandma's home the next evening when Mrs. Kim had not arrived home yet. Grandma looked so sad to tell us that the lady was likely to have made up her mind. She might have gone somewhere to bid farewell to her acquaintances. Ms. Thien Huong had not left the home the whole day. She looked heavily grief stricken.

Mrs. Kim got home about half an hour after we came up to BaNgoai's home. Upon seeing us, the lady came straight to us. Thien Huong later joined her mom.

"You look so neat today," My Le greeted her with a smile.

"The police told us the trip to NEZ may be within a couple of days. We're told to get ourselves ready," the lady calmly told us.

"You have made up your mind, haven't you?" I asked to find out about her decision after we had given her a night and a day to think it over.

"We have no choice."

"You and your daughter could opt to go back to your birth place. There, your relatives and neighbours may help you both mentally and physically."

"I did think about that. But I chose NEZ to speed up my husband's release."

"The two of you are but delicate females who have no knowledge of hard labor and agriculture; how can you start your life in the NEZ?" I guided her attention away from the possibility of an early release of her brainwashed husband. We knew that was only a bait to lure gullible people.

"It's hard, we know." She stopped for a sigh and then continued. "But that's how we hope to shorten my husband's days of misery."

"That's deceptive," I kept arguing. "First, you know they promised your husband and everyone a three-to-ten-day indoctrination session! Did they keep their promise? No. Tell me how long it is since your husband was incarcerated? Secondly, I have to tell you that this is but an extra punishment applied to families of our southern military officers. Don't you know that the state-run Saigon Giai Phong newspaper publicly indicated the first and the foremost category of people who must go to the NEZ are families of those who are brainwashed in concentration camps? The state-run newspaper has said it. NEZ is not for national economic development. It's for punishing family members of brainwashed people."

The lady did not refute my argument. She sat back and was in a contemplative mode. I turned to Ms. Thien Huong. She coiled herself up in the armchair at the dark corner in the sorrowful manner of a dejected wretch. Finding some way to bring her out of her mental distress, I asked Thien Huong, "Thien Huong, you may know of *Das Kapital* by Karl Marx. What did the father of Communists say about social struggle?"

"Teacher, I don't know much. Did they call it class struggle?" Thien Huong vaguely answered, not having fully come to her senses yet.

"You're right. Money exchanges, Bourgeois Attack, Price Reform, Reform of Industry and Commerce, brainwashing, digging our deceased relatives out of their graves, removing the names of our beloved landmarks, driving people from their homeland, burning our cultural works, and now the NEZ, all that have been done are but different steps in the process to erase our past and drive us blindly to proletarianism.

Those are premeditated practices taken from the Communist bible." Thien Huong showed signs of understanding, while her mother kept shedding tears without engaging in further conversation.

"Dear sister." I turned to Mrs. Kim. "In the USSR, Lenin established the NEP. Stalin sent Russians to Siberia under the pretext of economic development but simply to kill them by the cold. Those similar steps are now applied here. I have to tell you the New Economic Zone is a well-devised plan to extinguish the next generation of our southern anticommunist fathers. The New E Zone is simply the New Extermination Zone! Don't put your head into that noose."

My statement made Thien Huong feel creepy. She seemed to be thinking seriously about what I was saying. Realizing that the NEZ applied to families of brainwashed people and that it was but a further long term punishment to the direct relatives of the prisoners, Ms. Thien Huong looked terrified. She gave a serious look to her mom. However, her mother did not take those facts into account. It was understandable for someone in her shoes to try anything—self-sacrifice, self-exile, starvation, mortification, everything—to save her loved one from peril. To convince the desperate lady, I went on:

"Think about this. They were talking of moving people to a deserted, unproductive, uncultivated area to start a new life, but they didn't provide you with any tools, any seed, any help. Nothing beyond your own tatters. There's not a knowledgeable person to lead the group. You have no information of the wilderness you will be sent to. No health supports provided in such areas plagued with malaria and all kinds of tropical diseases. No building materials and no rudimentary equipment accommodated. Not even a little survival help before any food crops can be profitable."

"But we cannot stay here without a household register, without a food ration card, without recognition as legal citizens." The unconvincible lady stated her dead end to confirm her decision.

"But you and your daughter go there with two pairs of bare hands. How can you survive? Lots of illegal people with no recognized household, no ration card, and no civil rights are leading rather decent lives around here."

"Our hands are omnipotent. Laboring hands can convert gravel into cooked rice." To our incredulity, Mrs. Kim had repeated the liberators' slogan. With a worried look into the darkness shadowing the room and an indifferent tone, the unfortunate lady spoke softly in a whisper, to reassure herself more than to confirm a sincere belief. My Le and I ran out of arguments to convince her to have a second thought.

Mrs. Kim and Thien Huong left for the NEZ to our heartbroken regrets. We knew that Mrs. Kim and the other people who grudgingly joined the NEZ program desperately hoped their sufferings would pay for the early release of their loved ones. Restlessly waiting for any news of the two of them, we have never since heard about Mrs. Kim and her daughter.

Mrs. Kim and Thien Huong had left. The NEZ campaign kept going on. Not enough people applied for the voluntary agreement to relocate to the NEZs. The quota had not been met. The program then turned to be coercive. The Saigon Giai Phong newspaper clearly listed four categories of people who must leave for the NEZs. Included in the categories, as we had known, were families of government and army members who had undergone or were then undergoing reeducation.

There were densely populated areas around the country, especially in the northern delta, where residents were suffering from want of good living conditions to lead decent lives. It would have been a well-thought-out nationwide strategy if the responsible think tanks had conscientiously researched regions of the country with plenty of untapped resources. Strategists should have designed realistic and feasible plans to exploit these latent resources for national interests and for resolving the poverty of the country fellows. Wasteland reclamation and residential establishment agencies should have provided well-run guidance, initial and sustainable assistance. People from resource-deprived areas, especially people fully capable of joining the labor force, who wanted and had the ability to renew their lives—not the women who did not have suitable development and production capabilities—should have been not coerced but encouraged to knowledgeably and willfully migrate to such regions endowed with potentialities to start their better lives. New economic zones should have been planned under such a vision. NEZ should not have been a forced exile where family members of brainwashing prisoners must be sent, as the state-run Saigon Giai Phong newspaper reported.

In her article "Repression in the Socialist Republic of Vietnam: Executions and Population Relocation," Jacqueline Desbarats estimated that a total of 1.2 million South Vietnamese were forced to the NEZs. Seth Mydans wrote in the *New York Times* that about 1.5 million southerners were forcibly resettled in the NEZs, which simply were barren areas that were ravaged by hunger, illness and extreme poverty. After an automobile trip from Hanoi to Saigon in 1976, French journalist Jean Lacouture reportedly wrote that NEZ was "a prefabricated hell and a place one comes to only if the alternative to it would be death[23]." Unable to survive in the NEZs, the unfortunate residents left those deadly zones to become illegal residents in urban areas. It was a heartbreaking reality. NEZ people were our kindred but our hands were tied and we were unable to extend any support. Innumerable people were impoverished by the NEZ to the maximum extent. Finally, the NEZ establishments left their traces not on the fatherland map but in the nightmarish memories of people and on the saddening pages of history.

13. Uprise to lose freedom

Twenty-one years is not a long time in a country with four thousand years of history. From the date Vietnam was divided by the Geneva Treaty in 1954 that North Vietnam had negotiated and signed to the date they violated the treaty and invaded South Vietnam in 1975, the twenty-one-year-old Republic of Vietnam lived a prosperous life and established a flourishing culture.

Temples, pagodas, and churches mushroomed. Public buildings and monuments embellished the society. Spacious road networks and intertwined infrastructures rendered the communications of our Republic convenient. Numerous public and private universities around the South each accepted thousands of students of all academic majors into their different colleges. Works of multiple southern scholars were recognized internationally. In the early 1960s, neighbouring countries looked to the Republic of Vietnam as a model of development and prosperity.

Once the conquerors got a total grip on the Republic of Vietnam, in addition to their primary procedures of concentration camps, brainwashing, reeducation, money reduction, NEZ coercion, and so on, drastic measures were designed and carried out to totally wipe away all remnants of the Republic and its cultural heritage. The plans were devised to completely eradicate the history of the southern part of the country and remove from people's hearts the attachment to the lost bygone days. The realization of these fundamental measures was done skilfully in different ways at various locations.

First, in addition to the resettlement of a major segment of the population into unfamiliar areas, the original birthplaces with beloved names and memorable monuments the residents been so attached to and heroically sacrificed their lives to defend were washed off the country map.

Quang Tri is my hometown. It is the motherland where I spent the first years of my childhood among ingenuous peasants. That was the land where my forefathers entrusted their lives and their remains. My Quang Tri comprises not many but enough historic places to remember. Ai Tu, where the fabulous mother turned to stone while she sat waiting for the homecoming of her son. Tan So, where the young king Ham Nghi, after escaping from the imperial city, set his fighting base against the French invasion. Thach Han River, on whose bank the first Nguyen Lords established their headquarters against the Trinh Lords. La Vang, the national holy pilgrimage site where the Holy Mother appeared to the persecuted faithful in the nineteenth century. Quang Tri left its renowned marks in the book of history and in the hearts of numerous people around the world with the landmarks that evoke the brutal war page as Con Thien, Khe Sanh, Dong Ha, Lang Vey, Ba Long, A Shau, A Luoi, Ben Hai River, Lao Bao Pass, and Horror Highway.

Yet, the northern liberators officially signed the certificate, on September 20, 1975, announcing the death of my beloved Quang Tri five months after the Republic fell into their hands.

Thua Thien, on the southern border of Quang Tri, became famous in our history with its imperial citadel of Hue, where the historic Linh Mu pagoda reflects its image in the illustrious Perfume River. Mountainous sites of the province were scattered with tens of ancient royal tombs. Next to the notable Quoc Hoc High School on Le Loi Boulevard, the Dong Khanh Girls High had become an icon highly celebrated in national poetry and literature. Thua Thien and its imperial citadel of Hue suffered the same fate of death together with my piteous Quang Tri hometown.

Lying north of Quang Tri is Quang Binh, where My Le was born. She left behind her childhood full of angelic memories when she heartbrokenly bid farewell to her hometown in July 1954 on her run in search of freedom.

By signing the death certificate on September 20, 1975, the Central Communist Party Politburo issued its 245-NQTW Resolution to wipe out my hometown Quang Tri and the neighboring royal province Thua Thien, and to annex the two into Quang Binh to establish a new administrative province under the name of Binh Tri Thien. Trieu Phong, my original birthplace district, got deleted by the Resolution as well. Trieu Hai, the newly born district, spanned over Trieu Phong, Hai Lang, and the old Quang Tri citadel. My birthplace had thus gone from my birth certificate, and its disappearance left unrelenting regret in the hearts of innumerable local people. To dispel its presence from people's hearts, Quang Tri, Thua Thien and Hue, a large area of the country, was expunged into the nebulous past by the liberators.

Quang Ngai and Binh Dinh were another two former Republic provinces situated south of Da Nang. The two ill-fated provinces were also combined into the new single Nghia Binh Province.

Saigon, the capital of the Republic and the "pearl of the Far East" was the prime candidate that must be deleted from the love of the southerners. Together with its neighbouring Gia Dinh Province, Saigon was effaced from the country's map on July 2, 1976, to be replaced with a new name: Ho Chi Minh City.

The city My Le and I loved, where we spent so much time and our love life blossomed, and where we contributed our daily efforts into the building of its future; the City of Da Nang with its spacious seashore, active airport, prosperous land, and lovely beach was also eradicated after it fell to the hands of the newcomers. By the same Resolution No. 245-NQTW, dated September 20, 1975, and Resolution No. 19/NQ, dated 20 December, 1975, of the Central Communist Party Politburo, our beloved Da Nang City became part of the Quang Nam Province. According to the rearrangement, the new Quang Nam-Da Nang Province became one of twenty-one southern provinces and centrally governed cities under the Communist reign after 1975.

In Da Nang, the Second District, where My Le and I established our love life, although it was not such a prosperous piece of land or as well developed as the downtown, was renamed Thanh Khe District. The main street, Doc Lap, in the former Da Nang downtown, and on which were located the Champa Museum, the Han Market, the diocesan Cathedral, and numerous hotels and luxurious shopping windows, became Tran Phu Street. The shadowy Duy Tan Avenue, where I spent my first years in Da Nang, was altered into Nguyen Chi Thanh Avenue. Nguyen Thi Giang Avenue on the left hand side of Nguyen Cong Tru High previously bore the name of a heroine in the campaign against the French colonization; now the liberators gave it the name of Nguyen Thi Minh Khai, who was one among several mistresses of Ho Chi Minh.

In Saigon, Tu Do Boulevard, which means Freedom, got changed to Dong Khoi, meaning Uprising. Regretting the continuous uprising of the sympathizers to the North against the Republic in the past, which led to the fall of Saigon and the current absence of freedom rights, people mocked the ominous name-change of the main boulevard by saying, "Uprise to lose Freedom."

Monuments built around the former Republic in memory of Vietnamese heroes were pitilessly razed. Cemeteries, civil and military, were dug up. At the National Military Cemetery in Bien Hoa, the impressive Mourning Soldier statue was toppled and destroyed. The graves were ransacked.

My aunt, Ms. Thanh Duong, after having escaped to Da Nang from the Communist invasion of Quang Tri in April 1972, died of tuberculosis in 1974. Aunty Thanh never got married and had no children. In the remote village of Duong Loc in the former Quang Tri province, she led a poor and lonely life. When she luckily crossed over the Horror Highway to escape to Da Nang in 1972, because of her tuberculosis she was accepted to live in a hospice run by Saint Vincent de Paul Sisters.

When my aunty died in 1974, we could not bring her back to the occupied Quang Tri to be among her deceased relatives. We buried Aunty Thanh in the Tam Toa cemetery about two miles or so from our home. The cemetery used to be part of a wasteland before 1954. The barren sandy land looking toward Da Nang Bay had not been cultivated. When the refugees from Dong Hoi settled down in the area, the sandy piece of wasteland was chosen to be the resting place for the local deceased refugees.

A refugee in her life, my deceased aunty joined others who reposed there. The majority of families in the local refugee settlement were not that wealthy. They would not be able to build magnificent graves for their deceased relatives but only sketchy earthen tombs. From the burying place, those who were resting there might not enjoy the immensity of the blue ocean extending to the horizon; however, they were not far from their living relatives in the nearby hamlet and were able to listen to the endless murmuring of the waves slapping the nearby beach to lull them into the forever siesta.

Among other people who bade farewell to this world, My Le's father, in 1963, went into his eternal sleep at this hilly resting place as well. Later on, the prematurely born son of one of his nephews also joined Grandpa there. The nephew laid his deceased son in a humble slot at the foot of Grandpa's tomb.

Grandpa, Aunty Thanh, the son of Grandpa's nephew, and their sleeping neighbours were ordered by the liberators to move out of the sandy cemetery.

In her final golden years, lonely Grandma cried bitterly about unearthing Grandpa; she had his remains cremated and kept them on her ancestor altar.

Grandpa's nephew, a military captain, was held in a concentration camp when the graveyard was removed. The captain's father-in-law recovered the decayed remains of his poor grandson. The old gentleman kept the remains in a small jar and placed it on the little shrine he built in his front yard. The next day the captain's father-in-law came to BaNgoai and revealed, "Madam! Last night he returned and voiced his complaint."

"Who's he?" Grandma hurriedly asked in great surprise. "Who did you say has returned? My nephew? Did he escape from prison? Did he come to you last night? Where is he now?"

"No. No! You misunderstood. It's not my son-in-law. I wish he could. But no. It's his son!"

"Whom are you talking about? My nephew and his wife have no son. Which son?"

"It's his dead baby, whose remains I took home yesterday."

"I don't understand." Grandma was still in shock to hear what the old gentleman said.

"The baby was crying for a missing bone of his."

"A missing bone? The dead baby returned and told you a bone of his is missing?"

"Exactly."

"That's why you brought along a sieve, for filtering the dust for his missing bone?"

"I hurried up in this early hour for fear the tiny mound of dust dug up yesterday may get trampled by the crowd."

About noontime, the captain's father-in-law came back from the devastated cemetery with a tiny piece of bone carefully wrapped in a paper box.

The liberators designated a wasteland at the food of a mountain, tens of miles away from any inhabited area, for reburying the exhumed dead. Due to my home-arrest status I could not personally rebury my aunty in the remote field. Too old and unfamiliar with the mountainous area, my eighty-year-old mom was only able to follow the person we hired to bring the remains of my aunty to her new resting place. A refugee in her life, my aunty was also a displaced person in her afterlife status. We meant to put a gravestone on her new earthen tomb when I was out of my home-arrest situation.

Then we escaped out of the country to the free world. My mom died later. The old man we hired to rebury my aunt also passed away. Relatives of my aunt tried years later to locate her new resting place, but regretfully nobody was able to find where she was, after so many eventful years.

Half the world away, we were praying that our aunt's unrecovered resting place was her everlasting place. May she rest in peace! The body made from dust had returned to earthen substance while our souls would meet again in the eternal world.

While keeping our hope for the world to come, we had to witness the next heartbreaking events to evolve in the days of liberation.

14. Cultural heritage

Qin Shi Huang (259-210BC) was the emperor who solidified the multi-tribal country into a big China in the third century BC. World historians condemned the ancient Chinese emperor for the inhumane atrocities he performed in the solidification process. The ancient tyrant outlawed the educated class and burned ancient books. He also buried scholars and students alive. Owning a book of songs or a classic of history was punished especially severely. According to the book, *Records of the Grand Historian*, Qin Shi Huang had, besides students, some four hundred and sixty scholars buried alive for owning the forbidden books.

The Vietnamese Communist liberators were writing new pages of history by replicating the measures of the Chinese ancient tyrant. In a country with numerous dialects, like the primeval China, Qin Shi Huang might have a point in his strange unification measures. He might self-justify his carrying out the policy of "one nation, one single language" in such a lamentable way. It was one way, the hard and inhuman way, to unify a country torn by hundreds of tribes with different spoken languages and dissimilar traditions.

The people from the three parts of Vietnam—South, Central, and North—are believed to be descendants of the same ancestors. We speak the same language, use the same unified writing, and share the same traditions.

A Vietnamese folk song sings:

Cucumbers! Have pity on us, the pumpkins, we are here,

Even of different varieties, the same truss we share.

Vietnamese from the North, Central, and South areas may have some minor dissimilarities. However, we share the same fatherland, speak the same language, follow the same traditions, come from the same ancestors, and have built the same history. Myths about the origin of the Vietnamese population say that we all are descendants of the same one hundred children borne by Mother Au Co. For thousands of years, people from the three parts of the country fought side by side in wars against foreign invaders.

It was not the leaders of the Nationalist South but those of the Communist North who negotiated with the French colonists to win the Geneva Treaty to divide the country into two parts in 1954. The Geneva Treaty was signed on July 21, 1954, by French General Deltheil and Vietnamese Communist Prime Minister Ta Quang Buu. Foreign Minister Tran Van Do of our Nationalist Vietnam refused to initial the treaty. All that southerners did after the Geneva Treaty was to drive the French out of the South in 1955 to gain our independence as a Republic. Then the North, backed by Communist China, violated the 1954 Geneva Treaty and the 1973 Paris Pact they had signed to bring its troops to overwhelm the South.

The United States of America is a community made up of different races coming from diverse countries with dissimilar traditions, nonidentical cultures, and separate spoken languages. However, after the Civil War the more industrialized northern part neither imprisoned the defeated Gen. Robert E. Lee and his Confederate Armed Forces nor destroyed the cultural heritage of the eleven southern Confederate States which depended on the cotton industry and slave labor. The young history of three hundred plus years of the United States has been consequently enriched and augmented instead of being impoverished and destroyed.

Vietnam, unfortunately, has so many dark chapters of history. The dismal pages record multiple sinister acts carried out by foreign invaders. However, many regrettable actions have been the direct results of brotherly vindictiveness.

Despite having four thousand years of history, Vietnam did not have many masterpieces left in its libraries. In the fifteenth century,

Chinese Ming invaders collected and burned most of the Vietnamese cultural heritage. French colonizers later on seized many well-preserved manuscripts of ours and took them back to their homeland libraries.

Having been taken away by foreign invaders, those Vietnamese cultural treasures were still preserved in overseas archives. Upon taking over the North in 1954, the Vietnamese Communists self-inflicted a big loss to the national heritage by enforcing the elimination of cultural products. Books, magazines, music sheets, and copies of poetry written before 1954 were destroyed in their campaign. In his memoir *Hoi Ky Mot Nguoi Hanoi*, the author wrote about the 1954 book burning campaign:

"I had to cram three sacks. The checking team fumbled from the notebooks to other books for poetry, music, novels, and masterpieces. They brought and piled them up at the library on Trang Thi Street and burned them. Fire flickered a few days. In the excited belief, the secretary of the Youth Union, after chanting the word 'Determination,' said that the novels of Tu Luc Van Doan are extremely antirevolutionary!"[24]

During the 1954-1975 period, cultural groups in the North such as Nhan Van and Giai Pham were badly attacked. Writers were hunted down, prosecuted, and sent to labor camps.

During the same period, cultural activities greatly blossomed in the South. Thousands of writers, poets, song composers, journalists, and playwrights of different artistic vocations had their works distributed by many different publishers.

Not long after the April 1975 victory over the Republic of Vietnam, and after millions of southerners were sent into concentration camps, loudspeakers broadcast the official government "Mandate of Cultural Burning." The ruling powers requested every family and establishment to search for, collect, and burn indiscriminately every kind of existing cultural item: books, novels, poetry, magazines, other printed materials, manuscripts, music sheets, music records, and pictures. All cultural products were equated to the remnants of the US puppet. Youths wearing red sashes pulled books from the shelves of private homes and shops, brought them to appointed locations, and mercilessly burned them. Publishers were forced to close their business. Their cultural products burned.

Anyone caught concealing any piece of such material was accordingly punished. Local policemen were going around the village, entering into every household to enforce the compliance of the orders.

Generally speaking, most villagers, especially in the countryside, did not collect and keep many cultural items in their own homes. In the living rooms of most city dwellers, besides a religious altar, there usually was a display cabinet next to the coffee table and the surrounding armchairs. In the cabinet one could see nothing but shining glassware, china, and liquor bottles. Bookshelves were rarely seen. Most families owned shortwave radios. Some others had TV sets in their living rooms. There might be some hanging pictures of the family members. Military families might display some decorations.

Cultural works were not widely kept in private homes. As a result, most of the villagers neither paid much attention to the order nor realized the incalculable damage of such a measure toward the intellectual heritage of the country. By burning its culture, the whole past existence of the Republic would be irrevocably erased from history. That was what the new "Elimination of US-Puppet Cultural Products Campaign" attempted to do in the South after 1975.

Numerous southern authors were sent to concentration camps. Doan Quoc Si, Hoang Hai Thuy, Hieu Chan, all were put on trial on charges of being "commando writers." They were convicted on fake espionage charges and sentenced to years of imprisonment. Praised by French professor Pierre Chaunu of the prestigious Sorbonne University as "the great poet, the national glory," Duyen Anh, author of more than fifty masterpieces, was arrested, accused of being one of the ten most dangerous writers, and jailed for six years.

Having newly resettled ourselves less than ten years earlier in the beach home, my family did not have a big collection of cultural material either. Besides some classical books related to the material I was teaching, I had collected hundreds of musical sheets. On our bookshelves there were a couple of masterpieces from the Tu Luc Van Doan era, such as *Rupture* by Nhat Linh, *Half Way Through Spring* by Khai Hung, *Contemporary Writers* by Vu Ngoc Phan, *Vietnamese Poets* by Hoai Thanh and Hoai Chan, *History of Vietnamese Literature* by Duong Quang Ham, and so on.

Among a few foreign masterpieces I had collected were works in French such as *The Stranger* by Albert Camus, *The Plague* by Camus,

Nausea and *The Flies* by Jean-Paul Sartre, *Works of Love* by Søren Kierkegaard, and *Doctor Zhivago* by Boris Pasternak.

In her days of childhood innocence, our daughter Huong Giang loved to read the Vietnamese version of ancient Chinese martial-art-related stories such as *Water Margin, Journey to the West, Chu-Han War, Three Kingdoms*, and so on.

The mentioned books were our little literary fortune, which we so much treasured. Giving them up would be a dear loss. Taking the risk of digging the garden, I carefully buried the books in the hope they might be retrieved at a later time.

The sneaky digging in such a rush was hard and not well designed. Once the burying was complete, I realized it would be useless. The cultural treasures were not carefully packed with the necessary protective materials against natural destructive invaders. My garden got flooded by seawater almost every tempestuous season. The buried treasure would be ruined eventually. Moreover, the sandy land on which my house was built was full of termites. These ruinous insects could bite off that little treasure in no time. However, it would be better to let nature do its destruction than let my cultural treasure be burned in the liberation flames.

With a shadowy canopy hanging high, and trees nicely edging its curbs, Quang Trung in our Da Nang City was the best avenue any couple of young lovers had, at least once, hand in hand, wandered along. Le Loi Avenue, along which were lined four major Da Nang high schools, crossed Quang Trung Avenue at a charming crossroad. At the northern end of Le Loi Avenue, the National Adoptive Children School (NAC) faced Hung Vuong Boulevard. Going along from the NAC toward Quang Trung Avenue, a stroller in the sunshine on a weekday could come across thousands of young students. On the left hand side of Le Loi Avenue, the stroller would be amazed by so many glamorous schoolgirls in white garments. With shoulder-length hair streaming in the wind, the city's fairy girls were converging on Hong Duc Female Public High School.

Less than five hundred yards down the road on the right hand side was Phan Chu Trinh High, the most notorious public school of the city. Next to it was Phan Thanh Gian High, a private institution. In the neighbourhood of Quang Trung and Le Loi crossroads there were five other institutions. Among them were the newly established Da Nang

University and the neighbouring Lycée Blaise Pascal, a French college. Across the road was the semi-public Nguyen Cong Tru High.

Nearby were the Buddhist High and the Military Cultural High, on each end of the shadowy Quang Trung Boulevard.

Quang Trung and Le Loi crossroads therefore was selected by the liberators as the best cultural environment among the carrefours of our city for carrying out the main ceremony of the local burning of cultural heritage. Around the city, people were gathered by propaganda activists to witness and celebrate. Piles of cultural items were ritualistically set afire. The Han Market on the former Doc Lap Boulevard was another selected place for book burning. The book-burning campaign lasted for months.

Music and songs written during prewar days or by southerners during the war were characterized as "yellow music." One of the songs that brought back a melodious and affectionate memory of my school years was "Going to the Land of Cherry Blossom," Hoang Nguyen, the composer, was my high school teacher. During the French Resistance era he was one of the players in the shows under the leadership of a later-disgraced, resistant general. After leaving Nguyen Tri Phuong Junior High, the teacher-songwriter went to Da Lat, the land of cherry blossoms, taught Vietnamese literature at Tue Quang private school, and composed the above-mentioned famous piece of music. The song was a hit. I knew the song by heart, but would be heartbroken if I had to burn the music sheets of my former teacher.

Music sheets were burned. But the cherished songs could not be extinguished in people's hearts. Whoever was caught singing yellow music was brought to the police station for lengthy questioning and investigation. The involved person wrote a self-examination and could be released only after his written confession was considered appropriate and punitive action imposed.

During the cultural burning campaign, innumerable ancient and rare masterpieces from private collections and public libraries, if they escaped being burned, unfortunately ended up as wastepaper or as wrapping materials for grocery retailers along roadsides. Burned in piles or flying along the pavements were pieces of masterpieces from the Library of the Da Nang University, the Library of the French Lycée Pascal, the University of Hue's library. At the well-kept underground library of the Thien An monastery in Hue, the first rare manuscripts of the Quoc Ngu creators (Vietnamese writings in Roman alphabets) were collected and preserved under air conditioning for years. These rare works were dissipated in the liberators' cultural burning smoke.

In his notorious Vietnamese song entitled "Motherly Legacy," Trinh Cong Son, the sympathizer of the new regime and songwriter, should have added another verse, singing

> *A thousand years under Chinese colonization,*
> *A hundred years under French domination,*
> *After the end of the thirty-year civil war,*
> *The remainder of motherly legacy*
> *Was once again burned to tar.*

15. Life goes on

High above, the sky was brightly lit the whole summer. Rivers kept peacefully flowing day and night. Vibrant sunsets were still coloring the western horizon with vivid splendor. Birds were flying together in bevies to sing their endless melodies. In this splendid natural scenery, in remote jungles, in sacred forests of the motherly country, in distant mountains, millions of southerners, crowned with the puppet hats by their liberating brothers, were shamefully concentrated in the northern brainwashing labor camps by the abhorrent brethren.

City dwellers were forced from their own homes and sent to deadly-disease-infested New E Zones. Employment opportunities based primarily on the "Rather-Red-Than-Professional" principle had driven away much of the gray matter to the high seas, leaving the technically sophisticated southern part of the country in the hands of authoritarian party members. Monetary resources, purchasing power, and goods consumption were reduced to a minimum through repeated currency exchanges and Anti-Comprador Bourgeoisie campaigns. Rice distribution was erratic. A food scarcity policy was silently implemented. Cultural products were energetically destroyed by burning. Education simply focused on lessons learned by heart and was full of false propaganda. Manual labor was widely imposed on a national scale down to the immature hands of innocent school children.

By countless ways of manipulation, the entire population was unfortunately turned step by step into something resembling Pavlov's docile canines.

Within about two years, domestic pacification was somehow accomplished. Now it was time for the Vietnamese members of the Central Committee Standing Politburo to think and look beyond the country's borders.

Campaigns were boisterously running so southern youth—male and female—were, as the propaganda said, voluntarily enlisted for military training. Young adults of enrolling age who did not voluntarily enter military service were sent to forced labor camps.

As I had previously predicted about the what would happen after the Vietnamese communists came into power, the communists carried out their dream of creating an Indochina Bloc under their system of compulsory and permanent "friendship and cooperation." They started the Third Indochina War.

One hundred and fifty thousand soldiers of the People's Army of Vietnam (PAVN) under Gen. Cdr. Van Tien Dung blatantly invaded the Democratic Kampuchea in 1978. With ten thousand PAVN dead and twenty thousand wounded, Vietnam ousted the pro-Beijing Pol Pot regime to establish the People's Republic of Kampuchea, a proxy to the interests of Vietnam. Afraid of being attacked by Vietnam, Thailand—which shares most of its southern border with Kampuchea—sided with China against further Vietnamese expansion.

Being deprived of its Khmer Rouge proxy, China attempted to retaliate and "teach Vietnam a lesson." Chinese troops were dispatched along Sino-Vietnam borders to punish the Hanoi regime.

The 1978 Sino-Vietnam twenty-nine-day war cost each side tens of thousands of lives. The Sino-Vietnam border war brought a domino effect on the Vietnamese policy. The kingdom of concentration camps for brainwashing Vietnamese puppets in the northernmost sites of the country was hurriedly moved southward. The move was to avoid the possibility of the camps being liberated by the Chinese invading campaign. The "Lips and Teeth" bond between China and Vietnam turned bitterly sour while the Soviet-Vietnamese relations were significantly strengthened.

The Soviet military role in Vietnam increased. A number of momentous agreements were signed between the two countries. One of these coordinated the national economic development plans of the two countries, and the other called for the Soviet Union to underwrite Vietnam's Second Five-Year Plan. In June 1978 Vietnam joined the

Eastern block of Communist states' COMECON (Council for Mutual Economic Assistance) under Soviet leadership. That organization offered economic assistance to Vietnam for some of the projects abandoned by China. With the November 1978 Treaty of Friendship and Cooperation, the Vietnamese granted the Soviets access to the facilities at Da Nang and Cam Ranh Bays. The use of the bases represented a substantial regional strategic gain for Moscow. Soviet ships enjoyed friendly access to the harbors in the two bays. In February 1979, Soviet military aid to Vietnam rose to almost US$1.4 billion, while the Vietnamese national budget amounted to a modest US$2.5 billion.

Vietnamese districts along the Chinese border turned into iron fortresses manned by well-equipped and well-trained paramilitary troops. An estimated six hundred thousand Vietnamese troops were assigned to stand ready for another prospective Chinese invasion. The pro-Russian faction in the Vietnamese politburo was winning over the pro-Chinese section. Pro-Chinese cadres deserted. Truong Nhu Tang, former Minister of Justice in the Provisional Revolutionary Government of the Republic of South Vietnam, defected to France. Hoang Van Hoan, Vietnamese Communist Politburo member and Vice Chairman of the National Assembly Standing Committee of the Democratic Republic of Vietnam, deserted to China, where he charged that Vietnam's abuse of the ethnic Chinese minority was "even worse than Hitler's treatment of the Jews."

Vietnam started the campaign to expel the ethnic Chinese from the country in the early months of 1978. Ethnic Chinese were formally accused of "Hoa Comprador Bourgeoisie" and publicly denounced as "kings" of various market manipulations—rice-paddy kings, gold kings, paper kings, and so on. Ethnic Chinese living in Vietnam were registered to be deported out of the country.

Usually named "Hoa" people, the ethnic Chinese minority numbered around a million. They belonged to different groups. Among them were Canton, Teochew, Fukien, Hainan, and Hakka. Most of them descended from immigrants who came to Vietnam by boat hundreds of years ago. So they were commonly nicknamed "Nguoi Tau" in Vietnamese, which means Boat People. Many of them got married to Vietnamese. However, ethnic Chinese segregated themselves, kept their native languages and dialects, followed their own traditions, and confidentially protected their trade secrets. Most of them became wealthy and exerted a significant influence on the Vietnamese economy, especially in the well-developed southern part of the country. Some of them played an undeniably important role on the Vietnamese politic platform. Ethnic Chinese were everywhere in the country. The biggest Chinese concentrations were in the town of Cholon near Saigon and in the northern bordering provinces of Lao Kay, Yen Bai, and Hon Gai.

Having stripped the liberated southerners of their economic capabilities, the Communist liberators began to work against the ethnic Chinese community. Chinese minorities were to donate their properties to the State and to register themselves to be repatriated to China.

Some ethnic Chinese in the northern bordering areas simply walked across the border into the China mainland. The majority of ethnic Chinese had come to Vietnam by boat; they now were leaving Vietnam also by boat, not to return to China but as political refugees to Hong Kong. Wealthy ethnic Chinese leaders came to Da Nang, Vung Tau, and other Vietnamese seaside locations to purchase old motorized fishing boats for the one-way seagoing trips. Repatriated Chinese paid in gold to gain their seats on forced-homecoming boats. Each wooden boat had a crowded load of hundreds of registered ethnic Chinese. Several sailboats paid to be tugged along by a motorized vessel. Market speculation was, in every situation, the forte of Chinese businessmen. Owners of the outgoing boats made big fortunes by collecting bags of gold from the deportees. Most of the boats took months to sail the nautical thousand-mile voyage from the Vietnamese northern waters to Hong Kong. Many of them had to stop at Hainan Island for repair, food resupplies, and storm avoidance.

Taking advantage of the exceptionally golden opportunity to get out of the Communist domination, a multitude of people of Vietnamese ancestry, both in the South and the North, posed as ethnic Chinese. They paid the Vietnamese processing police with gold leaves to get pseudo identities so they could be happily deported out of their motherland Vietnam as ethnic Chinese. They paid the boat owners, also in gold leaves, to get seats to escape. In the South, authentic Vietnamese had to pay a dearer price to the police to be luckily banished overseas.

With the exodus of authentic Vietnamese, the repatriation of the ethnic Chinese campaign had initiated the second flux of the Vietnamese Diaspora.

Police supervision became much tighter along the coast, and particularly on me, and on my beach-home family. I was called up to the police station more often. Two topics were frequently brought into discussion.

"We called you up to ask for your cooperation." A policeman whom I had never seen before opened the dialog when I was irregularly summoned to the local police station.

"I'm cooperating. Policeman Thai may confirm my assertion. Did you see any sign of noncooperation? Did you?"

"We know you're working for your parish church. We need you to report on the activities of the parish priest."

"I concentrate on my daily work: delivering bread in the early hours of the day, going to the beach to purchase sea products for my fish-processing cooperative, working on bicycle frames, and laboring at Thanh Ha Company. My schedule is so full from dawn to dusk; I don't have time to spend at the church. I cannot attend weekday mass. How can I know if anything's happening there?"

"We know you train the parish choir, listen to the speeches of the priest, and attend the parish council meetings." The policeman enumerated activities in which he thought I might get involved.

Long ago, as a parish cultural councilor, I had actively been involved in many parish activities and taken charge of the parochial school. After the 1975 debacle of my country, Reverend Father Thai was replaced. Several parish councilors got brainwashed in concentration camps. A new parish council was established. As a home-arrested puppet, my involvement, if any, in the parochial business must be disastrous to the parish welfare. I had chosen to stay out of the new church management body ever since.

"Sir, I do train the church choir, once a week. I've composed some psalm melodies for the weekend masses. But I'm not a member to attend the meetings of the parish council," I explained to my interrogator.

"If you know any suspicious activities of the priest, or of the council members, do you report them?"

"Sir, our biblical teaching tells me: if you see any wrongdoing from someone then first you advise the wrongdoer not to do it. If the wrongdoer keeps following his erroneous path, tell someone else who can rectify him. If the wrongdoer doesn't change, make the case public. Was that clear to you?"

When telling the police of the bible teaching, I knew that the teaching aimed mostly at personal moral behavior. In the mind of the interrogator, he wanted me to report any possible political or antigovernmental activities of the priest or any other parishioner. I did not know if the police understood the biblical implication. The police interviewer did not make any further comment. He might not find any argument against my statement.

I was well aware that the police must also have requested someone else to do the same thing they had asked me to do. The police repeatedly summoned each of the parish council members and those who had a close link to the parish, frequently and individually. Repeated summonses created intense mental pressure on them. At some point, the police imposed spying obligations in return for a person's personal safety. Everyone knew there were three young parish members who had been most frequently questioned and challenged by the police. They were Mr. Hoa, his sister Nhan, and Mr. Cuong. Mr. Hoa was a diocesan student for priesthood. After the 1975 debacle of the South, the Da Nang diocesan seminary was confiscated; seminarians were not allowed to be trained to priesthood. Returned to his home, Mr. Hoa became an active parishioner. A very good singer, he assumed the music-related activities of our parish. Under very great pressure, Mr. Hoa and his sister Nhan died prematurely afterward.

Due to the new wave of the Vietnamese Diaspora the frequency of nightly police patrols around my own home increased significantly. Our German shepherd, Kino, growled the whole night. After about a month, Kino spewed up green and yellow bile, had an uncontrollable convulsion, and finally died from poisoning. My children and My Le cried bitterly. My Le became anorectic for a week because of Kino's pathetic death.

Kino had become one of our close family members after his previous owner, Captain Pilot Ton Ha, was killed during a mission. A big and robust canine, Kino was able to carry one of our children on his back. Once, Kino followed a female dog and ran away. My Le and the young live-in maid searched for Kino for days and finally found him at the home of a villager living in Thuan Thanh Ward, only about a mile from where we lived. Kino refused to go home. The owner of the female dog made an unreasonable request that My Le pay for the food he had fed Kino during his stay. My Le retorted, "Then you'd better pay my dog for having bred yours."

Despite being enticed to go home, Kino kept laying flat and would not budge. My Le had no choice than to lift Kino's head up while the maid hoisted his rear in order to carry the heavy Kino home along the hot sandy lane under the boiling midday sun.

The police poisoned Kino to keep their patrol unnoticed. My children and I buried Kino in our spacious front yard under the shade of a willow tree. The continuous sad hissing of the willow now replaced the nightly growling of the poor murdered canine. Without the presence of Kino, our beach home became a dark site silently haunted by the security patrol.

The police ordered me up to their station again:

"We know you speak English," the police interrogator matter-of-factly stated.

"I got my English when I was in high school, many years ago. My English may not be as fluent as you think. It got worn out after years unused. Do you need my language skill for anything?"

"No. We don't. But we know English-speaking people are plotting to escape overseas. Are you?"

"How can I?"

"You're infatuated by the alien scum."

"I don't know much of the overseas society. But even if I have some vague notion, it's impossible for me to go abroad. Seashores and borders are tightly guarded. I don't have a boat. I don't have gold to pay to any boat owner. Boat owners are strictly controlled. They are making big money and they're happily enjoying their lives. As for me, I have no seagoing experience. I'm too old to take the risk. I'm laboring hard to earn a living. If you know how to leave the country, please let me know," I discoursed, as I had prepared myself for such an encounter.

"I warn you that we're patrolling the beach. We have ships patrolling off the coast. And you're personally watched." The policeman raised his voice in a threatening manner. "If you try, you'll be caught. And you know what'll happen next."

"I've told you I'm well aware of what you've just reiterated. I don't worry about that. All I'm concentrating on now is building up the Tam Thuan Fish Processing Cooperative to be more productive. Co-op members rely on me. I hope that toward the end of this coming summer we will have a good report to present to the district economic conference."

I realized the fact that the special police had been tightly shadowing me since teacher Ngan, the former academic administrator of Sao Mai High, escaped from Da Nang by boat. At midnight, when there was somebody from the city escaping on the high seas, the local police came, knocked at my door, and woke me up in the middle of the night so they could be sure I was still at home.

No citizenship. Under home-arrest. Forced to submit a weekly written confession to the police. Frequently called up for interrogation. Repeatedly accused of being a puppet and an antirevolutionary. Taught that my offspring would not be eligible for further advancement in the Communist society. The kids coached to hate their puppet parents for being the cause of their obstructed future. Those mental pressures got heavier and heavier day after day. Educators in such a politicized culture had to bow themselves under the falsehood. The propaganda machine had intentionally distorted the textbook truths to poison the hearts and minds of the younger generation. We had laboriously struggled during wartime to live among the friendly people we had loved so much and in a society we had fought so hard to defend and develop. It now was so discouraging to live and serve a new world where people were managed to spy against each other, where education aimed at coaching the younger generation to hate, not to love. It was insurmountable to be an indefinite puppet in a new society where lies prevailed over truth, and deception was justified.

Overall, there was no future for myself. Neither for my wife. Not for my three children in this closed world behind the iron curtain, either. However reluctantly, I had shown my initial wish to cooperate for a better future for younger generations. My goodwill had been categorically pushed aside. Confronting the impasse in my life, my survival instinct prompted me to search for an exit. Even if I had to pay a very dear price for it, I would have to come up with a way out of the current dead end and into a livable future for us.

In the meantime, the fish-processing business was going very well, much better than My Le and I could ever have expected.

Back and forth so many times to the sites where fishing boats reported their catches to have them classified and weighed for fuel exchange, I befriended Mrs. Mua. The short lady was the head of the Seafood Buying Station (SFBS) of the Thanh Ha and Tam Thuan Wards in the Thanh Khe District.

Having come to Da Nang from North Vietnam, she had no specific knowledge of seafood-processing techniques. Mrs. Mua might have spent years fighting in the jungle. Her short, sturdy built revealed her days of hardship in the past. To recompense her battle time, the regime put her up to the management position. Contrarily to the conventional arrogant attitude of the victors, the lady seemed to be an ingenuous person, easy to deal and befriend. The seafood manager was ready to learn new fish-product-related money-making skills. My Le and I were invited to her home so we could show her some of the fish-sauce-processing basics.

Local government had provided the lady with a quite spacious brick home with a shadowy garden on a hilly side of the village overlooking the seashore. The site, previously owned by a local merchant, was so poetic under the morning sun. At the time, the home was not well furnished. The lady did not give the impression that she enjoyed her scenic environment. Perhaps she missed her years in the deep, thick woods. It was a pity to have such an elegant scene turned into a smelly fish-processing habitat.

The forty-some-years-old lady lived by herself. She never mentioned her relatives or her past. She seemed to be happy with her present life. When I proposed buying the by-products under her seafood management, I was surprised that she was willing to trade the fresh catches under her control for fish-sauce-processing secrets. We wondered why the lady had such a serious interest in the fish-processing field. As a high-level management cadre she should invest more time in strategic planning. She might advance her personal prosperity through various easier ways than dipping her hands in fish sauce making.

The lady did not have any equipment and did not want to spend money buying any apparatus. My Le and I knew what she wanted us to do. We hauled two of our big cement containers and set them up at her site, free of charge. We then actually loaded the containers with salted anchovies and showed her the next steps to extract the sauce with different levels of quality. We promised to come back every now and then to watch over the process for her.

The authority managing seafood products had stipulated directives to divide the catch of each fishing boat into different classes. Class I fishes, such as mackerel and tuna, were for export. Class II consisted of a variety of sea products and was for domestic consumption. Class III fishes, such as anchovies and cobias, were for processing mainly into fish sauce. Class IV, tiny and rotten fishes, were for animal foods and fertilizers. Anchovies were the best for fish sauce processing.

Mrs. Mua easily downgraded different types of Class III fish and sold them to us at a very low price as Class IV sea products. We did not know the reason the lady did so. We had no written contract. We assumed she acted in return for what we did to help her get into the fish-processing business. Fishermen and sailors did not care how the fishes they provided for their gas ration were distributed to the customers.

Fishermen submitted their catch to the management of the Ward's SFBS to get the fuel, proportionally to their catch, for the next seagoing trip. Unhappy with the way the fuel was evaluated against their seafood products, fishermen sold some of their valuable catches on the black market for bigger profit. They came only to the SFBS station to trade less-valuable nets for fuel in return. For the time being, the SFBS management had no way and made no attempt to control whatever fishermen did beyond the inland SFBS station.

Mrs. Mua's appointment to her position was but one of the many "Rather-Red-than-Professional" cases. She might have been a good jungle fighter in wartime but was not a skilled talent in the economic market.

In peacetime, strategists at the "pinnacle of human intellect," as the propaganda machine normally lauded, needed to have a broader vision on many aspects of the business. For the oceanic resource and fishing activity, many tasks had to be planned and carried out, such as organizing the fishing boats and owners into collectives; assigning them to different branches based on their equipment and customary fishing practices, training them in safe seagoing and advanced fishing techniques, supporting them with additional capital investments, providing the fisheries with specialized fishing gear and maritime and communication equipment, modernizing their seagoing facilities to increase productivity and safety, developing fish-raising farms to maintain product sustainability, aiming toward the industrialization of fishing, farming, and seafood processing on a global level, and so on.

Vietnam exposes its eastern side to the vast Pacific Ocean. The country owned many islands that had not been fully explored. Better known among them were Ha Long Bay Islets, Bach Long Vi, Cu Lao Cham, Con Son, Phu Quoc, Paracel Islands, and Spratly Islands. The Vietnamese continental shelf had so much potential for exploration and development. Deep-sea resources would be of very high value to an underdeveloped Vietnam. In August 1973, with help from the United Nations' ECAFE (Economic Commission for Asia and Far East), the two first Vietnamese oceanic oil mines Bach Ho and Dai Hung were discovered within approximately 125 miles to the east of Vung Tau. Pecten and Mobile started their oil exploitations of the two mines in October 1974.

Neighboring countries were hungry to claim ownership, even by illegal force, of the exploitation of the ocean floor of Vietnam. On January 19 and 20, 1974, Red China sent four People's Liberation Army Navy (PLAN) Corvettes, two Krohnstadt-class submarine chasers, and MiG jet fighters to start the Battle of Paracel Islands. They invaded the Paracel Islands, severely damaged four frigates of our Republic, and sank the Vietnamese Nhat Tao Corvette, killing our Navy Lt. Cdr. Maj. Nguy Van Tha and fifty-three South Vietnamese soldiers and capturing another forty-eight prisoners of war. Those aggressively invading activities by Red China after the two oceanic oil mines in the East Ocean were discovered showed the high interest of China and neighboring countries in Vietnamese oceanic resources.

While the resources from the two main deltas of the country had been long explored, long-term plans and activities had to be quickly designed and implemented to extend the existence and profitability of the country on the existing natural potentiality of the eastern shore. Strategists should not blindly work on one or two basins of fish sauce any more.

Unfortunately, freshly out of the jungles, the former fighters kept doing what they had done on their fighting trails: controlling the population's stomachs with scarce food rations; increasing food production by turning flower beds along city streets into vegetable-growing areas, or by planting cassava on vast red-soiled hills;

raising pigs in living rooms of newly acquired buildings; building up its war machine's strength; and so on. Instead of taking advantage of the rich maritime resources of the country, the party think tanks simply prescribed a limited fuel quota to restrict and thus control the fishing activities.

No strategic plan was seen in the near or far future of Da Nang City. Things did not come about any better on a nationwide scale, either. In his welcoming address to the newly elected National Assembly in 1976, Le Duan, the then General Secretary of the Vietnamese Communist Party, proudly said: "We have defeated the United States invaders. Our beautiful country has forever returned to the hands of our people. We are the complete masters of the immense and rich mountains, plains, and seas. Certainly, we will rebuild our fatherland, making it ten times greater and more beautiful than today."[25] In its victory nimbus, the country clamorously started its Second Five-Year Plan (1976-1980), aiming to rebuild the country ten times greater only by invading Cambodia in 1978. Financially, the Five-Year Plan did not reap any sizable result in ameliorating the living conditions of the country. In its 1980 report at the end of the Vietnamese Second Five-Year Plan, the World Bank wrote: "Vietnam today is one of the countries which have the lowest standard of living in the world."[26] Being one of the poorest countries in the world, "Vietnam is also one of the world's largest military powers. It maintains an army of over 1 million troops, a quarter of them stationed abroad, 200,000 in Kampuchea, 40,000 in Laos."[27]

The measures taken by the Communist cadres from the highest to the lowest levels of the party ladder could, at some point and by some reason, be tolerated only in an immediate short term for some selected fields. For an overall long-range vision the practices were unfortunately shortsighted.

Anyway, being a home-arrested puppet whose property, freedom, and civil rights were under full control of the police, I could not voice my viewpoint. Numerous goodwilled people initiated constructive schemes. Being puppets, their voices were unheard. Desperate, they ran away to the high seas. I was a puppet as well. All I could do was to hide myself under my restricted status. I was practicing the Good Labor policy in such a way to fill up the weekly report to the police and to earn a living for my second-class family. Fortunately, under the pretext of a Tam Thuan Fish Processing Cooperative, our seafood processing was a booming and profitable business.

Every day, loads after loads of the so-called class IV fishes, mainly from the twin Thanh Ha-Tam Thuan SFBS station under the management of Mrs. Mua, were hauled to Grandma's home for me to process. On foggy spring days, tiny fishes, especially the anchovies, by any reason I did not know, became abundant in the sea. The beach turned into a busy market with the fishermen unloading their catches and the buyers trying to get the fishes as cheaply as they were able to negotiate. We were so busy on those foggy days with loads after loads of fresh cobias and anchovies to process.

In theory, if the fish were bought at the government price from the seafood authority for processing, the final product must be sold back to the authority at a prescribed price. However, the local seafood authority either had no customers for Class IV end products or had no plan on hand for consumption. We were therefore tacitly allowed to sell them on free market. With abundant low-cost yet very good raw materials, we processed them into delicious commodities to sell on the free market for profit. We earned big fortunes while other fish-processing entities in the area could not compete against us.

Luckily, we enjoyed another advantage over our local seafood competitors. Grandma's home was next to the train station. Buyers coming from afar stopped by Grandma's home in the very early hours of the day to have their loads of seafood products ready for the early northward trip. Under the socialist reign, seafood trading, or any other type of individualist trade, was not officially approved. Traders had to load their merchandise at a very early hour to reach the market on time. Moreover, it was much easier for the early-morning traders to cover up their merchandise and avoid the inspection of the economic police force at the train station. It was also easier to exercise some ploys to have the early inspectors overlook their covered-up trade. Furthermore, the local police paid more attention to political activities than to our fish-processing and trading business. We got no trouble from the economic police for selling gross amounts of our products to the customers.

Seafood customers paid us in hard cash. Dawn was the busiest time for trade. Cash piled up in a closet at Grandma's home until the end of the day. When My Le was back from her health-care lab work, she was able to sit down and spend time counting and sorting it out.

Once the train was gone, the wholesale of fish products calmed down. Retail sales started later and lasted late into the night.

Before 1975, Mr. Chat was working for the United States consulate on Bach Dang Boulevard. His wife had just given birth to his firstborn child. Cooperating with the Americans at such a high level was a considerable antirevolutionary crime. Aware that someday the police would inevitably show up at their door for their capture, Mr. Chat and his wife were afraid to expose themselves to the eyes of the public. Their hideaway was in the back of the local church. Mr. Chat and other people in hiding only came out of their retreats to Grandma's home under the cover of darkness to buy fish products to feed their secluded families.

Our fish-processing business focused on three types of products: fish sauce, shrimp paste, and salted flying fishes. Materials for fish sauce were mainly from the so-called Class IV fishes, which the local district seafood management provided abundantly.

To produce the best quality shrimp paste, I had to be at the beach in the early morning hours during the first months of the year when prawns were in their plentiful season. Fishing boats caught tiny shrimps near the shore. I had to buy them fresh before anyone else might preemptively get them away. The best place to buy fresh prawns was at the Thanh Duc SFBS station. The SFBS was in the former First District of Da Nang City and more than five miles from our home. I had a very friendly contact at the site. Most catches of the best shrimp were traditionally sold at the Thanh Duc SFBS station. People who processed shrimp paste crowded at the SFBS to bargain for the best crop. The tiny shrimps must be fresh to bring forth the best paste.

Shrimp paste processing must be done quickly. The fresh prawns were pressed to extract the juice. The shrimp marc was then exposed to the sun to dry. The dried shrimp marc was finally brayed into fine powder before being mixed with its juice and salt and put in containers.

Fish sauce and shrimp paste processing did not need many labor workers or extra ingredients. Its products were, however, the most wanted and more profitable.

Springtime was the season of a special type of fish: the flying fishes. Many fishing boats dedicated themselves to catching this special type of fish. The fishes navigated in great schools. When a boat got among them, a multitude jumped out of the water and had a short fly. Many of them even landed in the boat. During the flying fish season each boat brought back tons of these Class II fishes to sell for domestic consumption. They were so abundant that they could not be sold directly on the retail market. They were sold in tons to be salted for later use. They were processed into products dedicated mainly for wintertime consumption, especially for localities far up in mountainous regions where fresh fishes were but a rare treat. Flying fishes were not tasty dishes. However, with her cooking skill, My Le was able to do magic by mixing selected flying fish with undetectable ingredients to make them into a very delicious dish for our family.

There were intermediaries who processed deals between the boat owners who caught flying fish and the inland processors of the fish. Before 1975, Grandma and my family had processed the flying fishes as a secondary activity for supplemental income. Knowing that we were back in this type of business after 1975, the intermediaries, during the flying-fish season, brought ton after ton of these special fishes to us.

In the early hours of the day, Mrs. Tho, one of our best-acquainted intermediaries, docked her small motorized boat near our beach home to call: "Mr. Tri! Mr. Tri! Come and get fishes!"

We could not predict which day the flying fishes might come. Once they came, they came in big amounts. I had to run around the hamlet looking for hand workers. Sometimes the news of the coming of flying fishes to my home spread so fast that many female workers who used to participate in our fish-processing works gathered by themselves without my invitation. Flying-fish processing provided temporary handwork for many unemployed local laborers. The local police and government seemed to be happy with our spectacular business for having contributed to the settlement of jobs for some local residents. When flying fishes came, I was busy with unloading the fishes from the boats, dividing tasks among groups of workers, getting the containers ready, and making the dedicated ingredients available. The echo of knives and cutting boards and the bustling voices and laughs from the group of fish-processing workers on the ground of our beach home created a vibrant and joyful atmosphere. With the prospect of a profitable future, and seeing the radiant faces of the workers—thanks to the provided work in a jobless situation—I also had a happy feeling in my heart.

While the intermediary was counting millions of individual fishes from the head-high piles, I myself jumped into big cement containers to arrange layers of fishes alternately with layers of roasted corn flour. It took me three or four hours to fill up one of the big containers with tens of thousands of flying fishes. A couple of other skilled and trustworthy workers filled the other containers that lined the shed.

The intermediary took time to count the number of individual fishes on the monumental heaps so we knew how much to pay the dealers. At the end of the processing season, when interested buyers for the salted flying fishes were found, the intermediary and we, the owners of the salted fishes, already knew the amount of salted fishes in each container to negotiate the appropriate sale price.

Spring was the busiest time for our fish-processing job.

To process fishes, we needed huge amount of sea salt. As I have mentioned previously, on May 2, 1978, the day prior to the curfew day for the 1978 money exchange, we luckily and unpredictably had spent most of our family cash to buy hundreds of tons of sea salt from the District Seafood authority at the reduced government price. Hundreds of 100kg bags of salt were piled as high as the roof of Grandma's shed. That amount of salt might be enough for two or more consecutive seasons.

The family fish-processing business, under the cover of the Tam Thuan Fish Processing Cooperative, was so profitable that we made bigger money than we ever dreamed of. The success of the business also built a good screen to shield me from the paranoid, suspicious eyes of the police.

Everyone in the family got somehow involved in the fish-processing business. BaNgoai, with accumulated experience and now in her golden years, was the technical advisor. She provided a spacious work area for processing and storage. She had related equipment and processing accommodation. She supervised workers when I was not available. She gathered trustworthy, reliable, and experienced workers for the business. The backyard behind Grandma's home was where we set up giant fish containers and where most of the processing work took place. The shed, after Thien Huong and her mother left, became the storage place for end products. Grandma had many long-term acquaintances with intermediaries and buyers and used to deal tactically with customers to get good purchase and sale prices.

My position in the process was of course the pivotal one. I dealt directly with the SFBS management and boat owners at the beach. On a daily basis, I was the main worker actually performing and overseeing the product processing activities. My Le, spending most of her daytime at the health-care lab, took care of the monetary side of the business mostly at the end of her work day. She treated poor and older workers with full compassion and kindness. Hand laborers were so thankful for her bountiful compensations.

Even our three little children played some interesting roles in the business. In early hours of the day and before going to school, our children used to gather at BaNgoai's home for breakfast. Huong Giang was interested in bringing some of the fish products to the retail spice-selling stalls in the local market across the road from Grandma's home. The lady vendors at the stalls loved little Huong Giang's fairylike beauty. They believed her presence at the beginning of the day would bring good luck to their retail business. At the end of the day, Huong Giang loved to go visiting the retail sales ladies around the marketplace to collect the money that was due. Sometimes she got treats from the ladies. Our little angel did the small job with some ruse. Huong Giang provided the lady vendors she liked with products of a higher quality than she gave the others. With higher-quality products, the selected retail vendors who received special treatment from Huong Giang attracted more buyers and enjoyed a better profitability.

Besides his inborn artistic talent, Nhi Ha, even in his early childhood years, had a special sensitive taste for the products we processed. With a couple of sips, he sampled the finished products, especially the fish sauce, and was able to advise us which one should be reduced or improved in quality to meet the customers' tastes. He was so good at singing in the children's church choir, at playing on the piano keyboard, in the watercolor painting, and in tasting the sophistication of our products.

The youngest of the family, Ky Nam, used to greet early customers with his childish joke, "No more fish sauce." He did not feel comfortable having people flock to Grandma's home, disturbing the tranquility of his early morning time. Patrons were not bothered by the innocent greetings of the little boy. They were confident that even without an appointment or preorder request we would have the amount of commodities they needed, no matter retail or wholesale, to satisfy their demands. Ky Nam's favorite product was shrimp paste. He could discern the paste we processed from the samples we got from other vendors in the area. His favorite dish was boiled pork slices dipped in shrimp paste specially mixed by his mom.

16. Tu Thuc syndrome

The repatriation of the ethnic Chinese minority had restarted the Vietnamese exodus. News of an escape's success or failure was the headline of the confidential daily conversations of people in the street. Tighter border security was imposed. Any unfamiliar face in the area was immediately shadowed by the local police. Blacklisted subjects were inspected openly and regularly.

Temporarily forgetting the shock of the early liberation days, people gradually regained their withered smiles. In the depth of their souls everyone was nostalgic about the bygone days. Watching the planes flying high in the sky, many swallowed their agonized sighs.

In the Vietnamese version of *The Wizard of Oz*, we have the legendary student Tu Thuc. Similar to Dorothy Gale, the straying Vietnamese student miraculously landed in the magical world of one of his scenic excursions. There he met, fell in love, and married the fairy Giang Tien. He was filled with happiness, and time seemed to stop flowing; his physical appearance did not age over time. However, love for his hometown and his relatives was still in his deepest soul. Homesick, Tu Thuc insisted on returning to earth. Leaving the magic kingdom despite the dissuasion of his fairy wife, he finally got to his earthly home. Touching down at the place he thought to be his hometown, Tu Thuc was disillusioned. Once he was back in his terrestrially meaningless world, he was brokenhearted to realize he has lost his wife and paradise. After the seemingly endless time he had spent in the fairyland, the mortal world he'd known had turned into an unfamiliar planet. Crushed by grief and struggling hard, Tu Thuc could not, by any means, find his way back to the lost charming fairyland.

Numerous pro-communist southerners got the Tu Thuc syndrome. The new generation of Tu Thuc, when they were in the heavenly southern Republic, dreamed of being in the Communist Eden. They fought against the Republic to be with their Communist fellows. After landing in the liberated paradise of their Communist dream, they were disillusioned about being strapped behind an iron curtain. The new generation of Tu Thuc was then striving hard in the hope of regaining the lost heaven. Never having fantasized about in living in the promised utopia of Communism, My Le and I were not among the deceived generation of Tu Thuc.

My Le and I belonged to the class of Dorothy Gale instead. Dorothy Gale happily went home after killing the bad wizards in her fairyland. Lost in the empire of Communist wizards, we by no means tried to kill any of such witches. Together with other human-rights-deprived puppets, we attempted to find the yellow line to free ourselves while we labored hard to survive.

Policeman Thai came to my home more often, sometimes in the early morning, sometimes at noon or when the sun was setting over the western ridge. From the day my German shepherd Kino was poisoned, there was nothing to alert me of the nightly police surveillance on my home.

After a rainy night, Mr. Tan, who lived about two hundred yards away at the other end of the lane leading to my home, came the next morning to work on his piece of land that lay alongside the western perimeter of my garden. I had grown a line of decorative yellow bamboo trees along the side of our front yard next to the piece of land Mr. Tan owned. Mr. Tan was not happy with my line of effeminate bamboos swinging in the afternoon breeze. It was not because the old gentleman did not have an artistic sense to enjoy the landscape. The invasive bamboo roots had turned his land, where the practical gardener grew potatoes, less productive. To prevent the bamboo roots from spreading any further into his potato garden, Mr. Tan dug a deep and wide trench along the bamboo line on his piece of land. The trench extended to the walls of our kitchen and dining room. On rainy days the trench was full of stagnant water.

When Mr. Tan came to his potato garden that morning, with an indignant look he called me over to complain:

"I don't know what you want to do to my garden. But why did you trample on my potatoes and my trench?"

"Mr. Neighbor! Please calm down. I didn't trespass on your property. What do you mean I've trampled on your potatoes? Show me."

"Come over this side to see for yourself," Mr. Tan invited, with an ironic half smile. "You want to destroy the trench or the dividing fence, don't you?"

"Why should I do such a silly thing? We're good neighbors." Looking at the trench against the wall of my dining room, I was suddenly shocked. "Sir! Come here and take a closer look. Something's very suspicious here."

"Don't sidestep." The old neighbor threw a suspicious look at me. "If it's not you then who else has done it? Don't blame the devil brats."

"Look! There are many shoe traces. These are the marks of military shoes. Some are old, many freshly new."

"Then who are those military?"

"You aren't. I'm not. You'd better ask the police," I blurted.

On the first days of liberation, Communist police and armed forces did not have military boots on. They were wearing handmade "bearded sandals" made out of cut tires. Only when the ammunition stores of the South were taken and opened, Communist police and armed forces in cities started putting on military boots. I was not surprised to know that the police were closely monitoring my home but I had not expected them to lay an ambush at the trench beside my home. One of the details that kept me thinking over and over was that they had left many different prints of military shoes in multiple sizes. Whoever came must have come in group of several persons. One or a couple of them must have stumbled into and perhaps got stuck in the trench right beneath the barbed-wire fence. Several of them must have tried hard to get the stumbled ones out. They must have been in such a hurry that they had no time to erase the tracks they left behind. Mr. Tan and I were looking at each other with amazement.

It was a sunny afternoon in April.

As I have mentioned, our beach home was at the end of the cul-de-sac. Whoever came that far, to the end of the lane, must be a visitor to my residence. Everyone knew that. The police did as well.

In my home-arrested situation, I was not enthusiastic in welcoming visitors or strangers to my home.

While taking a rest from afternoon yard work, I sat on the steps leading up to the front door of my home to enjoy the refreshing breeze from the bay. Romantic scenery at sunset over the western horizon and the moonrise on the bay evoke so many poetic feelings in a peaceful landscape. On that late afternoon I was in a great state of alarm when a gentleman leisurely walked up uninvited to my home. I could not identify who he was on first sight, although he looked somehow familiar. Dressed in a relaxed manner, the young gentleman greeted me and, to my surprise, behaved incautiously as if he were a close friend. After a few short informal words, and with a smiling face, he started talking indiscreetly about his reason for the surprise visit.

"We know, as patriotic as you are, you must be interested in doing something to serve our occupied country, mustn't you?"

"You're kidding me!" I jokingly replied, while the gentleman sat down alongside me. Both of us were warily looking out toward the street. The lane was empty.

"I'm serious. We're looking for people to join hands for serious actions." The gentleman went directly into the purpose of his sudden appearance. He might have been in his late thirties with a youthful and sincere demeanor. He had no specific bodily trait to easily identify him among a crowd.

"Being a teacher, I may be good only in unctuous flattery but useless in practical actions. You know, our ancestors have said: a scholar like me is just a sort of long dorsal creature who does nothing but eats and lies inactive." I assessed myself unfavorably in the anticipation that the surprise guest might happen to be a member of the police intelligence, who might try to set a trap to catch me. He did not introduce himself and I did not want to ask. If I asked, he might hide his identity for safety purposes. He kept on arguing:

"You know, being such an eloquent scholar, Mr. Nguyen Trai has contributed invaluable help to Le Loi's resistance and triumph over the Chinese invasion." The man invoked our ancient history to convince me, to which I replied:

"I'm in no way comparable to such a famous hero." I grew a little bit concerned about the gentleman's prolonged presence. Not seeing me at Grandma's home, policeman Thai might come to my beach home for an afternoon check. Anyway, I had to explain my case to get rid of this man as soon as I could. "You know, at my age I'm so worried about myself, my wife, my old mother, and my little children. These sentimental ties and concerns can only ruin any major endeavor. What you hope will be a useful contribution from me may end up being mainly embarrassing disadvantages, unwanted hurdles, and maybe a disastrous outcome for your group's efforts."

The visitor might not have seen my growing anxiety. He did not give any hint that he wanted to leave soon. The surprise encounter must not last any longer.

"I'm sorry. I have to pick up my children," I said. Hearing my statement, the gentleman might have realized that it was only an excuse to drive him away. He got up and said:

"We may contact you at a later time. Have a nice evening."

If I got caught by the police seeing a stranger, a lengthy interrogation would ensue, which I might not be able to cover up skillfully. I anticipated that the encounter, if it was not a trap, was but the first step to test the waters. Somebody might come at another time to convince me into joining their underground resistance movement.

To keep my home from being constantly shadowed by the police, during the day I spent most of my time at Grandma's home, where the fish-processing activities were evolving.

In the early morning I had the local market sweeper haul the sweepings to my yard. During the days when there was no fish-processing activity, I dug around the feet of the trees in my orchard to bury the market waste as green composting manure.

When I built my beach home, the home was so exposed to the high wind from the ocean. I grew willows and a special type of big coral trees around the garden perimeter. Some of the coral trees were also close to the home for shade and shielding. The willows gave an endless whistling sound in concert with the fluttering waves all day and night. The towering coral trees shaded the home with their evergreen foliage. Schools of songbirds loved to build their nests on the tree branches in the springtime. Birds gathered under the foliage on sunny afternoons to enjoy the breeze, singing their lovely melodies into the evanescent wind.

Word on the grapevine was that ghosts, dressed in fuzzy white, appeared on the branches of the coral trees around my beach home at nighttime. Many nights I was so busy at Grandma's house that I went home late in the night. I never saw any such ghostly image. Neither did My Le nor any of my children. But the grapevine kept growing. They said the ghosts were singing saddening songs all night long. The grapevine even said the police were afraid to come close individually to my home at nighttime.

I have never had any encounter with ghosts. In my childhood, my mom told me strange stories of ghosts. I listened to her interesting stories but did not wholly believe they were real. She told me that while my dad was working for the City of Quang Tri, about ten miles from home, he was only able to bike home late on Fridays to be home for the weekends. When he left the asphalted provincial route 64 to veer to the dirt road leading home, it always was night. The dark road wound through a deserted cemetery where there were big coral trees. My dad was a very religious person. On his way home he always prayed his rosary. Once, my mom told me, my dad encountered an immense group of wild pigs. Coming out of nowhere on the deserted road, the pigs were hysterically running in front of Dad, behind him, on all sides making a whistling noise. My dad did not care. He kept biking through.

On another occasion, while Dad was riding home late on a summer night, it was dark and rainy. Dad had to ride quite slowly while he held the umbrella with one hand. After several days in a row of boiling sunshine, the ground flared up a screen of suffocating steam under the rainstorm. The road became hidden in the rain. When my dad reached the dirt road leading to the graveyard, it was totally dark. However, a mysterious light brightly radiated under my dad's umbrella.

Mom told me of many other ghostly encounters. Some were very scary. She said there were little girls who went around the village looking to pick up ripe wild berries to eat. Some of the girls were caught by ghosts and pushed deep into the dense bushes; their mouths being stuffed with mud, they died of suffocation.

After our brother-in-law, Captain Pilot Ton Ha, was killed, his younger sister An went to consult a psychic lady about her dead brother.

"What did the lady tell you?" My Le asked Ms. An afterwards.

"The lady, mimicking my brother's voice, recited a Latin prayer my brother learned when he attended a parochial school."

"Did you believe that your brother was speaking?"

"It was him. The lady is not a Catholic. She knows no Latin prayers; how she could have recited the prayer without any mistakes? The lady knows nothing about us; how she could tell me things that happened when my brother and I were young?"

"You know, your brother was living with us for so long. Did your brother say anything about us, via the psychic lady?" My Le curiously asked.

"I did ask my brother, and he told me: Tell sister My Le that I came to visit her often at dinner time. When I came I made the light flicker on and off and my K9 was chasing around after me."

While stationed at Da Nang Air Base, on his off-duty days Captain Ton Ha used to come to our beach home to have dinner and to take care of Kino, his German shepherd. His wife was living in Saigon. My Le and I recognized that for several months after the death of our brother-in-law, at dinner time electric lights in our home kept flickering for a while and the canine was running around as if he were chasing after some invisible thing.

Besides the flickering light in my home, I never had any explicit experience of a ghostly encounter. All were but hearsay. I knew that the dead were still alive in some form. They exist in a transcendent dimension. They may be around us. They may watch over us. But most of us may not see them. I never saw one.

People in the neighborhood spread a rumor that while a police officer was monitoring my home, ghosts tried to drown him in the trench and his comrades had to come to his rescue. I knew my German shepherd had been poisoned to keep the police monitor from being noticed. I knew the police did come close to my home along the trench in the neighboring garden. But I could not prove right or wrong the ghost-related rumor. When Mr. Tan drew my attention to the multiple suspicious traces of military shoes on his trench next to one of my coral trees, it puzzled me.

The trunks of the coral trees were big and thorny. Some of the trees were up to fifty or sixty feet high in the sky and created a lot of shade over my orchard. The trees deprived the healthy orchard of sunlight. Their roots might have been eating up the nutrition needed by the plants as well. Sitting under the shade of a coral tree on a hot summer day listening to the birdsong was very pleasant. Reluctantly, I decided to have some of the coral trees cut down for the benefit of the orchard.

I hired Mr. Luong, the local grave digger, to fell the unwanted trees. Grandma used to hire Mr. Luong to split firewood for fish-sauce-processing purposes. He was a little bit old, but his strength and skills were so undeniable that he was wanted for hard work in the area.

The grave digger came to my home at an early hour of that day with his bulky tools. First, he started digging a big hole around the root of the designated coral tree right next to our home and several yards from the orchard. This was the tallest tree towering over the east side of our beach home. The hole he dug was wide and about knee-deep. Once the hole was deep and wide enough, the grave digger was able to jump into it to swing his hammer to cut the base of the big tree. The wood of coral trees is quite soft and easy to cut. Climbing up a long ladder, the grave digger carefully tied a strong rope to the top of the tree to hold it from falling on the roof of my home. It took the grave digger several long hours of preparation while I was working at Grandma's home.

Around midmorning, to my surprise, the grave digger came up to Grandma's home with a sad appearance.

"I gave up! I gave up!" he babbled as he saw Grandma and me.

"What's wrong with you, sir?" both Grandma and I asked him at the same time.

"Something's strange! Very strange! Something must be mysterious."

"Please tell us what's happening. Did you hurt yourself?"

"No."

"Have you downed any tree yet?"

"None. I couldn't do the job. Any time I chopped the coral tree you showed me, my hammer bounced back mysteriously. I couldn't cut into the soft tree trunk. I tried over and over again, and the bouncing hammer missed me by tiny distances. I was so scared."

"Hey! Were you drinking before you came?" Grandma asked.

"No. I only drink a little bit when I dig people's graves. Not this morning for this job."

"Did you check your hammer?" I could not help inquiring about his tools.

"I've sharpened two of them and brought them along. I've tried both. Coral wood is soft to cut. Why did they both always bounce back?"

"Are you telling us a superstitious story?" I teased him.

"I've tried on the two coral trunks you showed me this morning. Both hammers didn't cut any of the trees but kept bouncing back." The grave digger asked Grandma for a bowl of hot tea, which he drank eagerly, and then continued: "I have a hunch about something scary. Let me tell you about it."

"What?" Grandma took the empty bowl from the old gentleman.

"The big rope I bound securely to the top of the tree fell right on my back and hit me hard. It almost struck me down into the hole I've dug."

"B'cause you didn't tie it correctly."

"I knew what I was doing. I've made several loops around the tree trunk. I've tested it to be sure it holds solidly."

The report of the grave digger and his worried face had me uncertainly fumbling for words.

"Sir! I know there are angels, guardian angels for example, but I'm not sure about ghosts. Do you believe in ghosts?"

"They may be the ghostly souls of those fishermen who perished on the high seas last typhoon season."

"You're Catholic, aren't you?" Grandma asked, breaking her silence, although she knew well that the gentleman was a good Catholic.

"Madam! You know me. I did say a prayer before I tried again to cut the tree. It's thanks to my prayer that the hammer didn't hit me and the falling rope didn't kill me."

When I told the grave digger that I did not understand what was happening, the gentleman posed a question.

"Didn't you hear the rumor that people saw ghostly images on your trees?"

"Who told you that? Who has spread around that silly gossip?"

"They said even the police were staying away from your home. They won't dare to come at night."

"That's interesting. I'll ask the police officers."

"You go and ask them."

"So, you give up? Thanks for your help, and for your interesting story. Let me pay you."

"Don't pay me. I've failed to do the job."

"If you couldn't do the job, I don't think anyone else can do it. I may have to do it myself. I have to cut some of them to clear space for my growing orchard."

"Do whatever you think you can do, if you think you have a better power over . . ."

"Over what? Just kidding. I know what you meant! Sorry about what happened."

I was at Grandma's home almost every day, especially during the fish-processing season. At home, my own old mother was alone. She might do some laundry for our children or do some light yard work to kill time. She was in her eighties, but her back was straight. She woke up very early every morning and walked to the church to attend mass. She was even able to carry buckets of water from the well to water the orchard. Otherwise, she used her spare time for prayers. At noon, I brought lunch from maternal Grandma to my homebound mother.

The police officer monitoring my home-arrested plight, Mr. Thai, came to Grandma's home almost every day. Most of the time Grandma chatted about nonsense to kill the time with him. Every now and then she gave him some pocket money. He never refused to take it. Grandma did so for my own safety, and the policeman kept coming on the pretext of monitoring my home-arrest status, but who knows, perhaps it was simply because of the sum of cash he got. Once, when I came for a chat with Mr. Thai after he'd taken the money from Grandma, he gave me a lecture:

"We, the revolutionary police, are taking good care of people. Don't you see that? It's not like the police of the old regime; they extracted money from the people they were supposed to be protecting."

If Mr. Thai did not see me during the day, he might come to my beach home around four or five in the afternoon when My Le, my children, and I were home for dinner. It was only when there was news that somebody had escaped to the high seas that Mr. Thai, with at least another policeman, came knocking at the door at night to check me out.

It was to my surprise and great fear when I was summoned to the city police headquarters on Gia Long Street. I was put in a waiting room and left alone for almost an hour. The room was not spacious but clean and well lighted. Its wall had several dark small rectangular openings. I was the only person there that day. I had the feeling that I was closely watched until, to my surprise, a police lieutenant colonel appeared.

"Good afternoon lieutenant colonel." Standing up, I saluted the high ranking police officer with much worry in my heart. "It's a surprise that I have the high privilege of seeing you today."

"We invited you to ask for your help." The officer, who might have been in his late forties, smiled invitingly. He showed me to one of the three armchairs in the reception room. The lieutenant colonel neither showed the customary cold appearance nor uttered the usual harsh language of Communist cadres.

"Sir! I'm afraid I may not of any help to you," I said, finding a pretext for refusing.

"Don't be so fast to refuse when I haven't told you what we need your help for." On the coffee table, as in any northern home, there was a tea set. A thermos bottle containing hot water was on the floor under one corner of the coffee table. While replying to my negative response, the lieutenant colonel grabbed the thermos with one hand and uncovered its cap with the other. Without looking at me, he poured the hot water into the teapot slowly, as if he were prolonging the time for me to worry and get into a troubled state of self-examination. While waiting for the tea to brew, the lieutenant colonel continued:

"You have close contact with our service at the lowest level, so you may give us some valuable feedback about how we should do our business, improve our service, and even eliminate those individuals in the police organization who don't do a good job."

The high-ranking officer's statement was unexpected. The police captain of my district had once accused me of being an international spy working on postwar strategy. So, being called to this high level of meeting, I had anticipated the subject to be counterespionage. The lieutenant colonel, with the decisive voice of a powerful authority, went on:

"You're an educated person. First, please tell me with specific details if any police down there cause any inconvenience to you or to other people."

"Thank you for asking for my observation. I'm home-arrested, so my domain of activities is somewhat limited. I can't be fully aware of what's going on all around."

"Does any policeman ill-treat you?"

"The ones that I have frequent contact with are Mr. Tuong and Mr. Thai."

"How are they?" the lieutenant colonel pressed on.

"Mr. Tuong is a soft-spoken person. He has not come close to me very often. When I saw him he advised me to lead a good life, to contribute to the common good, to carry out the Good Labor policy, to be honest in my declarations, to help the police in removing the antirevolutionary elements, and so on."

"Did he ever yell, menace, or anything?"

"No, never. As I've told you, he's a soft-speaking guy. He hasn't created any hostility among the local population."

"You did mention Mr. Thai."

"Yes. I see him almost every day. He is an outgoing person. His everyday presence in the hamlet keeps the homes safe and the life peaceful. We joke when we come across each other on the streets."

"All you've said are good things to hear, but we need to find out the inadequacies to correct and improve."

"Maybe I'm not a good observer. To me, any police officer who comes to me seems well-behaved. I think they're well trained to do their jobs. If there's anything to be improved, their supervisors may know the code to straighten them up before we may notice. I don't know their private lives, but they're leading very good public lives."

The police lieutenant colonel might not have been satisfied with what he heard from me. Or he might not have cared about it. I got the impression that the questions he asked me were not his primary goal when he demanded my presence at the city headquarters. I could not believe that I was summoned to this level of investigation just to answer a couple of trivial questions about the behavior of low-level police. It was hard to understand why such a high-ranking police officer, who dealt with strategic issues, would spend time with me simply to inquiry into personal matters. I knew there were one or two local underground groups of resistance being uncovered. Several death penalties were announced and executed. Being summoned to the headquarters of the citywide police force, I had anticipated they might suspect of my possible involvement in the resistance activities. I even was afraid that my name might be on the list of contacts the underground groups had kept and the police had confiscated. During the long wait time, it could be that behind the walls several people were painstakingly screening me to identify if I was one of the people the secret police were looking for.

When the lieutenant colonel let me go without any word of intimidation, threat, or advice, I was still wondering about the purpose of calling me up to see the deputy head of the city police headquarters. I had prepared myself in such a way that I would not put my head into their strangling noose, but my being sent home without any further measure still puzzled me. I knew that even if the secret screening failed to identify me as one of their suspects, the secret police might do away with me according to their famous policy "better to kill in error than fail (to kill) by omission". It was hard to believe I was spared. I was fully conscious of the fact that the noose was still dangling over me. I could not be optimistic; I was really worrying. Nothing happened to me that day. However, that night or the next night they might come to quietly lead me away at gunpoint without any given reason at all. I had better get away before it was too late. In my prayers I petitioned for some sign showing me whether it was good and safe for my family and me to find a way to get out of the country.

In the hamlet where we lived, besides a couple of families who specialized in iron and bronze casting, the main occupation was fishing on the high seas. I thought that was why from the very beginning the refugee resettlement agency had selected the sandy waterfront to set up homes for refugees from Tam Toa in 1954. The area used to be a desert-like uncultivated sandy beach open to Da Nang Bay. During the Vietnam War, most of the youth were drafted. Only a small number of local people, mostly outside of the mandatory military service age, were involved in the fishing business.

In the fiery summer of 1972 when the Communists invaded my hometown, some of the local fishing families fled farther to the South. I was told that only three boat owners took the risk of staying back in the local fishing business. Professionally, I had been completely engaged in the education of the younger generation. I had therefore missed the opportunity to communicate closely on a daily basis with all levels of local residents, including the fishermen, and to personally know them well.

As for the three fishermen and boat owners who stayed behind, I had heard about Mr. Thao when he was selected to be among the athletes of the national Olympic team. He did not win any medals internationally, but we were proud to have him in our neighborhood. He was young, athletic, and handsome. I could not quite specifically remember, but I might have met Mr. Thao several times at Grandma's home.

The other boat owner was Mr. Phap. He ran a very successful family business. He might have been in his fifties. He had grey hair but looked very sturdy. His younger brother, Mr. Thanh, and his son, Tuan Anh, were the main sailors of Mr. Phap's team. If I remember correctly, the third boat owner in my hamlet was Mr. Thuc. Sailors working for the three boat owners, most of whom I was not familiar with personally, were among other families in the hamlet. Working on the high seas with rudimentary equipment, and exposing themselves to the unpredictably tempestuous weather to earn a living, was quite a risky endeavor. However, they were among the families in the area who led rather financially decent lives.

After the black April of 1975, local fishermen became quite wealthy, partly because they were the few workers not being stripped of the best-equipped facilities, and partly thanks to their repeated rich catches of fish. Furthermore, fishermen were not strictly shadowed; the government provided them with fuel rations to perform their profession on the high seas. Some of them even fled away with the large amounts of gold paid by the escapees; they were free to work as much as they chose to, wherever and whenever they wanted. There was no one on the high ocean to force them to pay blackmail. While all types of food were strictly regulated by ration card, most of the fishermen's catches were sold on the free market at the fishermen's self-regulating price. They were an unsung privileged class of citizens. Fishing families led luxurious lives. Fishermen were the frequent viewers of soccer games at the local stadium. When the repatriation of the ethnic Chinese was at its peak, leading to the second Vietnamese exodus, the price of a fishing boat increased at a dizzy pace. Boat owners were sought after as people's lifeline.

Mr. Thao—the young, athletic fisherman—was a close relative of Mr. Phong, the former village chief officer who had been brainwashed for a while after 1975. Having no children, Mr. Phong adopted a boy and a girl. They were living in a decent brick home on the north end of the same lane where my family lived. I thought Mr. Phong might be thinking of leaving the country in search of freedom. I ventured to suggest to Mr. Phong that he could act as a broker and approach Mr. Thao, on my behalf, about an escape. In my evaluation, Mr. Thao was a young athlete who knew well the outside world and the social misery of the current living conditions; he must be the best candidate, the candidate of my choice.

As I have described previously, Grandma's home was facing the local market across Tran Cao Van Street. With Grandma's consent, Ms. Y and her boyfriend, Mr. Due, set their sewing machines in the front porch of Grandma's home, looking out to the busy market. Clients and friends stopped by the couple's open sewing kiosk, especially in the late afternoon when the market was busiest. Most of the time they stopped by for a chat, or simply to watch people going back and forth, rather than to order anything. It was at Ms. Y's sewing kiosk that all the grapevines were told, all the news of what was happening in the locality was discussed. When I had a break from the fish-processing business, I also joined them there.

Boat owner Thao stopped by one afternoon at the sewing kiosk. It was about three o'clock. I happened to be standing idly in front of Grandma's home. Some gossipers gathered around the kiosk at this early hour of the afternoon. I did not really know if the presence of Mr. Thao was just coincidence or intentional. Mr. Thao and I leisurely engaged in some conversation. I had the feeling that Mr. Phong might have conveyed to Mr. Thao my intention to buy my escape from him.

Without addressing me directly, Mr. Thao told everybody at the kiosk, although nobody had asked him, "Wealthy people from the city want to buy their escape from me."

"Do you have the guts to do that?" I asked nonchalantly.

"Probably. If they pay me good."

"How good is good?" somebody from the kiosk inquired.

"Someone offered me twenty-five taels of gold per head." He spoke openly while he stepped one foot on the first step leading to the sewing kiosk. Facing the road, I leaned on the left cement pillar of Grandma's front gate.

"Did you agree?" somebody behind my back asked.

"It's a risky endeavor. I have to think twice whether I should risk my life for only twenty-five taels of gold."

"But if you have a hundred escapees on your boat, you'll collect 2,500 taels of gold, won't you?" another listener commented.

Most of the people who happened to be there that day heard what Mr. Thao was saying. He talked nonchalantly as if was not specifically addressing anyone. Somebody astonishingly made a suggestion:

"Thao! Go ahead, it's a big fortune I could never dream of."

"Then you should own a fishing boat now," somebody responded to the unknown speaker.

"Thao! You're fishing! Go ahead, catch people instead of fish, and you'll make huge fortune," the unknown speaker continued after a short silence. "With a single catch you can throw away your equipment and have an unbelievably huge treasure to enjoy for the rest of your life."

That kind of back-and-forth talk lasted for a while. Some people sounded serious, others were joking. The price Mr. Thao indirectly mentioned was far beyond what anyone but very wealthy tycoons could seriously consider. Because I had contacted Mr. Phong as a broker to test the intention of the young boat owner, I guessed this was the way Mr. Thao indirectly told me the escape price. To buy eight escape tickets for our family, we had to pay him two hundred taels of gold. If we wanted four more tickets for My Le's siblings from Saigon, we had to have three hundred taels, or twenty-five pounds of pure gold. It was way, way beyond our financial capabilities. Darkness invaded my vision of such an escape, at Mr. Thao's disclosure. The escape avenue via Mr. Thao's door—which I had very high hopes of opening when I took the risk of asking Mr. Phong to broker—Mr. Thao had just completely shut off. My Le asked me several times about Mr. Thao; I elusively digressed into something else for fear the news would dissipate every hope in her.

One afternoon, as I was roaming the quiet beach on the other side of my home under the setting sun, I came across Mr. Ve, who was a retired military officer. Mr. Ve was repairing a small bamboo-knitted sampan. Curious, I derisively asked him, "Are you going to run away across the ocean with this tiny boat you're fixing?"

To my surprise, he did not look away from what he was doing but simply replied, "This may bring me to the bigger boat waiting out there."

I was enough of a seagoing person to know how they were able to manage such a tiny boat, or even a round bamboo woven basket spread with tar, in the immense sea with its endless engulfing waves.

"Are you about to start your adventure soon?"

"When the time comes."

Mr. Ve did not hide his intention to run away. However, he sidestepped from saying anything specific in response to my exploratory question. I could not blame him. In a society where everyone is expected to spy against the other, alertness is the golden rule. Mr. Ve was the same age as Mr. Thao. They were distant relatives. Seeing what he was doing and the way he responded to my inquiry, I suspected Mr. Ve might team up with Mr. Thao in an escape plot to come.

17. The Cao Dai gentleman

People were running away from our homeland in such a torrential flood that the police increased their nightly patrol along the beach to a very high frequency. Brainwashing camps became more crowded. More jail camps were hastily established to imprison captured boat people.

Stories, true or false, about such and such people in town having escaped on the high seas became more and more epidemic. The news, day after day, aggravated the annoyance in everyone's heart. On the street, acquaintances exchanged hesitant looks, as if it might be the last time they would see each other.

Police came knocking at my door at night more often. I was in a high-alert mood, partly because I was afraid they might round me up in concentration camp, and partly because I anticipated the price for an escape might greatly increase as the demand went up and the boats became scarce. Eventually the price per head might reach the point that we could only look at it with so much dying envy, but could no longer afford it.

I went to work at Thanh Ha Seafood Company as usual. I was less interested in working to earn a living than in looking for a chance to get connected to some boat owner. One Monday morning, on my way to the Thanh Ha Seafood Company, I ran into the former head of the local Hung Dao Youth Group of the Cao Dai Trung Thanh church. The local Cao Dai temple was at 35 Nguyen Hoang Avenue. We biked to work along the same village road and saw each other almost every day but had not traded any conversation. We both knew we were subjects of police tracking and did not want to be caught seeing each other.

Today, upon seeing me on my bike, the gentleman sped up to catch me and asked me to stop for a quick chat. Reluctant to stop for fear of being closely watched and easily caught, I went on biking ahead of him for another half mile without saying anything. I got the impression that the gentleman had prepared to intentionally pick me on my way. He came close and repeated his request.

I was looking for somewhere to hide. Outside the residential area I spotted a sandy slope away from the street. The spot was partially hidden with some low shrubs fluttering lightly in the wind. Although sparse, they provided a thin shield for anyone smart enough to hide from the prying eyes of passersby. Unable to elude the gentleman, I veered out of the road, hid my bicycle behind bushes, and walked up the slope overlooking the glittering bay under the first warm morning sunlight. This part of the less-traveled road and the scenic beach were quiet at this early time of day.

Cao Dai is a locally grown monotheistic religious sect founded by Mr. Pham Cong Tac (1890-1969) who officially established its Holy See in the city of Tay Ninh. The church group had an active tradition of political and military struggle against the French colonists in the nineteen fifties and more recently against the Vietnamese Communists. One of the prominent Cao Dai anticommunist figures was Gen. Trinh Minh The, who has gotten killed in May 1955. The church's opposition to the Communists was a factor in its repression after the fall of the Republic in 1975.

The Cao Dai gentleman I came across that Monday morning was a high school teacher dismissed from his teaching career by the liberators. We had been associating with each other in school-related social activities, but I was not close enough to him to know his personal identity. Having been kicked out of the educational system, he was working for a rice-milling cooperative while I worked for Thanh Ha Seafood Company. The two establishments were but several hundred yards apart. I knew of the gentleman's anticommunist political views but was not sure whether he has engaged in any political or military activity. I did not know if he had been given probation status either. In my home-arrested situation, I kept myself away from any unnecessary contact. Being stopped for an unusual chat, I had a hunch of what the gentleman was going to talk about. Without beating around the bush, he started talking when we had barely sat down:

"Did you think seriously about what my friend told you the other day?"

"Did you mean the youth who came to my home asking me to join the underground activity?" I asked, to be sure about whom the Cao Dai gentleman referred to and what subject he actually talked about.

"Our envoy reported that you're reluctant to join the endeavor. Are you?"

"Then I know your group plans to do something."

"Do you?"

"Not specifically. But I should reassert that I'm reluctant to join your plan of action."

"Don't tell me you have to take care of your family."

"I do. But I have other reasons not to get involved in your strategy." I took the chance to put forward my opinion.

"I want to personally hear your opinion."

"You may not appreciate what I'm going to tell you."

"I'm listening." Looking far away, the gentleman spoke resolutely.

"To my estimate, it could take your group at least thirty years or much more to come up with any sizable result, if you were lucky enough not to get caught like Reverend Father Vang and his fellows from the Vinh Son church. Did you know Reverend Vang's case?"

"I didn't know him personally, but I'm aware of his case. However, you cannot subdue yourself to the victors simply because somebody had been caught."

"I do not and will not subdue myself or side with them."

"But you're running away, aren't you?" The Cao Dai youth abruptly changed the topic to personally attack me.

"That may be an option. I know. It's not the best one," I calmly stated.

"What I'm going to say is harsh. But you're about to run away from your fatherland. To run is to lose."

"We're all losers."

"If everyone runs away, who will fight for the good cause? Is it an irresponsible behavior? Or is it a crime against history?"

"But you should also know if we start a struggle for power by military means—I repeat, *struggle for power by military means*—we need at least a thirty-year span."

"Rather long than never. We cannot use the length of time as an excuse to avoid our responsibility." With the same convincing voice, the gentleman gave his curt response without looking at me.

"Length of time is not the issue. The issue is, during the long struggle millions of our compatriot lives will perish. The whole nation will be put back to the Stone Age again."

"The current situation is worse than the Stone Age," the gentleman retorted.

"Let me recount some facts from our history to clarify my point." I felt a little bit uneasy but tried to draw his attention to our Vietnamese historical realities to elucidate my opinion. "You know, the rulers of the two antagonist dynasties Mac and Le struggled against each other for more than sixty full years without anyone coming out as winner."

The gentleman seemed struck at what I had said. Not leaving him to think for long, I continued:

"You know that the conflict of the Trinh Lords against the Nguyen Lords took 150 years, and both sides vanished with their countless dead victims."

The Cao Dai youth stayed silent. I took the chance to further attack his position.

"The fight for power against Tay Son by Nguyen Anh cost millions of lives. And you already know the recent thirty-year war between North and South, from 1945 to 1975, consumed so much time, many lives, and innumerable country resources. And unfortunately the bad side came out as winner."

"But—"

"Military struggles for power between brotherhood antagonist ideologies have been disastrous, as you know. And now you want to start it over again! Don't you?" I interrupted the gentleman to finish my statement.

He tried again, saying, "But no cost no gain. That's the rule of thumb. And we cannot simply subdue ourselves to the evil invaders. Le Loi, Quang Trung, and many others have fought to drive invaders out. We should follow their paths."

"To fight against foreign enemies as Le Loi and Quang Trung did, military campaigns are legitimate and should be done at any cost. I'm for it." I felt a little bit arrogant trying to argue and distinguish between the war against foreign invaders and civil war, but I could not help continuing to express my thinking. "However, you know, to change a political authority and its ill policy, our best recourse should be political actions, not a civil war on military battlefields. Our history has proven that."

"That's illusion," the gentleman said, with a half-mouth laugh.

"That's reality. The dynasty transitions between our Dinh and Le, between Le and Ly, and between Ly and Tran were done without any civil war, without sacrificing millions of lives. It was greatly beneficial to the national interests that way."

"Do you condemn the heroic struggle that we southerners have engaged in with so much of our lives and blood? Do you?"

The gentleman grew somewhat hysterical at what I had said. I cooled him down by saying, "Our South Vietnam was cut off from the whole country against its will and was given away to the French by the Vietnamese Communists in their 1954 Geneva Treaty." I reiterated the facts that had often haunted my mind. "Inheriting half of the miserable country, we southerners drove the French out of the South in 1955, gained our independence, and established the South into a Republic. Our Republic was recognized by the international community."

"The Republic of Vietnam is a country."

"It is an independent country under international law."

"Backed by their Communist Allies, the North brought huge army troops into our territory to invade our independent Republic." The Cao-Dai gentleman cut me short to say exactly what I had been about to tell him.

I added, "We had no choice than to fight to the death. We didn't invade their northern People's Republic. Their armed forces came to our country. We had to go to battle simply to defend our own Republic from being invaded."

"Why didn't we come up with a political solution, as you've said, instead of engaging in a hellish war?"

"It's a long story. I should simply say that, after having driven the French out, completed the pacification of separatist groups, and strengthened the South into a prosperous Republic, our president via foreign ambassadors such as Mieczyslaw Maneli from Poland and Goburdhun from India had contacted Pham Hung, the then leader of the Communist Central South Bureau, and Ho Chi Minh. When we were strong enough we did negotiate a political solution. Negotiations between the two regions toward a federal solution to stop the war had been actually started."

"Don't you think it was only a trick by Ngo Dinh Nhu to win American support?"

"No. It was a serious and sincere negotiation with planned political, economic, and social steps."

"Then why did it fail?"

"It didn't fail. Ho Chi Minh showed his goodwill by sending a branch of peach flowers to president Diem for the 1963 Lunar New Year. The process stopped owing to the assassination of President Diem and his brother Nhu by the treasonable generals."

"Then we had to go back to war, didn't we?"

"We did, because of the North's invasion."

"Then we should continue to fight."

"We should, but not on a military battlefield anymore."

"Fight but not on a battlefield? Then where? France established its democracy by overthrowing their king by civil war. The northern part of the Unites States won over the South's segregation also by its civil war. Why shouldn't we?"

"We shouldn't do anything simply because France or the USA has done it. We should follow the examples of our dynasties Dinh, Le, Ly, and Tran in their peaceful political transitions. While the Le, Ly, and Tran fought heroic battles to drive the Chinese invaders out, they didn't sacrifice lives of our countrymen to transfer power from one dynasty to the other."

"It's interesting! Your historical point of view is appealing. But I'm not convinced."

"It's admirable that you're standing up to confront the dangers you're exposed to without fear. I wish you safety. But I don't see it an appropriate solution to the national interests."

The gentleman did not look happy and stayed silent. Letting him ponder a little bit further, I watched the rising sun above the blue ocean. It was beautiful and peace-inspiring. The undulating ocean stretched immensely to the sparkling horizon far away. Nature was so calm, not showing any concern with our worrisome situation nor with the hopeless plight of our countrymen.

It was getting late in the morning, but I wanted to take the last chance to give my friend another view of our national interests. I continued by saying, "To grow your group up to a nationwide fighting scale, besides time and human sacrifices you may need some allied support."

"That's why we need people like you."

"Don't interrupt me; I couldn't contribute anything but simply a couple of instigative ideas. You know, you have to depend, to some extent, on foreign allied help. Do you know what happens next?"

"What happens?"

"History has taught us its sad lessons. To fight against the Ho dynasty in the fifteenth century, the last king of the Tran dynasty asked for Chinese reinforcements. Eighty thousand of the Ming's troops came. The result was that the Tran king became a toy in the Chinese hands. Tran Ngoi had to organize resistance against the Chinese domination but failed. It took Le Loi ten years to drive the Ming's troops out of the country and regain independence."

"Damn it!" The Cao Dai gentleman could not hold his impatience.

"Lately, in his struggle for power against Tay Son, Lord Nguyen Anh had recourse to the French aid. The result was that we got eighty years under French colonization."

"Doggone it!"

"The Vietnamese Communist regime gave up Paracel Island and part of our northern bay to China simply to pay back their debt to Red China for invading our Republic."

"They betrayed the country for their dirty ambition."

"But that's history. Things kept happening that way. Loans, even from allies, must be paid back. You don't have much chance to win the war against the victors without getting some type of outside support. And you don't want to pay the debt, do you?"

"I hope it's not the ostensible reason you're claiming just to cover up your propensity for uninvolvement. It's impossible to sit and passively wait for change to come out of the blue!" He sounded cynical with the elegant terms he used.

"No. We should fight, real hard, and all kinds of sacrifices are needed. The issue is that you should not kill each other on the battlefield. You should fight on a political platform."

The Cao Dai man left with thoughtful look as the sun rose high and hot above the horizon. He might have been thinking poorly of me. It was not easy to shake up a man's strong, established political convictions in such a brief encounter. My impromptu discourse might have seemed unorganized and confusing. He came with the disposition to persuade me, not to be won over.

I did not see him ever again. Several months later, the bad news came. Betrayed by an insider, the underground group was uncovered by the Communists. The gentleman and his friends stood heroically in front of the court of hate. They were sentenced to death and publicly executed by the Communist firing squad.

FLYING BIRDS

1. If the lamppost knows

The work at Thanh Ha Seafood Company did not reap tangible benefits. The concurrent bicycle-frame-filing business took much time and effort. It was also damaging to the health. And the bicycle market was saturated. Having quit the business, I was still suffering its side effects, which was a severe, lasting cough. I had to see a lung doctor to cure my health problem and to keep me from being embarrassingly detected by my coughs whenever I was around.

The clinic at the north end of Le Dinh Duong Street used to be run by the Sisters of Saint Vincent de Paul. It was where My Le gave birth to our three healthy children. After our Da Nang City fell to the Communists, the Sisters were expelled and the building was confiscated to turn into a state-run pulmonary clinic. One of the young doctors I knew got a temporary assignment to work there. I made an appointment to see him.

I came to the clinic quite early, ahead of my appointment time. Unfortunately the waiting line was so long that it kept me out of the waiting room. In the serpentine waiting line, I came across an old acquaintance who was the husband of one of my second cousins. The gentleman ran a pharmacy on Quang Trung Boulevard in the city of Quang Tri before the city was totally demolished by the Communists invasion in the summer of 1972. With the pharmacy business, he made big money. Having run from Quang Tri to Da Nang with a fortune, the gentleman and his family, in my expectation, must have bought their escape tickets and left the country long ago.

Astonished at the sight of him, I could not help saying, "I cannot believe you're still hanging around. Why? I thought you've must be overseas by now."

"You know, my combined family was a big one. My wife's side and mine. It's not that easy to have every member of such combined families leave."

"I know."

"We lost a big part of our fortune when they came to Quang Tri. Furthermore, risking the whole big family to the high seas on the same boat was—what do they say ?—putting all the eggs in the same basket. Too risky!"

"Why don't you depart in separate groups? Are you still looking into that direction?" Upon this question of mine, the gentleman signaled me to exit the waiting line. In the open corridor, he lowered his voice to answer me:

"Of course I do. If a lamppost knows how to move, it will run away as well."

"Everyone is saying the same thing. If a lamppost knows . . ." I repeated the unusual sentence, as if it were the voice of the subconscious. Everyone was looking for some way to get out of the country, even those who had supported the Communists for some time and were now suffering from Tu Thuc syndrome.

Like Dorothy Gale, my family and I were trying hard to find a surviving channel to free ourselves from the unwanted paradise. And so were others. My cousin was right. "If a lamppost knows how to move . . ."

New patients kept coming to the waiting line. My second cousin's husband and I strolled to the end of the corridor away from the crowd and the gentleman disclosed, "I know somebody who is in the process of organizing an escape. If you want, I'll introduce you."

"Why don't you put your family on the boat? You don't trust the organizer, do you?"

"I do. The source is reliable. For now, the price is simply beyond my reach for our big family."

The gentleman did arrange an encounter for me, as he told me. The mentioned boat-organizer came to the appointment on a bicycle two days after I met my relative at the clinic. The organizer was a young adult, clad in a rather filthy outfit as if he were a worker coming home from hard, dirty work. I came out from a road-crossing next to the railway along Dong Da Street. I had not specifically known the guy. We recognized each other mainly via cues from the descriptions given us by my second cousin's husband. The young organizer stopped biking on the side of the road and sat on his bicycle, his left foot on the ground to balance his bicycle, as if he was ready to run away at any time. The road in the afternoon rush hour was humid and noisy. The humidity was unbearable. On the corner was a small shop that sold flavorsome noodles. The shop got crowded with customers during evening time. The organizer and I were to rendezvous there. Upon seeing me, without any introduction, he started:

"You're Tri, aren't you?"

"The pharmacist told me about you."

"Tell me. How many people?"

"Six in my family. Another six siblings of my wife."

"Twenty-five taels for six persons."

"Sir! I can only afford twenty for my family. That's all I have."

"Forget it! You're a niggard!"

He biked away without any further word. I felt sorry about my privation. My Le and I had invested most of our resources in our fish-processing business. My Le told me we only had less than twenty taels of gold. Compared to twenty-five taels per head as the fisherman Thao had once informed, twenty-five pieces for six persons was a reasonable price. Unfortunately, My Le could not trade anything to have five extra pieces beyond what we had. We might borrow a couple more from one of our friendly neighbors. However, borrowing five more pieces was beyond our capability to repay. And how could we repay once we had left? The neighbor lady was an underground gold trader whom we had dealt with before by pawning some of our valuables. It was in the first months of the year when our fish product was not ready for wholesale and we needed money. I had just told the prospective organizer of my family's inability to pay. Without offering me any room for further consideration, he left the scene with a curse.

I went home in the hope that the organizer might rethink to offer us seats on his boat. Several days later, through her gossip, the lady who was our fish trading mediator told everybody that the so-called organizer guy did not own any boat. He just collected money from escapees and then hijacked somebody's boat and ran. Unfortunately, he was caught, together with his escapee load and the sum of gold he had collected.

Although being home-arrested, I was not strictly confined to my own home. Day after day, by experience I knew I could travel within the borders of the three districts that made up the city of Da Nang. Prior to the 1975 catastrophe, I rarely went beyond the periphery of the three districts either.

Within the boundary of the three districts, under the shield of working for my Tam Thuan Fish Processing Cooperative, I went to the two main boat-landing ports, one in Thanh Ha and the other in Thanh Duc, to fetch material for my fish-processing business. It was where I got needed information. There, I tested waters to see if any boat owner was reliable and was in the process of escaping overseas. It was a surprise to know that most people I did business with, seamen and those who were not fishermen alike, had all looked for or talked about a way to leave the country.

Most boat owners were searching for somebody who had seagoing experience and owned such equipment as a compass and shortwave two-way radios. None of the fishing boats had any such technical equipment. They also hunted for mechanical technicians who might fix the problems of motorized equipment. Former navy officers who had experience in traveling to international waters were in very high demand. English-speaking escapees were preferred partly because they were well-educated people who could deal with foreign ships in international waters and with the authority at the port they might come to. English-speaking people might be of much help in the new world that boat owners were not so familiar with. The boat owners were willing to let these preferred escapees travel free of charge.

The information was so encouraging to me, but its reliability was the number-one concern. Some boat owners were simply cheaters. Some might work for the secret police. After collecting money and gold from escapees, on the night the escapee load was onboard, the owner might signal the police so everyone but the boat owner was caught and sent to jail. The escapees lost their freedom and their fortunes. Their homes were confiscated, their household cards taken away, their citizenship revoked. If they were released from jail afterwards, they had nowhere to lead a normal live. Nothing on hand to support themselves. Their future was but misery while the cheaters got the big share in the collected sum of gold and the trust of the security police. Some other boat owners asked for a very high seat price. Having enough gold, they bribed the border security guards to buy a safe escape.

After the failed contact, with more thinking and discussion between us, My Le and I decided to try other prospective directions.

Grandma had an old acquaintance, also a boat owner, who reported to the Thanh Duc SFBS station. The station was more than five miles from where we were living. The gentleman, Mr. Dung, was living with his daughter-in-law and his grandchild. Anytime I saw the gentleman at the SFBS, he always caringly asked about Grandma's status. The old gentleman was very religious and sincere to win our trust.

I came to the Thanh Duc SFBS station one early March morning looking for shrimp. Seeing me, the old gentleman stopped washing his fishing nets and came to greet me. Seizing the opportunity, I ventured, "Everyone is trying to leave the country. You're a boat owner; they may pay you a very high price if you help them out."

"I know. I know." The old seaman did not conceal the fact, saying, "I've been contacted so many times."

"Then why are you still here? You can make a big fortune transporting escapees overseas."

"My son, Captain Hoang, do you know him?"

"Somewhat."

"He's still being jailed in concentration camp. I'm waiting for his release."

"When do you expect to have him home?"

"I don't know. Last time I visited him in Tien Lanh camp he told me he planned to escape from the camp. But I told him not to take such a serious risk."

"I don't think Captain Hoang knows enough about the area surrounding the Tien Lanh concentration camp to successfully escape. Several detainees did escape, but got caught or killed. Are you able to wait for several more years for your son's release?" I inquired deeper into the possibilities.

"I've waited for almost five years. I can keep waiting. He's my only child." The worrying father shed light on his expectation. "My son was not a high-ranking combat infantry officer. Several friends of his have been let out. I hope he'll be out anytime soon."

"What happens if Captain Hoang is home tonight?" I got directly to the point.

"Then we may be out on the high seas before daybreak," the old sailor confessed seriously. "My son did tell me to be in ready mode."

"Are you?"

"Surely. I am."

"Don't you have to load food and gas for such a surprise trip?"

"Only my family members."

"How about food and gas?" I insisted. My concern was to know how to accumulate and safely hide those prohibited items.

"It's our secret." The old man cleverly avoided revealing his confidential matter.

"May I join you?"

"If timely information can be established between us. I know your wife's mom and family. I'll do anything I can to help."

"May I contribute to the cost?" I expressed my curiosity as to the price issue, which Mr. Dung categorically refused.

"No. No! I won't take anyone else along but your family and mine. I won't take anything to have your family with us on our boat. All I need is your prayers and God's help."

It was a cordial, generous, and trustworthy offer. The problem was that we had to wait for the release of his son from jail. Captain Hoang was being brainwashed at the Tien Lanh camp. As far as I knew, not many detainees got released from the camp. Could we wait for his release? And for how long? Furthermore, living far away from the old gentleman, we had to find a reliable liaison to keep close contact for timely information. It was a life-and-death situation to depend on a third party whom I did not know, in this world where even school-age children were taught to spy against their very parents and siblings. Parents could not even dare to treat the children they loved with a delicious dish. Otherwise, in the regularly submitted confessions at school, the children could mention such a treat and the family would be accused of living a condemned lavish capitalist life. In such a society, who could be trusted? My frequent appearance at the Thanh Duc SFBS, especially outside of fish season, and my direct contact with the boat owner could not elude the watchful eyes of the border guards.

Meanwhile, as we were anxiously waiting for some good news from the old gentleman in Thanh Duc Ward, we turned our search toward Mr. Thanh.

The mentioned fisherman was rather young, friendly, and jovial. His wife had given birth to twin girls about a year earlier. The twin sisters were not very healthy. They were suffering from severe whooping cough. Besides the twin sisters, Mr. Thanh had several other children, I was not sure how many. His wife had a twin sister as well. The twin sister and her family moved to the Central Highland in 1972.

Tanned and muscular, Mr. Thanh had a healthy look and a humorous manner. He liked to blend himself among younger people. This type of person could be quick thinking, fast in action, and more interested in the life of the open world. His big brother, Mr. Phap, owned a fishing boat. Mr. Thanh and several other sailors were teaming with Mr. Phap in their fishing business. When he was not on a fishing trip, Mr. Thanh joined young people at the sewing kiosk of Ms. Y. His presence turned the group into a lively get-together.

In 1954, when fleeing from North Vietnam after the Geneva Treaty to resettle in the Tam Toa refugee hamlet, Mr. Thanh and his family got significant help from Grandma's family, so he had deep respect toward BaNgoai and her family. Knowing of Mr. Thanh's dispositions, My Le and I were somehow confident to open this door while we kept the old fisherman in Thanh Duc Ward as a backup plan.

At first, we had Grandma do some initial exploration to pave the way. BaNgoai had some of the diplomacy tactics. Although she was in her late sixties, the way she talked and joked lured people to her side. She tactically dealt with policeman Thai to conceal me and our family. She usually sneaked out of the home in a way nobody could detect. I was processing fish products in the backyard of Grandma's home. When I needed her expertise, sometimes I could not find her anywhere around the home. After My Le confided our intentions to Grandma, she dealt with Mr. Thanh or with his brother whenever necessary. Feedback from Grandma was very encouraging.

Recognizing the favorable way things were going, I was on the direct thread with the prospective collaborator. Mr. Thanh and I saw each other frequently. He came to the seamstress kiosk almost every day when he was not on a fishing trip. However, it was only after getting favorable feedback from Grandma that I did not hesitate to tentatively sound out his mind by beating around the bush to pick up the story. I was surprised and very pleased that Mr. Thanh, without any hesitation, went straight into the issue of planning the escape he had dreamed of for so long.

Having once fled from his birthplace in 1954, Mr. Thanh did not have much attachment to his existing settlement. Furthermore, having been a commando who had infiltrated the North to work behind enemy lines, he also feared that someday the police would hunt him down to punish him for his past. Mr. Thanh informed me that his brother, Mr. Phap, was very reluctant to leave for overseas. We discussed how to convince his brother to join us in the perilous plan. That was the hard part. Mr. Phap was the boat owner and the leader of the fishing team. The escape plan could not be carried out without his voluntary management. The next hurdles to overcome were the guard of border police and the impediment of the crew. My Le and I badly needed the insider help of Mr. Thanh. For the time being, neither Grandma nor My Le and I wanted to deal directly with his brother.

In addition to the bond of brotherhood and his workmanship, Mr. Thanh might have contributed a significant financial share in his brother's business. We were not sure, but we hoped that Mr. Thanh had a high influence on his brother. Mr. Phap was rather old and might not have any interest in leaving his profitable business for overseas living, which he did not know or appreciate. The two brothers had an old mother who was deep-rooted in the locality and whom Mr. Phap was reluctant to leave behind. They also had an unmarried younger sister who took direct care of their old mother.

One of Mr. Phap's weak points, which we hoped to exploit, was the military-service ages of his children. Mr. Phap had two grown-up children. The boy, Tuan Anh, was the main mechanical technician on his dad's boat. The boy was one of the most active and intelligent sailors of the team. Tuan Anh had a sister a year or so older. Both of them were approaching military service age. The police might enlist them anytime soon. Tuan Anh was in love with a lovely girlfriend whose name I should have better known. The sister was a close friend of Uncle Su, My Le's brother. We vaguely heard that the girl was in love with a local youth. My Le and I talked Uncle Su into strengthening his relationship with the girl to establish a better connection with her family.

The fishing team working for Mr. Phap consisted of about ten seamen. Their boat normally was out in the ocean for a one-week-long fishing trip or so. Before sailing out, they had to stock enough food for ten robust workers for more than ten days. They also needed enough gas for the long journey. The boat did not have a freezer. The owner bought and stored enough big ice cubes in the lower deck storage of the boat for fish freezing. Like most of the fishing boats at the time, Mr. Phap's boat was not equipped with maritime instruments. There were a couple of rudimentary life buoys. There was no mariner compass, neither weather forecasting equipment nor two-way communication radio. Once they were on the high seas they were all alone, totally separated from the rest of the world and at the mercy of the ocean. They might look at the color of the sky in the afternoon to have some type of rudimentary weather forecast.

In order to secure enough gas and food for the perilous journey, owners of prospective run-away boats had to surreptitiously buy gas incrementally on the black market, and save it and hide it somewhere. Some people dug the seafloor to bury barrels of gas for their secret need.

When the boat was home, the seamen took turns keeping a vigilant eye on it for fear it may be hijacked or the owner may run away, leaving them behind, jobless.

As the spring days became nicer, many people were clustering at the seamstress kiosk of Ms. Y, especially in the early evening and during the days when young fishermen were off duty. Evenings were also the time most of the local young people had nothing to enjoy or to work on. They came to the seamstress kiosk for joking, for watching passersby, for gossiping, and for killing time.

The seamstress kiosk was on the other side of Grandma's living room wall. From the wide open window of the living room, whoever sat inside the living room was able to see and directly exchange words with people in the open kiosk. When there were too many people, they felt free even to go into Grandma's living room. Grandma did not care and was willing to let them do so. She considered them somehow to be her relatives and wanted them to fill her empty nest. Sometimes Grandma brought something for them to drink or eat for fun. They used to volunteer a helping hand with Grandma's odd jobs around the home. On nice evenings, Grandma's home became noisy with jokes and laughter on both sides of the open window of her living room.

As I have said, Mr. Thanh frequently joined the early evening gossips. Compared to most jobless youngsters, Mr. Thanh was more financially stable. He could run to the open market across the road in front of Grandma's home to buy some liquor or a piece of roasted meat or cake to share among the group of gossipers. They were not heavy drinkers, but most fishermen used to have some drink to warm them up when they were out in the windy, chilly open sea.

Most of the people who gathered at the seamstress kiosk were out of work. Some were former professionals with a situation similar to my own status of a home-arrested educator. Others were former government employees who were now dismissed puppets. Or they were low-level members of the former Republic of Vietnam Armed Forces who might have just been released from concentration camps and had to report to the local police every week. They could be local youth who had just finished high school and were not eligible to apply for higher education because they were children of puppets. Those people could have applied for work but by declaring themselves Catholic in the required religion question on the application form, they were simply denied any employment.

Those people might be doing any occasional odd job they could find to earn an insipid living. Some were selling bread door-to-door in the early morning to earn some extra loaves for the survival of their families. Some were paid-by-load porters for early traders and travelers at the nearby railway and intercity bus stations. Some of them woke up at three in the morning to get to the baker as early as they could to pack hot and crispy loads of bread to deliver to customers. I was among them. Some owners of cyclos—three-wheeled pedaling taxis—parked them along the road in front of the local market and joined the group while they were waiting for prospective customers. Some were in the wait mode for new loads of bicycle frames to work on. Some set up their fishing nets in the Da Nang Bay several hundred yards from the seashore to catch some fishes at night. Their wives sold their tiny catches at the morning market to buy food for the day. A couple of them were seminarians who were sent home when the seminary was nationalized and religious institutes were banned. This group of people from multiple social classes and with different backgrounds were gossiping and noisily joking without caring much about their obscure futures. When there was an airplane flying high in the blue firmament, leaving behind a long streak of white smoke, everyone looked up. Some sighed as if they were missing something very dear to them from the recent past.

Mr. Thanh and his brother lived on the same lane leading to the beach where they usually anchored their fishing boat when they were home. The boat was a motorized wooden one. Its dimensions were about 16 x 5.5 yards. It had a covered chamber on part of the upper deck. The chamber was for the boat driver and had some space to house sailors. Nets, big ropes, round bamboo-woven fishing baskets, oars, and other fishing equipment was piled up on the uncovered part of the upper deck. A bigger room on the lower deck was for fish storage and extra sleeping quarters. The storage cellar was temperature controlled with piles of big ice cubes. The boat was driven by a Japanese-made gasoline Kubota engine. I did not know its series, horse power, or nautical speed.

The homes of Mr. Phap and his brother were on opposite sides of the same lane and were within about forty yards from each other. From the front doors of the homes the two brothers and family members were able to talk back and forth without any difficulty. Children of the two families, even the youngest ones, ran to and fro between the two homes without adult supervision. The homes of other sailors working for Mr. Phap were in the same neighborhood.

Prior to sailing out for a multiple-day fishing trip, the two brothers and the sailors spent much time on the beach mending their nets, fixing their equipment, putting more tar on their round bamboo-woven fishing baskets. They use the baskets to transport food, gas, ice cubes, fishes, sailors, and equipment back and forth between the boat and the shore. On the high seas, sailors got into those baskets to row in different directions to fish and to collect the fishes that had gotten trapped in their nets. The female family members of the sailors were seen around the beach providing drinks and treats. Most of the women knew how to row the baskets to bring supplies to the big boat. Occasionally, when there was a shortage of hands on the boat, some women could join the team to go to the high seas.

Our first trials with Mr. Thanh were very promising. My Le informed her younger brothers and sisters in Saigon to get ready. We wanted to leave the country as soon as possible but were not yet able to negotiate with the boat owner to come up with a specific time frame. Mr. Thanh informed us, bit by bit, of the direction and promising intent of his brother, such that we had a lot of hope and put ourselves in the ready mode. Mr. Phap had not yet given us a formal agreement for the escape. We had no details of the getaway, the seat price, or the escape date. However, we were expecting that it must be some date in the early summer when the ocean was less hazardous. We hoped that we would be able to sell our first fish products soon enough to have the money to pay for our exodus.

Less than a month later, Grandma said we had to bring My Le's siblings from Saigon to Da Nang.

"Mom! We haven't had a commitment to any specific date yet. It's dangerous to hide so many of them in my home." Both My Le and I informed Grandma of the undecided situation.

"Mr. Thanh just let Mom know that we have to buy something for the boat," Grandma said (referring to herself as Mom as in the Vietnamese culture, *see reference 3*).

"What is that something?" I asked worriedly.

"I don't know. You'll have to ask him. He said something like, the cylindrical rotor to propel the boat."

"How do we know what to buy? I'll tell him to buy and fix anything that is deemed needed; we'll pay for it. It must be expensive. Did he mention how much the cost is?"

"He said we need the best for the safety of the trip."

Mr. Due, who was Ms. Y's boyfriend, was residing very close to the homes of Mr. Phap and Mr. Thanh. Mr. Due and Mr. Thanh were friendly neighbors of the same age. Through the connection of Mr. Due, whom we trusted as our secret liaison to the boat owner, My Le provided Mr. Thanh with the sum of money he asked for. With the intermediate of a third party, we hoped our advance money would be well honored by the receiving end. We had no direct way to know if the equipment was actually bought and the boat was refurbished as planned for the risky journey. However, we felt assured that the boat owner was committed by the fact that he asked us for such an advanced contribution.

For a while after we paid the sum, we did not hear anything, either directly from Mr. Thanh or via our agreed-upon channel of communication. The prolonged no-news condition made us very anxious. When asked, the liaison let us know that Mr. Phap was still regularly sailing out for fishing trips and he made big money thanks to big catches during the favorable season.

One afternoon during the last week of April, when My Le stopped by Grandma's home after completing her regular business day, Grandma told her:

"Mr. Thanh told Mom he'll pay a visit to his wife's twin sister in Ban Me Thuot sometime next week."

"Mom! What's going on?" The news stupefied me, and I grew much disturbed. "We're expecting our siblings to arrive from Saigon any day now. And he leaves for the highland! Mom! Did he say when he will leave for Ban Me Thuot and for how long?"

"Be patient, son! We have to depend on them, and we cannot push them hard." Grandma seemed to vaguely see something indescribable. She told us, "Mom has filled a twenty-liter can of shrimp paste for him to bring to his wife's sister as a gift. He may leave in a day or two. He has applied for his temporary absence permit."

"Mom! Did he tell Mom what he's told the police about the purpose of his visit?" I grew more worried as I heard that Mr. Thanh had applied for his absence permit at the police station. He obeyed the rule, but I wondered if he was clever enough to dispel any suspicion.

"Mom did ask him."

"What did he say?"

"He told the police that he and his brother are getting old and may not be able to be fishermen much longer. So he's going to Ban Me Thuot where the family of his sister-in-law lives, to see if he and his brother may move their families to the New Economic Zone."

"Did he say how the police reacted?" I kept bothering Grandma with my questions.

"He said that upon hearing his intention to go to the NEZ, the police approved his permit without any further question."

"Shortsighted!"

"Who's shortsighted? Me?"

"No, Mom! I meant the police, who else?"

"Why?"

"You know, Mom. Mr. Thanh and his brother were the last real producers in this village of poor consumers. If they stop fishing and leave for the NEZ, sailors working for them will be out of work; their families will starve. The local economy will be crippled."

"Why do you have to worry about that?"

"Just a thought. Anyway! Thank God he knew how to manage."

When we contacted our liaison he explained that Mr. Thanh had gone to pay his last visit to the family of his wife's twin sister. What Mr. Thanh told the police upon applying for the temporary absence permit was but a disguise. That meant Mr. Thanh was resolute about leaving the country. It was a good omen meaning the two brothers had come up with a decision. The first steps Mr. Thanh took were to bid farewell to his relatives far away.

Another month of anxiously waiting passed by. In the meantime I took the risk of contacting the old gentleman in Thanh Duc to see if there was any hope on this lead. Upon seeing me at the beach, the old gentleman hurried to speak with me. He told me he had just come back from another visit to his imprisoned son. The son told him there was no hope of a near release and the son was hiding food and knives, on his way to labor, for a planned escape from the prison.

"But how can I get in touch with you on the day?"

"Don't try to see me. Let your Grandma do it."

To our relief, Mr. Thanh came back after more than a week. The weather was very favorable for seagoing. No typhoon was anticipated in the near future of the monsoon season. And Grandma conveyed a new request from Mr. Thanh to My Le:

"Mr. Thanh suggested that we must store up canned milk and seasickness medication. He has two one-year-old twin girls who are suffering from very bad whooping coughs."

"It doesn't sound good."

"You have to look for cough suppressant drugs or sleeping pills for them." My Le felt uneasy upon hearing request after request.

"Mom, we're talking about escaping and you're talking about milk and cough medicine, seasickness medicine for him to feed his children? Did he ask us to buy gas and such?"

"Sorry. But you understand what I meant? We have to satisfy every one of their requests."

"OK. I'll send for our relatives in Saigon."

Grandma then reminded My Le: "Ask them to contact the pineapple farm director Huynh Tuyen for valid travel documents."

"Mom, I know it. Milk and medicine I'll have to buy little by little on the black market. There's no problem. But nobody has mentioned about the price per head yet. Can we afford it?"

"I forgot to let you know. Before leaving for Ban Me Thuot, Mr. Thanh let Mom know that Mr. Due will be our contact. He will be among the escapees. Through him we'll get more details."

"We already knew that." My Le cut short Grandma's statement. "Mr. Due and my husband have contacted each other on several occasions. But we must see Mr. Phap at least once. We cannot simply rely on the mediator."

"Both of you must be very careful."

Da Nang Bay, stretching beyond our beach home, was so peaceful and calm in the very early morning hours. The air, filled with morning fog, caressed the skin giving an extremely fresh feeling. The busy flying-fish season was long over. No more boats were coming to unload tons of sea products at our beach home.

That morning, to my big surprise, I faintly heard a sound as if someone was calling my name. Hearing a familiar female voice, I looked to the street but could not see any one around. Running out to the front yard, I spotted a tiny boat at the beach. A little lady was standing up on the boat hood and waving at me.

"Lady! You caught me by surprise. What is this for?"

Coming on a tiny motorized sampan, Mrs. Tho, the lady who used to bring loads of flying fishes to us, whispered her offer when I waded closer to her boat:

"An organizer hired me to transport people to his big escaping boat. I thought of your family."

"Really?" Stupefied by her unexpectedly friendly attention to the difficult circumstance of our family, I could not react immediately with an appropriate decision to her surprise proposal but said, "Thanks for your cordial considerations. Could you reveal some additional details?"

"B'cause of my sympathy, I brought this matter up. All you have to tell me is yes or no. Else you and I should keep it a dead secret. I'm leaving now."

I kept thinking for a couple of seconds without answering the lady. She restarted the motorized sampan and left in a hurry. The lady and I had dealt on fish business for a couple of seasons. She ate meals with us at our home several times. My Le and I had never mentioned to her our political situation and aspiration. The lady did not seem to be inquisitive into our personal issues. She must have had a good sense of observation to know my family and my political status to some degree and to be highly sympathetic. We knew the svelte lady gave our family a lot of priorities and ease in business. However, I did not know whether My Le was on good terms with her or not. As for me, I had no clue of her real whereabouts, her political trends, her family, or her social orientation—I certainly didn't know enough to get committed to her surprise offer on the first hint. I knew the lady did it out of her goodness and her concern for our plight. I had no doubt about her heartfelt sincerity. In fact, I was touched by her thoughtfulness. And the plan sounded trustworthy. But I did not know the organizer and his plan. Was he reliable? Who could know the unexpected? After Mrs. Tho left, I felt a little bit uneasy for not having seized the opportunity to find out more to appropriately respond to her kind offer. When I told My Le about the offer from Mrs. Tho, My Le assured me that it might be a blessing for our family when we did not follow the lady's lead. Moreover, running after two hares we may catch neither.

That afternoon, policeman Thai came to Grandma's home. He gave me a lengthy lecture on how to carry out the Good Labor policy, how good the new revolutionary treatment of the population was, and how bad the puppet government was. Policeman Thai left Grandma's home only after she had tipped him with pocket money. Mr. Thanh might have been waiting for some time before Mr. Thai left. He hurriedly stepped in.

Not having sat down yet, Mr. Thanh rushed back to the market across the road saying he had to find something for a sip. The seamstress kiosk was not crowded yet. It was still early for jobless gossipers to gather.

Coming back, Mr. Thanh happily explained, "I pretended to rush to the market just to make sure the policeman didn't follow me. I came more than fifteen minutes ago in the hope there were not many people around, but Mr. Due warned me of Mr. Thai's presence."

"He stops by almost every day to give me lectures."

"I came to nail down some details of our plan." Mr. Thanh spoke of the purpose of his visit, which I was so anxious to know.

"Did your brother inform you of a date?"

"No specific date yet, but in the very near future."

"How do we manage to avoid the police?" I expressed my concerns about how to stuff the boat with needed fuel and food without being detected, how to safely load so many people into the boat in a hurry, how to keep other sailors from watching over the boat, and how to blind the border police to avoid being arrested. "Do you have any scheme?"

"That's what I want to ask for your inputs."

I could not thoroughly and seriously think about a disguise trick to distract the border guards and keep the sailors away from the boat. All the steps to start the trip and safely get out of the harbor must be well orchestrated and cleverly executed in a timely manner mainly by the boat manager. I was so concerned that I did suggest an idea:

"It seems to me that Tuan Anh has a girlfriend. Does he?"

"He does. But what?"

"Why don't we organize a wedding ceremony for them? Only a pseudo wedding."

Mr. Thanh proved not to have understood the suggested plan. He did not pose any question but looked questioningly.

"We invite guests, for example, to a restaurant away from our living area; we invite the local police to a night reception with treats and a music band. Don't forget to invite the sailors. Do you have any sailor you can trust?

"Sure. We have Mr. Loi. We'll let him join the escape."

"Then let this sailor watch over the boat during the reception. And make sure all the other sailors are at the reception to keep them away from the boat."

"That can be arranged. All sailors will be invited."

"While the guests are enjoying the night, we'll steal out. We may have to add a little bit of strong sleeping pills to their drink."

"Let me talk to my brother about your suggestion." Mr. Thanh stopped for a few seconds and then said, "But it sounds slightly familiar, as if someone else has carried out such a trick." Mr. Thanh sounded doubtful.

"Wedding receptions take place all the time, they may not suspect anything. Anyway, we may have to devise another scheme. What's important is that you and your brother must master the details and the option of improvisation. In the meantime, it's better for me to know how much we can contribute to the expense of the escape so we can be ready."

"My brother decided that only four families will be loaded. Our two families, yours, and the family of sailor Loi. Roughly about forty people."

"How about your parents?" I asked.

"No. My brother won't let old people onto the boat. Neither my parents nor yours. He specifically insisted," Mr. Thanh said threateningly. After a short pause, he continued: "They might die through the rough sea travel, and it will be fatal to the whole group."

"How sad it is!"

With the short comment, I thought of my old mother. Would I have to leave her behind? How could I? BaNgoai was younger than my mother and she had other children whom she might rely on. Seeing me shuffling uncomfortably in the armchair, Mr. Thanh might have understood what I was anxious about. He continued his menacing ultimatum:

"Either you accept the condition or there's nothing."

"How about if we spend an extra sum for our parents?"

"We don't bring our parents along." Mr. Thanh killed any hope in me for negotiation by categorically saying, "Either you go without yours or you stay back. No deal. That's the ultimate condition. You know my brother's character. When he says no, that means no. That's how he leads our sailor team."

I sat silent at hearing the ultimatum. Outside, the sky looked as if it were spinning around. Mr. Thanh woke me out of my short insanity, asking, "Should we have any cue just in case?"

After a few seconds, I resumed my alertness and wondered,

"What is the purpose of a cue? We know each other. We communicate directly."

"It's just in case we need to communicate through a messenger or we have an emergency and need to communicate when there's somebody else or the police around."

"If that's the case then . . . one side should ask the other about something, such as 'Is it going to rain tomorrow?' Just any meaningless question."

"Then what?"

"The other side should answer, 'Thanks for asking!'"

"That's it?"

"No. Upon hearing the 'Thanks for asking' response, the first one should ask another question, any question. And the other side should reiterate exactly the same answer: Thanks for asking! The questions and the identical answer must be said at least twice. But the cues should be used only when we cannot directly communicate with each other."

In his younger days, Mr. Thanh joined the army special forces. I did not know the exact name of the military unit. Members of the unit went through rigid physical, military, and cultural training for daredevil underground activities. The unit sent their agents to infiltrate the North for secret political and military actions. Mr. Thanh had worked behind the northern line on several occasions. In such a working environment, agents might not know each other individually. They could recognize each other only through secrete catchwords. Information could be indirectly communicated via the so-called mail boxes, which were secret hidden spots the agents continuously changed and the receiving end could only identify by following complicated cues. Mr. Thanh and I were in a hidden plot. However, we knew each other. I did not anticipate any occasion in which we would need a catchword for communication. Anyway, by second nature, Mr. Thanh suggested we have cues; I took it to be good forethought.

Four of My Le's siblings from Saigon finally reached our beach home. Two of them, Aunty Uyen Duong and her six-year-old son, Tam Giao, came by train on a hot Thursday night. Two others, Uncle Binh Duong and his sister, arrived two nights later. Aunty Uyen's husband was a pilot who had been killed in 1972. She was granted a sum of money on the death of her husband and a monthly amount for widows and orphans. She saved the money by purchasing gold to avoid the uncertainty of the value of monetary paper notes over time. When Saigon fell under the Communists, all her monetary supports were cut. She did not own a home but stayed with another sister. The pineapple farm director, Mr. Tuyen, provided Aunty Uyen with a paper certifying she was an employee of the farm who wanted to bring her son to Quang Binh to visit her mother-in-law for the first time after the war ended.

Uncle Binh and his sister had just finished their higher education prior to the Saigon debacle. They were jobless and living among other siblings in Saigon. Certified by Mr. Tuyen as his farm employees who were on the trip to look for better seeds for the farm, the two of them caught another train to Da Nang.

To divert the night vigilance of the police, the five members of my family—My Le, me, and the three children—set up a spacious mosquito net in the front porch outside our front door to sleep under at night. In the early nights of summer, sleeping out in the porch or even in the open front yard under the magical moonlight was a way most families tried to enjoy the night breeze during their sleep when none of the houses had cooling systems or air-conditioning. Our home was on the beach. There was plenty of fresh air, a mild atmosphere, and the mellow purr of rippling waves lulling us into peaceful sleep. We did not need to expose ourselves to the breeze and fog at night. But that was the perfect way to hide our relatives sleeping inside the home in case the police eventually came for a surprise house checking.

The next day, when stopping by Grandma's home after eight hours at work, My Le requested our liaison to fetch Mr. Thanh as soon as possible. Mr. Thanh did not show up until several days later. Upon seeing me, Mr. Thanh asked, "Any emergency?"

"Our relatives from Saigon are available," I informed him. "We're anxious about a date."

"Not tonight. Neither tomorrow."

"We cannot hide them too long, you know. The police may search my home anytime as they've done before."

"My brother has just loaded provisions for a fishing trip." The information startled me. Mr. Thanh continued, "This is the season for catching fish. We want to gain some more money for our parents. We'll sail out at the beginning of the week. You'll have to wait."

2. The twenty-fifth hour

Spring was in full bloom. The blue sky was scattered with migrating birds flying north in spectacular formation across the immense firmament.

In late afternoon the ocean breeze nicely caressed soft skin. Looking out from the living room window of our beach home, I scanned the surface of the water in the bay. That was the most risky area on the escape trail. Near-shore fishermen were setting up their fishing nets everywhere for night catches. They could earn credits working for the police by warning them of any suspicious boats sailing out at nighttime. At the mouth of the half-moon bay, border guards had their patrolling ships on twenty-four-hour watch; it was up to them to search any boat leaving the bay for the high seas, or at least to check the fishing trip permit or count the people on board. With their speedboats, the border guards were able to chase after boats trying to run from them. The weather was so calm these days. Escapees willing to risk the rough high seas could not have asked for a better time than these storm-free days when the ocean was peaceful. These were the last beautiful days of a serene spring.

Unfortunately, Mr. Phap was planning for more fishing trips and more delays for his money making, while My Le's siblings confined themselves in dark rooms waiting for the unknown. It was very discouraging and risky. The adults could somehow patiently hide themselves indefinitely behind the closed doors, but six-year-old Tam Giao could not be kept out of sight for a prolonged period of time, especially during the beautiful daytime. Tam Giao was the same age as our youngest son. The latter was enjoying the freedom of a free kid under the sun, running around among the playful innocent youngsters of the area, while Tam Giao became more and more irritated in a restricted gloomy corner.

Keeping our relatives hidden was a constant source of worry. We never knew when someone might show up unexpectedly. When honeybees had built their combs between layers of the walls of my wooden home, an old gentleman in the village had helped me build equipment to house the bees for honey extraction. The gentleman came to my home when I invited him for help. However, he might also come unexpectedly for a follow-up check.

His next-door neighbor, Mr. Phong, the former head of Tam Toa Ward, had been strolling leisurely along the alley to the beach every day since he was released from concentration camp. He stopped by my home for a chat anytime he saw someone around. He knew well our nephew Tam Giao and his mother.

One afternoon during his stroll, Mr. Phong detected our nephew around. The old gentleman could not help asking me, "Why is Tam Giao here alone? Where's his mom?"

"His mom meant to take him along to Quang Binh to see his old grandma."

"Is his grandma living in Quang Binh?"

"His grandma has three sons. The two older ones got killed in the war. She brought the little one back to live in her native village of Quang Binh after 1975."

"Why didn't Tam Giao join his mom?"

"That was their initial plan. But the journey from Saigon to Da Nang was so tough. The Da Nang-to-Quang Binh railway is much more inconvenient and troublesome. The weather is detrimental to the delicate health of the boy. His mother had to leave him here and go there by herself."

"The boy is growing up fast. He looks very healthy!"

"His mom gave birth to him only several months after his pilot dad was killed. It's over six years."

"Poor boy!"

"You know, for the time being, he's the only grandson in his dad's family. His mom was so afraid of anything happening to him. So she left him under our protection to go to Quang Binh by herself."

"So sorry for both of them!"

To distract Mr. Phong from the presence of little Tam Giao and the absence of his mom, I led the conversation in another direction to avoid his alarming inquiries:

"Did you ever contact Mr. Thao for a trip overseas on his escaping boat?"

"I'm too old for escaping. Moreover, I have been released from concentration camp. They won't touch me anymore. I hope the situation will change in a favorable direction."

"But do you know if Mr. Thao has any such plan?"

"I think there must be someone who is interested in his boat. But I didn't ask. Do you want me to ask him for you?"

"I had a conversation with Mr. Thao some time ago. I thought you'd talked to him about my intention and so he brought up the issue to me in response."

"I don't remember if I ever mentioned your case to him," the old gentleman vaguely told me. Mr. Phong was about to leave my home. He looked out to the empty street and suddenly asked:

"If Thao is leaving soon, tonight or tomorrow, do you want to join him?"

The unexpected question made me jump. Did Mr. Phong actually come to convey Mr. Thao's urgent message? Did Thao really want my family to be on his boat? What was the price? Was he about to leave tonight or tomorrow? I was struck dumb at the unforeseen situation. Mr. Phong looked calm and serious. The former village head used to be as lively as a cricket. Seeing me overcome with embarrassment, Mr. Phong went on to ask:

"If you leave tonight, will you bring little Tam Giao along?"

"Sure. We'll bring him along."

"Without his mom?"

"His mom will accept the situation. Sir . . ." Seeing Mr. Phong was ready to leave, I anxiously stopped him. "Did you come to inform me of Mr. Thao's invitation?"

"Seeing Tam Giao here, I felt softhearted." Mr. Phong did not directly respond to my inquiry.

"Thanks. Should I be ready for something?"

"I know people are contacting Thao about leaving. Why don't you contact him directly?" Mr. Phong turned away from my insistent questioning.

Mr. Phong's ambivalent answer disillusioned me. To probe further into the situation, I asked him:

"Do you know if Mr. Phap or Mr. Thanh has any such contact or plan?"

"That I don't know. If they plan anything, how can I know? Maybe they do. Maybe they don't. Diligent fishermen do not care about a world so strange to them."

"Is Mr. Thao in the same shoes?"

"They're enjoying the huge income they earn in their fishing business. They may not want to risk doing anything now. I don't know."

Mr. Phong's statement put me back in a hung mode. Had he really conveyed an invitation on behalf of his relative? Had Mr. Thao vaguely heard or suspected anything of our involvement with Mr. Phap that he wanted his hands on? Or did Mr. Phong simply speak spontaneously when he suddenly saw Tam Giao? I was really confused. Moreover, the old gentleman seemed to believe in what the Communists had repeatedly promised: a peaceful life for him. He had not learned from what Mr. Nguyen Van Thieu, former President of the Republic, said: "Don't listen to what the Communists say, but look at what the Communists actually do." Flies were easier caught with honey; the old gentleman should know that. As for the potential of working with Mr. Thao for an escape, I needed more information to weigh the pros and cons when we had halfway hooked ourselves to Mr. Phap.

With the pressures from My Le's siblings, who grew anxiously irritated while they were hiding behind closed doors, I had to talk to our liaison to clarify some critical details.

Our liaison, Mr. Due, was in his late forties. He was a healthy unmarried man and was well known to be the boyfriend of Ms. Y for such a long time. We did not know why the couple did not get married. One of Mr. Que's brothers, a fisherman and boat owner, had gotten out of the country in 1975 and resettled in the United States. Mr. Due applied with Mr. Phap to get away on his boat. He suggested to Mr. Phap that once they had reached a refugee camp, he would ask his brother to sponsor Mr. Phap's family to the United States. It might be the way Mr. Due wanted to pay back Mr. Phap in return for his seat on the escaping boat. My Le and I never asked Mr. Due whether he was asked by the boat owner to pay by gold. Mr. Due was also a close neighbor of Mr. Phap. One of his relatives was the girlfriend of Mr. Phap's son Tuan Anh. In my work environment, I was separated from Mr. Due only by an open window. We agreed that he was the best person to play the reliable role of a liaison.

When I addressed him that afternoon, Mr. Due listened attentively.

"We want you to get the answers for several critical issues," I said.

"Let me know them."

"Do you know if Mr. Thao is going to escape soon?"

"That I don't know. If he does, as you heard the other day, he'll ask for a very high price. Can you afford it?"

"I just want to know. This is the situation: If Mr. Thao escapes before we do, it will be very difficult for us to move. The beach will be tightly controlled. Mr. Phap will be strictly shadowed. So you should look into Mr. Thao's possibility and warn Mr. Phap to act fast."

"I see. If Thao leaves, we'll be in great difficulty. I'll track Thao down. What else do you need?"

"I want to know about my family's share of the expense. We need to know, to weigh our capability. Is Mr. Phap asking for more or less than Thao did? We need a specific amount so we can be ready."

"I see your concerns. Me too. I need to know how much I must pay him. Anything else?"

"The next is the specific date. We cannot be put in such a hanging situation. And as I've said, we must sail out before Mr. Thao may do."

"As far as I know, Mr. Phap is ready for a fishing trip next week, and maybe for several more trips." Our liaison showed sign of impatience when he uttered the observation. He stopped to swallow a sigh and then added, "I know. Nothing will happen within at least a week or so."

"Did you get yourself in a ready mode?"

"Sure, I'm ready. Ready anytime. In the meantime, I'm just enjoying my last days in this country."

"You always look relaxed. I see you laugh all the time. That's why you have such a healthy body. Do you have good appetite and sleep?"

"Appetite for barley and manioc! Are you kidding me?" Mr. Due burst out laughing, and then continued, "To make up for my loss of appetite, I sleep well. Very well."

"I can tell."

"You know, once I slept under the open sky. Around midnight it rained, but I didn't wake up until I was drenched."

"People said you sleep so soundly that mosquitoes may carry you away asleep."

"That's me!"

"But be vigilant to let me know what's going on. Don't let the opportunity slip away unnoticed."

"I'll keep a close contact with them, and I'll let you know of anything I know."

"I need a clear answer on the details I mentioned. You know, I cannot let the grass grow under my feet. Furthermore, do you know what the statement 'Thanks for asking' means?"

"Ha ha. Thanks for asking! You think I have no clue of the cues?"

"Good!"

We did not hear anything for a while. April was over, and we were two weeks into May when the mediator came to me for the price of the escape.

"Mr. Phap needs two taels per head to leave behind for his parents. He told me that your mother told him there will be ten from your side. I thought there were only five or six."

"Thanks for the details." Knowing the price they set, I felt much relieved. However, I was so afraid that we might not be able to fully afford the price for my five-member family. My Le told me before I went to negotiate with another organizer several months ago that we had only twenty leaves of gold. I did not know whether My Le's siblings could afford it either. My Le and I had carefully avoided mentioning to the siblings the delicate issue of a contribution to the escape cost. Seeing me deep in thought, the liaison sat back, his long right arm spanning the couch, in a waiting mode. I continued:

"Did he mention any specific day?"

"Mr. Thanh has insisted everyone must be ready. The time is coming. He won't let anyone know until the very last minute."

While Mr. Due and I were discussing the details, My Le stopped by after work. A young guy, who used to be a military private and was out of work after the fall of Da Nang, sneaked in silently after My Le. He used to play the drum set in my talent shows. He might have been in his early thirties and was a very quiet guy. Over the years I could not even remember his name. My Le knew his parents well. Taking a seat, uninvited, next to our liaison, the young guy broke his usual silence by addressing My Le as if something had caught him by surprise:

"Sister, I see something strange on your face. Come here, let me see your palm."

My Le was caught by surprise as well. The guy was not a fortune teller. Nobody had ever heard about his palm-reading skill. My Le pulled a chair close to him, sat down, and curiously opened her left palm to him without saying anything, while still holding her bag with her right hand.

"Not your left palm. Your right one, please."

While examining My Le's palm, he straightened himself up and looked at My Le again from top to toe, to My-Le's great curiosity.

"Why do you look at me like that? What's up? Why won't you tell me? Am I going to hit a jackpot?"

"Why are you here?" the palm reader asked My Le in return. "Your face and your hand told me clearly you must have gone away! Far away!"

"What? I'm still sitting in front of you."

While pretending it was a joke, both My Le and Mr. Due were awestruck. Their four eyes met in stupefaction. To see if the young guy was a reliable palm reader, My Le leisurely suggested with humor, "Why don't you read Mr. Due's palm? To see if he's about to get married to his girlfriend."

"OK. Let me see."

Mr. Due enthusiastically extended his right palm out to the young guy, but the latter said, "Not the right one, your left one. Male's left, female's right. OK?"

Having intently observed Mr. Due's palm while My Le waited anxiously, the guy didn't say anything. Then Mr. Due could not help eagerly asking him, without being fully awake to remember that walls have ears, "Am I destined to go anywhere? Overseas, for example?"

"In the twenty-fifth hour, sir!" the palm reader coldly replied.

His response alarmed My Le. Mr. Due, who was an approved applicant for the planned trip and was the chosen connection for communication between the boat owner and ourselves, seemed not to understand the full implication of the palm reader's statement.

Anticipating that our exodus would be very near, I tried to resolve two thorny and heartbreaking issues. We had to get twenty-five taels of gold ready to pay the boat owner. My Le and I had invested most of our financial resources in our fish-processing business and the products would not be ready for sale soon enough to have money to buy extra gold for the whole group. If we collected all the precious metals we had accumulated during several years in the fish-processing business together with our wedding jewelry, we still might not have enough to cover the expense for our family and the siblings. My Le could not keep this critical matter unknown to her siblings. Finally she brought the thorny issue up among her brothers and sisters. Two of My Le's younger brothers had nothing on hand to contribute. All that the uncles had brought along was the clothing on their backs. And so had the youngest sister. Realizing the impasse of our financial status, Aunty Uyen broke the silence to assure My Le, the two uncles, and the youngest sister that she would cover the deficiency for the whole family group.

My Le and I had paid dearly for the boat repair, for the milk, for the medicine, and for some pocket expenses of the owner and his brother. We had taken the risk of negotiating the escape. I had told Mr. Thanh, "If something happens, you should tell the police: it's Mr. Tri who devised everything. You were simply lured into the plan. You just wanted to have some extra money. It was because of the little sum of money that you acted blindly." What I brew, I must drink.

But both My Le and I felt so uneasy about spending the savings that were meant for Aunty Uyen's orphaned son, to cover our escape. We were the elder siblings but were unable to cover financially for our younger relatives. Upon the offer from Aunty Uyen, I felt guilty for my own family. Facing the unforeseeable future, I blurted out the anxiety of my heart:

"Aunty Uyen! You've offered to cover for all of us. I don't know what to say. If we're lucky enough to reach a free port as we plan, I don't know whether I'll be able to do anything even to feed my children. How can I reimburse your generous gift?"

"Don't worry about that! Don't think about repaying me. I want to make it clear: you won't owe me anything."

My Le and Aunty Uyen tried to put together the sum of gold to pay for the ten-member group. It was about two taels short. My Le was to find a way to fill the deficiency.

But the most heartbreaking issue for me was that Mr. Phap had decided not to let my eighty-four-year-old mother come on the boat.

I was her only surviving child. What ingratitude I would be showing to leave my old mom alone behind. I expected that after I left, the police would confiscate my home and kick my mom out. Should I stay to be with her in her last years? "Oh Mom, what should I do?"

Mom had led such a sorrowful life. In her childhood, she went through traumatic experiences under the reign of the Can Vuong movement (Aid to the King) and the Binh Tay Sat Ta campaign (French Pacification and Catholic Persecution) between 1885 and 1888. Her native Catholic village got surrounded. Militants of the campaign fired handmade rockets to burn the little parochial church and thousands of Christians who took refuge in it. My dad's grandparents were massacred in the anti-Christian campaign. My grandfather ran away from his village, sought shelter in a non-Christian hamlet, survived, and got married to a local girl. Dad ventured to set up a plantation in an unexplored mountainous area. Struck with malaria or typhoid fever, Dad died when my mom was in her early forties. Without Dad's helpful hands, Mom labored hard to feed and raise three children. Mom played the role of a home teacher; she taught my sister and me to read and write, while my big brother was caught by the Communists and sent to jail hundreds of miles north. Mom cried bitterly day and night, and she sold her rice fields and family treasures to go searching in vain for the whereabouts of my brother. He was liberated by the Allies only later. Then my poor sister died of being frightened during the war. My sister had just been buried when my brother got killed. Mom was crying bitterly over the repeated losses. Worried about me being forced by the Communists into insurgent activities, she sent me to the city, far away from home, for education. She stayed alone in the remote countryside working to support herself and me. Anticipating her last day without anyone around, she bought a coffin for herself and put it next to her bed.

Eventually, when the Communists broke the New Year truce in the 1968 Tet Offensive to invade my birthplace, Mom escaped the hellish battle to join My Le and me and her grandchildren in Da Nang, as I have said previously. Mom took care of our children while both My Le and I were working. We had a live-in nanny, but Mom preferred to fix delicious dishes for her grandchildren herself. My children and I owed her a lot, while I had not done anything significant for her. Now I was going to take her cherished grandchildren away from her. My Le and I were about to run away from Mom, leaving her without any support. "Mom! How could we do this? Oh, God! Should I stay back with Mom instead?"

I brought the lamentable issue directly up to my mom, who comforted me by saying:

"Son, I love you and my grandchildren. I don't want the lives of my grandchildren and yours to be miserable. I had the worst experiences with the Communists. Don't let my grandchildren suffer as I did. Take my grandchildren to a good life. I have lived by myself for more than thirty years. Don't harm yourself and my grandchildren because of me. Mom loves all of you very much!"

Mom did not cry in front of us, but I knew her heart was broken and she might wipe away her tears silently. I spent many sleepless nights thinking of my miserable mom and of the disloyal son who was about to leave his mom unsupported. When My Le talked to her about the tragic circumstances of ours, Mom encouraged her not to worry about Mom and ruin the plan. Mom also gave My Le her last piece of gold to contribute to the escape price. "Mom! Nothing's left for you. Neither your son nor your grandchildren. Not a penny. There's no home for you, either!"

I kept weighing the deplorable decision to leave or not to leave. I understood the decision of the boat owner not to let old people take the risk of a long journey on his boat on the rough high seas. But his decision broke my heart. What should I do? Was it feasible to let My Le and my children leave on their unprotected escape while I stay back with my lone mom? Or should I leave Mom unsupported to shepherd my little children on their way to the unknown future? I fell into the dilemma of the painful separation of lovers as described in his epic "New Heartbreaking Sound" by our great poet Nguyen Du:

> The moon being divided into two halves,
> One half shines on the pillow of the one who stays behind,
> The other sadly illuminates the departing beloved's path.

After my mom spoke her words, I could not face her to talk to her anymore. I thought I might not withstand the delicate situation.

"Dearest Mom of mine, I felt so guilty betraying you, Mom! You love me to the point you sacrifice your own life for my survival, for my little children's livelihood, for staying behind empty-handed and alone in your old age among an unfriendly universe!"

The boat owner kept loading provisions and applying for fishing-trip permits, making us wait day after day in frustration.

That night, after retreating from the seamstress kiosk, our connection, Mr. Due, came back in a hurry.

"Is there any good news?" I asked, upon seeing him at the doorstep.

"Unexpected happening!" the liaison answered curtly and stepped into Grandma's living room. He looked back to the street to make sure his appearance at such a critical hour was not noticed. Then he continued, while sitting down in the armchair against the wall:

"The police have served summons to Tuan Anh and his sister to register for military service."

"That's great!" I rejoiced at the news about Mr. Phap's children. "It's also an ultimatum to Mr. Phap to act, isn't it?"

"Mr. Phap was thrilled at the summons. He didn't say anything, but I know he's made up his mind. Nobody saw him outside his home the whole day. You should get yourself ready."

"God bless us!" I said, while our liaison sneaked out of the room hurriedly, as if chased by an invisible onlooker, without saying goodbye to me.

3. Last supper

I
t was May 28, 1978, three years and two months after the 1975 Black March. Numerous painful events had happened ever since.

We were suspended in agonizing anxiety.

Mr. Phap and his team were all out on the beach that sunny afternoon busily preparing for another fishing trip. The weather forecast was favorable. Our liaison told us the aching news that Mr. Phap had just gotten another permit from the police for his next fishing trip. They must have planned for a long expedition in such an advantageous season since they had loaded more gas and food than usual.

"Did you try to ask Mr. Phap if we're about to leave?"

"Your concern is also mine," Mr. Due sadly said. "I did ask him last night."

"What did he say?"

"You won't believe what he told me."

"What did he tell you?" I grew anxious.

"He's crazy. I thought he was half drunk. He chased me away and yelled at me, 'I'm not going anywhere. Nobody goes anywhere. Understand? Get away from me!'"

"I can't believe it! Didn't you remind him of his children's summons to military services? Did you put that pressure on him?"

"I brought the issue up to his wife the day before."

"What was her reaction?"

"Oh! She told me she'd asked her husband. And she said he showed sign of being persuaded."

"Then why didn't he act?"

"I don't understand. He's gone crazy."

"Did you probe Mr. Thanh?"

"I stopped by yesterday evening but he wasn't home. His wife told me he was visiting somebody downtown. But I did see an interesting sign."

"What?"

"I caught his wife packing up clothes and stuff for her twin babies."

On the beach, Mr. Phap's team was loading a large amount of huge ice cubes. Each cube might have weighed forty pounds or so. Tanks of gas, bags of rice, cans of fresh water, and other provisions had been stacked in the fishing boat until it was full, the previous day. The boat was well reconditioned for many days of seagoing. The whole team of sailors were mending the nets and completing the last work on their equipment along the sandy beach next to the big boat. That part of the beach was cluttered with nets, all sorts of miscellaneous equipment, and the fishing team. They were noisily talking, joking, and laughing. Some were scanning the early afternoon sky. They had everything ready for sailing out early the next morning. The blue sky was in harmony with the gentle, quiet ocean stretching to the horizon far away. The men looked happy about the favorable weather and a promising outcome of the fishing trip.

I felt discouraged upon hearing the very bad news from our liaison. Leaving Grandma's residence, I hurried home early to share the unfavorable news with our hiding relatives. In the discouraging situation, we might have to move our relatives to another hiding site, away from the surveying eyes of the police, or even send them back to Saigon. Otherwise the relatives, my family, and I were at a very high risk of being caught. Previously I had brought the issue up to My Le and the siblings but we could not decide which way to go. There was no safe hiding place available. Saigon was too far from Da Nang; the communication could not be timely. Travel between the two cities took time and was strictly controlled, especially when the exodus was at its highest point. The siblings were so reluctant to think about going back to Saigon.

The short lane I traveled every day seemed today to be an endless route leading me to nowhere. I was thinking hard of a solution to the current impasse and thus did not pay attention to the passersby. I knew every face living along the lane leading to my beach home. Most of them were not wealthy but were very friendly and communicative. Each time they saw us or any of our children they reached out to have a quick talk. We often exchanged a few cordial greetings when we came across each other. Today many were surprised to see me a little taciturn.

At the locked front gate—the front gate was locked when I was at BaNgoai's home—I encountered the policeman Thai, unpredictably. A sense of uneasiness invaded my heart. Mr. Thai did not tell me why he had come to my home at this early hour. He knew I had been at Grandma's home but had not stopped by to see me there. Since he did not say anything, I was thinking he might be just strolling by. But who knew, maybe he suspected something and was ready to enter my home for inspection. Had he seen little Tam Giao running around? Had someone—Mr. Tan for example, or teacher Hoa from the wooden chalet opposite to ours—suspected something and reported it to the police? Was it possible that Mr. Phong, fulfilling the obligations of his probation after being brainwashed, had informed the police of the suspicious presence of little Tam Giao around my home? Had the siblings hiding in our home become impatient and made a regrettable mistake? Mr. Thai looked sinister. He did not greet me as he saw me. My heart skipped a beat.

To buy time, I did not try to open the front gate. I called BaNoi as if she kept the key for the gate. After a couple of calls, my mom appeared at the kitchen door and looked out to the front gate.

"Mom. Get the key to open the gate for Mr. Thai!"

I called quite loudly to alert my relatives, but I was so afraid that they might not be able to hide themselves if Mr. Thai actually got in. The back door of our kitchen opened to the backyard, which was more than an acre wide and led to a narrow, shallow stream. The backyard was divided by a barbed-wire fence that we built to keep our German shepherd Kino from wandering too far from home. I had shown the relatives how to hide away beyond the fence in emergency cases. I bought time for them by calling my mom to open the front gate.

My mom turned back into the home as if to go get the key to the front gate. She came out after several minutes. I unlocked the gate and it swung open. I hesitantly set my foot in, but was stunned as Tuan

Anh, son of Mr. Phap, ran over at his fastest space shouting, "Mr. Thai! Mr. Thai! Come quickly. Come for rescue!"

The policeman turned abruptly toward Tuan Anh and asked repeatedly, "What's the matter? What's the matter?"

"Come. My uncle Thanh!"

"What's the matter with him?"

"He's beating up my dad. Please come!"

"Beating up? Why? Where are they? At home? Tell me."

"No! They're at the beach!" Tuan Anh said breathlessly. He was gasping as if he had been running for a while, looking for police help. His news made me jump. I was wondering if they intended to ruin the plan we had painfully designed. Why did they get into such a stupid dispute and let the police get involved? Or did they want to get out of the plan that way, as Mr. Phap had told Mr. Due?

A bitter cold ran up my spine. Despair invaded my soul. I imagined our plan to escape had been dissipated like smoke in a cyclone.

"Calm down. Take a deep breath, and let me know what's going on," Mr. Thai eagerly asked Tuan Anh.

"What happened?" I attempted to calm down my discontent and resentment to ask Tuan Anh.

"Uncle Thanh let a fishing basket drift away, leaving no trace behind. My dad blamed him. Damn it! Then they had a ferocious fight because of it."

"How could a fight for such an odd thing happen between brothers?" My hidden grievances had not subsided in me, and I asked Tuan Anh the somewhat insensitive question.

"Where were the sailors?" Mr. Thai turned around to ask, as he started hurrying away.

"They're there, but couldn't separate the two. Please come, else he'll kill my dad!"

Policeman Thai hastily took the shortcut to the scene. Feeling desperate, arms hanging at my sides, I looked at the two of them leaving. I hesitated, and then chased Tuan Anh as he ran after the policeman. Anxiously I asked, "Sorry. But was anyone hurt?"

"Thanks for asking."

"What did you say?"

"Thanks for asking." To my surprise, I suddenly realized Tuan Anh was repeating the cues we had agreed upon. Tuan Anh did not look back but slowed down a little bit to mutter a quick answer to me:

"It's a ploy. It's time! We'll leave tonight!"

"What did you say?"

"I'll pick you up. Tonight!"

"Oh, God! Tonight? We'll be . . . in the front . . . porch."

I was so thrilled at the unexpected news that I stammered out the words nervously. I could only let Tuan Anh know in such a short phrase where we would be. I could not know if he caught my broken sentence.

Informed of the big news, My Le's siblings almost burst from joy. I left home right away in such a hurry to fetch My Le home for last-minute preparations. There was not much time left, while some critical things had to be done.

Along the way to the health-care office, I became mentally confused. Pedestrians were dimly flickering along like disappearing pictures. Many questions sprang up in my mind. Is something about to come to an end quickly? Should it really happen? How should I behave? Am I about to leave my miserable mom? And the home we live in? And the fatherland we love? Is tonight the night of no return? Is My Le willing to leave Grandma? Lots of questions popped up in my troubled mind.

I did not realize I had gone past the Malaria Eradication office. Upon coming back, I shocked My Le with the news. I saw My Le's hands shake and her face turn pale upon hearing the information. She fixed her gaze on her coworkers with a nostalgic look. I signaled her to leave for fear she might lose her calmness and burst into tears. We hurried home without saying anything, to the surprise of her coworkers.

We had to get at least another two taels of gold to complete the requested sum. We had to be personally confirmed by Mr. Phap. We must deliver the sum to him before the boarding time. All the things we needed to bring along, we'd had ready many days earlier. Not much. Just our personal papers, family pictures, and clothes for our children. Milk, medications, and food had been step by step delivered to Mr. Thanh a while ago.

The quarrel between the two brothers was dragging on. Mr. Phap wrathfully broke a couple of other fishing baskets, kicked his brother, beat those who dived in to intervene, tore off his shirt, chased the sailors and their wives away, tumbled the mended nets from the stands, and furiously called off the fishing trip. He kicked sand dunes, waved his hands to the sky and screamed chaotic sounds, and no one understood what he actually said. Female workers were crying bitterly and calling for help. Yelling wrathfully, Mr. Phap, with unkempt hair and bloodshot eyes, left the scene sprawled with destroyed equipment. The police followed him home. Sailors ran away one after the other. Mr. Thanh called sailor Loi back and asked him to watch over the loaded boat while other sailors vanished from the scene in a depressed and discontented manner. They could not believe their eyes. The two brothers never had any quarrel. Mr. Phap had a loud imposing voice. On the boat floating on the rough sea, his voice, as loud as a speaker, sounded stronger than the roar of the waves. But the sailors never heard any exchange of strong words between the two brothers. The sailors left the scene in disbelief.

From the front doors of their homes, the two brothers kept yelling at each other. Their wives were trying unsuccessfully to talk them out of the tantrum. Mr. Thai left. Several other policemen came, and they stopped on the thresholds of the two brothers' homes, trying to keep them from disturbing the neighborhood. The policemen left the scene when Mr. Thanh rushed to the market for liquor. People and kids in the area gathered along the lane out of curiosity until the day went dark.

The night fell. Electrical power was down. The hamlet and surrounding streets grew somber.

Our contact, Mr. Due, came to Grandma's home. My Le brought all our jewelry, wedding rings, and gold leaves so Grandma could deliver them to Mr. Phap for us. Two more taels were needed and we were short. Mr. Due came to confirm what we had already been notified.

"Around midnight tonight Tuan Anh will pick you up. Be ready."

"Thanks for the news. You'd better go home and get ready, too."

In apprehension of the potential Communist offense to my family's worship icons, I moved some of them to the nearby chapel and destroyed and respectfully buried the remaining debris. Waiting until the night was dark, My Le and I brought two bicycles to the local gold dealer whom My Le used to deal with.

"Sister! Could you lend me two taels of gold?" The lady gold dealer was several years older than My Le; both of them addressed each other in a friendly manner as 'sister.' Gold dealing was a covered-up business, so night time was appropriate for such type of contact. We did not know whether the police were aware of the lady's business. If they were, the lady might have to buy their closed eyes and deaf ears. For safety, we had to wait for the darkness of night to show up at the door of the gold trader.

"You're my good neighbor. No matter how many of them, I'll get them for you as they're available. No need for both of you to come in a pair. Come on in."

"I'll catch the early train to travel to Saigon tomorrow morning," My Le said. "I've just got the temporary absence permit this evening. There's no electricity. It's so dark that my husband had to come along. With two extra taels from you, I may trade them for some things we need. Please take the two bicycles as a warranty. If I won't be home soon enough and you need your loan back, please contact my mom."

"Sister, don't be so formal. Your mom and you are our neighbors. Our acquaintance is the solid warranty. I won't take the bicycles. Please keep them for yourselves."

"If you don't take the bicycles, I may have to go empty handed."

"I guess you may want more than two taels. Don't you?"

"Thanks for your offer, sister! But only two, please."

Reluctantly, the lady underground gold trader kept the bicycles as we insisted. My Le got what she needed. She handed the borrowed gold leaves to Grandma. To deliver the sum, Grandma came to Mr. Phap posing as if she were the last person trying to reconcile the two brothers.

"Lady! Go home. It's my family business. I don't need any of you to poke your nose into it." At his front door, Mr. Phap chased Grandma away after she had completed the delivery.

Grandma brought home the final pieces of information. It would be midnight or later when the beach was clear of patrolling border guards. Tuan Anh would put ten of us on a fishing basket and row to the motorized big boat.

BaNgoai skipped her dinner and was sitting on an old chair against the back door looking out toward the ocean, emaciated and sorrowful. We were so sad as we tried to find words to comfort her. Our daughter came around nine o'clock to kiss Grandma goodbye. Our older son brought some of our last valuables to her. Hugging our children, Grandma cried bitterly and silently.

My Le and I did not eat anything until final preparations were done. Heartbrokenly kissing Grandma goodbye, both of us drove to the mini cake shop a mile away from home on Tran Cao Van Road to taste the last supper. We sat on two low, shabby stools next to the oil lamp, under the sole unlit lightbulb. We were alone without any other customers around in the out-of-electricity night. In the badly shaped, dimly lit shop, my heart ached to think of the dark conditions my country fellows would go through for the rest of their miserable lives.

It was the last supper on the land we loved and were about to leave.

4. Double five celebration

It was a moonless night. A few faint star-lights hardly pierced the cloud screen.

I was wondering if any ghostly soul did come crying on the luxuriant branches of the surrounding trees. It was the longest night we had ever experienced. While our three children slept soundly, My Le and I were in the wait mode inside the mosquito net at the front porch of our beach home. We could not lull ourselves into sleep. The murmuring waves sounded as if ghostly souls from the dark world were wailing in the endless ominous night.

Facing our beach home was another chalet built by My Le's brother and later sold to Mr. Hoa, a high school teacher. Mr. Hoa's chalet and ours were very much similar in shape and were built one on each side of the lane. There were times my students had mistaken the opposite home for mine in full daylight. Tonight, it was a dark night on the fourth of the fifth lunar month. The moon was but a faint arc on the horizon that did not shed any light.

It was past 12:00 a.m. A new day had started. The overcast Tuesday came with no breeze, signaling the start of a gloomy May 29, 1979, day. The atmosphere turned a little bit hot. Or it was because we were burned on the inside with the tense situation and we kept turning and shuffling around endlessly. It was past twelve o'clock, the agreed-upon time. Each minute went by as slowly as an hour.

My wrist watch showed 1:20 a.m. In summer time the daybreak would be quite early in this country. Local people might wake up very early to start their labor days. I felt a burning inside for not having seen the appearance of Tuan Anh as we were promised. As time went on, I grew much more worried. Did something go wrong? Or did he get caught? Night remained silent and was slowly drifting away. What might have happened? Were the fraternal fight ploy and the whole escape plan discovered and broken? During the evening, the police did not seem a bit suspicious. Or were they also playing games, pretending to naively believe in the frivolous family dispute? Was it possible that the police would show up to catch us all here?

Five more scary minutes had gone by without Tuan Anh's coming into view. I nervously counted every passing minute. It was 1:30 a.m. At this time, the local bread maker would be up to bake the first batch of new bread for the day. He might have filled a full bag of hot loaves for me to deliver to the barrack at the farthest end of the city. I constantly stared into the dark for any movement.

Time kept clicking on. It was way past 1:30 a.m. Like a panther, Tuan Anh, in dark outfit and coming over the shallow canal behind my backyard, swiftly sneaked along the low and sparse hedgerows. I felt my whole body chill. He had reached the lane in front of our home. I woke my children up while My Le went inside to alert the siblings.

Rushing, prowling in the dim light, instead of turning to our front porch, Tuan Anh headed toward the opposite chalet. Oh no! It must be a fatal mistake. At the minute Tuan Anh was about to climb onto the porch of the other chalet, the owner of the chalet, holding an oil lamp in his hand, opened the front door of his home, stood hesitating a second as if he had caught a glimpse of some unfamiliar movement. Heavens! Tuan Anh must have been uncovered! The teacher then disappeared into the back of the house; it was likely he was chasing after something.

It must have been a strenuous night for Tuan Anh. Over the night, ambushing along the shore, Tuan Anh and sailor Loi evaluated the situation, observed the frequency of the police patrols, and monitored the beach for a safe window. Seeing the police patrol go past the boarding area at the critical time, sailor Loi ran to notify Mr. Phap and Mr. Thanh while Tuan Anh first raced to get his girlfriend and then rushed to fetch our family.

To be sure, Tuan Anh could safely get all of us away; Mr. Due had asked Tuan Anh's girlfriend to stay with him that night. Under the moonless sky, they were sleeping on a double bed in the open-air "Thousand Stars Hotel" in the front courtyard of Mr. Due's home. Tuan

Anh reached the courtyard and stealthily climbed over the sleeping body of Mr. Due to sneakily wake his girlfriend and leave without disturbing Mr. Due. It was incredible that Mr. Due could sleep so soundly through such an anticipated event. Two persons slept on the same bed, one got picked up, and the other was left undisturbed.

While he left his girlfriend hiding in the bushes next to the shallow canal behind our home, Tuan Anh mistakenly approached the home of Mr. Hoa, almost being detected, prior to sneakily climbing back to our front porch. He must somehow have gotten confused in his rush to complete several critical tasks in a hurry when the patrolling border guards had just passed by. The move of the escaping families must be prompt and neat, else it could be easily uncovered.

The foot patrol covered several miles of the beach, and it was about half an hour before they came around again. Lately, due to the high volume of escapes, sometimes there were two patrol groups going in opposite directions, which would cut the time in half. Our forty-some escapees had only a narrow fifteen-minute window to quietly leave home, quickly gather at the beach, get in round baskets, row to the motorized boat, manage to board the high boat in darkness, and rush out of the immense bay.

At the beach, Tuan Anh had a hard time getting his girlfriend and our ten-member family safely into a single fishing basket. It was the first time we had bustled into a round bamboo-woven fishing basket on the undulating waters in the night with bewildered hearts and uncontrolled limbs. Our children clung hard to My Le and me, while my heart was broken thinking of my mom being left behind. I did not wake my mom when we left; I knew she was not sleeping but simply did not want to ruin our plan with the emotional attachment of the painful separation.

The basket was too narrow for our eleven-member group. Seawater was almost getting into the heavily loaded basket. But Tuan Anh skillfully managed to paddle us to the big boat, where he had to help the kids climb, in the dark, up to the deck way above their heads. Within ten minutes or so, my family and the families of Mr. Phap and Mr. Thanh were all safely onboard. We were anxiously waiting for sailor Loi and his family. I did not see Mr. Due around.

About another ten minutes passed by. We did not catch sight of sailor Loi. The critical twenty-minute clear window closed. We could not wait any longer. The next police patrol might come back in minutes. Mr. Phap made the decision to start the engine. The boat roared and shook strongly. Like an arrow coming off the bow, the fleeing craft rushed out in the dark. All passengers were down in the obscurity of the lower deck, next to the chilly ice-cube storage.

I was trembling. It might not have been due to the chilly chamber we were in but to my inner suffering and my fear of the innumerable anticipated dangers lying ahead of us. The chance that seamen operating the fishing nets along the bay would warn the police to catch us. The uproar of the starting boat that could sound the alarm to the border guards. The border-patrolling ships at the port that could stop and search our boat. The risky wide ocean that we were to travel. Imminent typhoons and storms along the journey. Pirates prowling around. Red Chinese patrol forces along the maritime route. The possibility that sailor Loi and Mr. Due, being left behind, could react unfavorably against us.

The sailing team's ignorance of the travel direction—a route they had never taken before—was another imminent danger. I wondered whether the boat owner was heading to Hong Kong as we had intended. If he was, we hoped that as we came within several miles of Hong Kong at night we might recognize it by its colorful illumination. If we came during daytime, we would see the tall buildings stacked up on its mountain slopes and even Victoria Peak, the highest mountain. But without the guidance of a maritime compass, neither two-way radio communication, nor experience of the sailing route, we might go astray, heading to nowhere on the boundless ocean.

Confined in the darkness of the lower deck, time in my troubled mind reeled as slow as through centuries, while actually it took about half an hour to get out of the Da Nang Bay safe and sound. Everyone was allowed to turn up on the upper deck only about two hours after we left our beloved Tien Sha seaport. We had gone through the most challenging episode of our escape from the prison-like country. Everyone exhaled with relief. It was still dark, and we were too far away for my strained, tearful eyes to look back to the homeland and the beloved grandmas we had painfully left behind.

"Dear Mom! From now on, I will be thousands of miles away from you! The ocean expanse will make it impossible for us to be close!" The lost homeland was fading into waves of separation. Loving memories of home would turn into blurry, cluttered-up images of bygone days.

As the first yellow rays of the rising sun illuminated the eastern horizon, the kids, recovered from the terrible moment, started shouting noisily at the glorious sunrise over the immense ocean. Dolphins, tens of them, were swimming alongside our boat as if they were racing against the fugitives. We were but a lone tiny spot on the vast, undulating body of water.

"Mr. Thanh! Which way are we going now?"

"We're going to heaven!" Mr. Thanh jokingly replied.

"Don't be so optimistic. I haven't brought the issue up to any of you before, but I want to know where we are actually heading."

"I've said it. We're going to heaven!" Noticing my seriousness, Mr. Thanh went on: "Don't be nervous. Right now we have to go as far from the shore as possible. Border guards may chase after us."

"What next?"

"We won't go to hell, as I said."

"What do you mean?"

"We won't go toward Thailand. That's the road to hell. Pirates are waiting there to rape the females, plunder the wealthy, murder people, and sink the boats."

"Are we definitely heading to Hong Kong?"

"That's the way to paradise. We are."

Some high-rolling waves tossed our tiny boat up and down like a floating leaf. My Le began to be struck down with delirious seasickness. I felt an inexplicable irritation whirling up in my guts and in my soul. The sailors' wives did not seem to worry about the boat floating back and forth as if on a swing line; they began preparing the farewell breakfast.

I was worrying whether the sailing team did actually know the gateway to Hong Kong; I talked to Mr. Thanh again about my concern. Taking a prepared long coil of rope with a round stone tied to one end, Mr. Thanh gradually lowered the stone into the water. The stone silently dragged the rope about twenty yards down to the dark ocean floor. Mr. Thanh then explained to me that it was the way the seamen knew how far they were from the seashore. When asked how they would know they were heading in the right direction, Mr. Thanh replied:

"We haven't ever reached Hong Kong before. But we have been fishing close to the Chinese Hainan Island. We looked at the sun during the daytime and the stars during the night to locate our whereabouts. If we reach Hainan, we're half way to Hong Kong."

The crunching sound of the waves and the monotone noise of the engine made my head swim. Tremendously sad for the loved ones left behind, very much bewildered by the uncertain future ahead, so painfully attacked by seasickness, both My Le and I could not stand on our own feet. Nothing could be put in our mouths. We left our three little children to the mercy of the sailors.

At the end of the first day on the high seas, the eastern horizon was a gloomy gray color while the western sky was a horrifying pink. The boat owner warned everybody of a possible coming hurricane. The ocean was unusually calm, as if nature was accumulating its strength for an upcoming explosion.

Massive dark clouds poured in to cover the firmament. Around nine o'clock, the ocean began tossing its aggressive waves in the darkness of the night. Howling gusts hit the boat and threw seawater against its sides and over the deck as if it were raining rocks. Our small boat was tossing and rocking like a hammock swaying out of control.

"Don't move around. Don't rush to one side of the boat," Mr. Thanh warned everybody.

The lonely security oil lamp went out. All was dark in the rain. Salty water splashed up into the boat. Exhausted, My Le could not react when being drenched. Holding her from being hit against the surroundings, my worn-out hands were shaking. The boat driver slowed the boat speed down to somehow synchronize the forward movement of the boat with the oncoming waves. Every time a voluminous wave struck the boat, I felt heartbroken to hear the kids' screaming. Waves after waves like aggressive wild elephants struck the tiny running boat mercilessly. Shielding myself against the water-soaked wooden wall, I witnessed the horrific happenings. Seawater ran all over the deck and siphoned out through the holes along the sides of the moving boat. Should we have left our homes to die on the screaming ocean and get buried under the ferocious waves?

Loaded escaping boat on the high sea

Source: Vietnamese Boat People Monument, Westminster, California

This is the same type of boat on which we escaped.

The sea rage lasted, unfortunately, for about three long hours or so, more than enough to put us into a horrible state of terror. The youths took turns bailing water out. I thanked God for letting us survive the experience. I deeply appreciated the boat manager for having calmly and skillfully balanced the boat to keep it afloat in such a terrible encounter. After the fleeting furious storm, the splendid sun rose the next morning. The ocean returned to its peaceful ways.

A tempestuous long night and two risky days had passed. Lying in a gloomy corner of the boat, fully seasick and deprived of seeing the daylight, My Le and I got the impression that a week had gone by. Sometimes the kids' cheering with joy vaguely rang in our ears when the dim silhouette of a shoreline appeared obscurely on the horizon. On their first long journey on the rough high seas, our three kids and My Le's siblings, like the fishermens' families, happened to experience no health problems. However, confined by seasickness, My Le and I were not able to watch over our children to be fully aware of their welfare. Mr. Phap and Tuan Anh alternated their turns at the steering wheel, skillfully managing the boat through the stormy period. Mr. Thanh kept up with the fuel, entertained the kids, calmed our anxieties, and caught fresh fish from the sea to feed the escapees. His wife fixed the dishes for the passengers who had lost their homes. The savor of freshly cooked dishes, dissipated in the salty smell of the ocean atmosphere, brought nostalgia for the soulful meals spent among family members in the cozy home left behind. Bruised and seasick, My Le and I could not put anything in our mouths except a couple of sips of fresh water for survival.

A third day came. It was sunny. The blue ocean extended calmly to the glorious horizon. At noontime our boat came across a fishing vessel. Coming close, we recognized it as a Chinese fishing craft. People from the strange vessel were speaking Cantonese. I could understand a smattering of the words they spoke. They might think sympathetically that we were ethnic Chinese being repatriated by the Vietnamese government. The Chinese boat approached us and in a friendly way handed over drinking water, cigarettes, and special cakes we called "ash cakes." The cakes reminded us of the "Double Five" day, which was the fifth day of the fifth month of the lunar year. Chinese and Vietnamese commonly celebrated the Double Five with ash cakes. Not delicious ones, the ash cakes were but a traditional and symbolic ritual. On that unforgettable Double Five day, we were so moved by the sharing of cakes and kindheartedness of the unexpected strangers. We were not sure if we and the friendly boat really understood each other. When asked about the direction to Hong Kong, the comradely fishing boat driver waved his hand northwards as if suggesting we keep going ahead.

The weather was favorable. The quick encounter on the immense and deserted ocean raised everyone's spirits. My Le and I felt somehow better. Then came the fourth evening.

After four continuous days of running, including several long hours on the stormy ocean, the boat did not show any sign of overworking. The engine sounded mild. That reminded me that the owner had tuned up the engine; they had asked us for money for it. The ocean was calm. Sea gulls were spanning the waves peacefully, signaling the mainland was not far from us. The kids started pointing their fingers. Hong Kong slowly appeared on the horizon, at first as a dark line slowly growing into a gloomy bluish island, then in its multicolor display of flashing lights, and finally with illuminated stacked-up high-rises. The noisy celebration woke My Le and me from our killing seasickness.

It was twilight. Mingling among fleets of incoming vessels, our boat reached one of the Hong Kong piers, undetected. Flustered with joy, we looked at each other without yet knowing how to deal with the situation. It was night and we were in an unfamiliar country. Get ashore, or find a nearby police station to show ourselves? We had not decided yet. Considering the different spoken languages, we might have to wait for daylight to find the appropriate channel to communicate with the island's authorities and see what we could do and how we could do it. All we knew was that we were safe. We had reached our destination. The Communist world and the risky high seas were retreating far behind our backs. Our souls were relieved and our hearts full of joy.

5. A grain of salt

The sun had gone behind the island's peak.

Gazing absorbedly at the nightly beaming magnificence of Hong Kong, we were exhilarated by the impressiveness of the island, without our boat even having successfully lowered its anchor to moor yet.

Filled with the joy of having safely reached our destination after such a long, life-threatening passage on the Pacific Ocean, we were not yet ready to cope with our situation. Everyone was still looking up at the brightly illuminated city and wondering about what we should do next.

Suddenly, in the dim twilight, a Hong Kong two-story patrol boat flashed its red light and in a few moments drew alongside our tiny boat. The shape of our boat and the identification numbers on its sides were clear enough for the patrol guards of the island to spot us among numerous local boats converging to the pier. The patrol police did not take time to talk to us; they silently tied our boat to theirs and towed it to the Western Quarantine Anchorage. I got the feeling that the Hong Kong border police were so familiar with refugee boats coming to the islands that they did not bother questioning them. We were kept overnight in the middle of the water, away from the piers.

With fishes caught along the trip, Mr. Thanh's wife fixed a big dinner for our group. Even though not wholly recovered from seasickness, My Le and I had a good sip of the soup. The rest of the boatload savored the dinner jubilantly. They attempted to consume as much as possible of whatever food and drink was available in anticipation that finally we would have to surrender the boat and everything left on it to the mercy of the police guards. Carrying on with high hilarity, My Le and I momentarily forgot all the travel misery to join in the celebration of our group.

Boat People sailed into Hong Kong Harbor

We did not know whether we would be able to sleep that night. Everyone was up early the next morning in the animated vitality of the busy harbor. The sun rose gloriously—or our beaming hearts saw everything in its brightest glory. The bay was filled with its glinting rays as boats and crafts crisscrossed the dark-blue ocean at daybreak.

Under the splendid rays of the morning sun, we spotted the tall ship Skyluck anchored less than two hundred yards from our left side. The ship deck was swarming with about 2,600 refugees; many of them were women and infants.

The Skyluck came from Vietnam to Hong Kong on February 7, 1979, four months ahead of us and three months after the Huey Fong, crowded with over 3,300 refugees on board, arrived on December 23, 1978. We had no idea why the Skyluck's passengers were not allowed to come ashore. Several weeks after our arrival in Hong Kong, on June 29, 1979, some refugees cut the Skyluck's anchor chain, causing the 3,500-ton ship to drift into the rocky Lamma Island and sink.

Not long into the morning, a patrol boat came and towed us to the Government Dockyard. We could not believe our eyes. Thousands of people, males and females, clad in olive khaki, crammed the long and vast landing quay. Their outfits reminded us of the northern Vietnamese Communist soldiers when they came invading the South. We ran away from them to confront their likeness here. Their resemblance to the hated soldiers hurt our eyes and hearts.

We were called to the Hong Kong police processing tables set up in the open dockyard. Questions were asked. Individual identities entered in the register. Bodies searched. No stone left unturned. On that memorable late morning, the first day of the fully sunny month of June 1979, our boat group was officially registered to be on the threshold of the free world as three separate families.

Necessary formalities completed, we were shown to a corner of one of the four large warehouses. Innumerable people were lying and squatting at sixes and sevens on the bare floors of the warehouses. Records of the Hong Kong Government Office showed that, in the middle of the year we came to the island, the dockyard's transit center held more than 12,000 people at a time.

At noontime, two porters arrive carrying a big wooden container full of cooked white rice. The porters distributed to us cooked rice in individual plastic bowls. Steam from the rice container evaporated very attractively in front of us. Another two porters shouldered a container of hot vegetable soup. They poured a scoop of the soup onto the rice in each of our bowls. That was our welcoming meal in the new haven.

The Government Dockyard transit center was managed by the prison staff. Twice a day, we, prisoners of the center, stood lined up in groups. The prison staff came calling the name of each person on the roster for checking. No movement or word was allowed during the check. The prison staff might not hesitate to act with violence to maintain discipline.

At this point, we started feeling all the fatigue of the rough sea journey. Worn out, we lay down on the dirty cement floor of the warehouse, to sleep or to wait, with nothing underneath our backs.

Most ethnic Chinese minority boat people coming from North Vietnam had gotten used in the past to the frequent abrupt moves during wartime. Each of them, young and old, possessed at least one wide piece of plastic sheet. It was a multipurpose handiness. With the piece of synthetic fabric, they would wrap all their personal belongings and put it on their shoulders to move. If it was raining, the sheet got turned into a convenient provisional raincoat. At nighttime, the multipurpose piece of cloth was spread on the ground to lie on and to wrap up in, to warm the body in the cold. Those ethnic boat people came to Hong Kong with the magic pieces of synthetic linen. Southerners as we were, we had not familiarized ourselves with those practical circumstances enough to accommodate ourselves with such rudimentary conveniences. In the current difficult circumstances, we learned, quite late, the poignant lessons from these people. My Le, our children, everyone else in our group, and I lay barebacked on the floor next to thousands of other boat people to lull ourselves into dog-sleeps.

Next morning came. At the sound of the siren, confounded, we were amazed to see everyone from the warehouses, male and female, young and old, hurriedly bustling out to fill the open dockyard, half naked. The prison staff turned the fire hoses on the huge crowd. Every Tom, Dick, and Harry washed, brushed his mouth, and enjoyed the early group showers. Each one must act fast, very fast, before the fire hoses were turned off, unannounced.

Detained at the Government Dockyard transit center, we were fed two meals a day, rice and vegetable soup unchangeably for every meal. Days later, most of the members in our group were not able to eat as much as we should. The same vegetable soup over and over; we all were too tired of it to consume it. The daily soup was not salty at all. It was far too light and tasteless to swallow.

Again, we should say the refugees repatriated from North Vietnam had far more foresight. Besides the multipurposed plastic sheet I have mentioned, they also brought along to the more civilized world a vital item, sea salt, either carefully wrapped in banana leaves or contained in tiny bottles.

In the closed transit camp, nobody was allowed to go out or to associate with anyone beyond the fence. Prison staff, however, allowed newcomers to write home. The letters must be either in Cantonese or in English so they could be inspected by the prison staff before being sent out. Most of boat people coming to Hong Kong from North Vietnam were ethnic Chinese. Their primary spoken languages were various Chinese dialects. Vietnamese was their second language. Nevertheless, the majority of them could not write either in Cantonese or English as required. I did not know how to speak and write Cantonese fluently either.

However, I volunteered to compose letters in English to help those in need. In return, they had nothing to pay me. Sympathizing with our salt deprivation, some generous and sympathetic ethnic Chinese opened their well-kept containers to kindly share a very small amount of the sea salt we craved. The whole group of ten of us survived those days in the closed camp thanks to these tiny grains of salt. We appreciated them more than any cheer. In the context of tribulation, a grain of salt was extremely precious.

In search of freedom, nobody wanted to be interned in the closed camp, strictly guarded and disciplined by the prison staff. Only later I learned that during the June 1979 peak days there were thousands of people coming by boat each day to Hong Kong. Hong Kong Immigration records showed 68,700 boat people were in Hong Kong Harbor during the 1979 peak time. Among them there were many people who had come from the Chinese mainland. They took the rare opportunity to illegally pose as Vietnamese boat people to seek asylum overseas. The Hong Kong Immigration agency had to detain every newcomer at the prison camp. With the collaboration of the United Nation High Commission for Refugees (UNHCR), Hong Kong Immigration agents did their best to filter out the economic escapees from mainland China. The UNHCR would not recognize them as refugees. They were sent back to the mainland.

In one of the filtering sessions, we were among several boatloads gathered in one separate room of the hangar. At the start of the session, every person was requested to submit any type of metal, precious or not, sharp or dull, to the custody of the prison guard to get a receipt for later account. While the attendees submitted their wristwatches, cigarette lighters, knives, etc., an ethnic boat owner coming from North Vietnam poured out onto a small table—in front of the perplexed eyes of hundreds of refugees squatting on the floor—a mound of glittering gold the owner had brought along in two bags. There was no account informing us whether the owner had gotten his incredibly huge fortune back when he was released from the prison camp. There was an unconfirmed rumor that some owners of refugee boats who came to Hong Kong with bags of gold leaves had been killed by robbers.

On January 19, 1979, when the refugee ship Huey Fong entered Hong Kong Harbor, the police discovered caches of gold leaf valued at US$6.5 million in the engine room of the ship.

Leaving our beloved homeland behind, we had become illegal border trespassers. We were detained in the prison camp for a while for investigation until we were recognized as real Vietnamese boat people by the UNHCR. Our group was then transported out of the prison camp to Twen Mun in New Territory. Some refugees who had come earlier told us that we were very lucky to be detained in the closed camp for such a short time—less than a week. Others were cooped up for there several weeks and even months.

Several multistory buildings were newly built in Twen Mun, north of Kowloon, for the business development of the area. One of the high-rises was a twenty-three-story unoccupied factory building. The high-rise was temporarily used by the UNHCR to house 16,000 refugees.[28] Unfortunately, I cannot remember the name of the street or the number of the building. Our family was among the first occupants. About six hundred refugees were allocated a vast empty floor. Each of us was given a narrow piece of reed mat. Designated as a family unit, My Le, her siblings, our children, and I got our small lot on the floor against the eastern wall of the building, separately from the two other families who came on the same boat. Our nearest neighbor was an old, slim man with a severe endless cough. Not knowing his real name, we nicknamed him Mr. Cough.

Our family of ten were up on the fourteenth floor of the building. The UNHCR provided the refugees in Twen Mun with canned food. Twen Mun was an open camp, meaning that residents were free to be in and out of the building day and night. No restriction. No supervision. We got the chance to meet, among the other occupants, some musicians from the Hanoi Philharmonic, an engineer graduated from an Eastern European university, an ethnic Chinese physician, and several former North Vietnamese soldiers who came to Hong Kong with framed Honor Citations signed by Ho Chi Minh. Some even showed us their Communist Party membership certificates.

I was told that among refugees coming to Hong Kong from North Vietnam, the Hanoi Government had inserted many death-sentenced criminals and infiltrated the flux of deported ethnic Chinese with secret agents for their shady purposes. There were reliable reports from a couple of refugees who did underground intelligence work for the Hong Kong security agencies in refugee camps. When I worked for the refugee newsletter *HOPE* the reports came to me saying the inserted criminals committed armed robberies in the camps and even in the open Hong Kong camp. Some boat owners with huge amount of gold were also the victims of those criminals. The Hong Kong police had the criminals' felony records. However, the police did not prosecute them, simply because if they were officially prosecuted, no countries would accept them for resettlement. The criminals would then become a permanent social burden for Hong Kong.

Tens of thousands of refugees were in a high-rise, and many of them had never before used the advanced facilities of a modern building. Overload and misuse turned the building's elevators and restrooms into nonfunctioning rubbish after a week or so.

The labors of the escape journey had severe consequences for the bodies of our family members. Our youngest son was suffering from heavy measles. I was stricken with a serious bronchitis. To climb more than two hundred steps to reach our floor, the fourteenth story of the building, I had to stop more than ten times to sit on the stairs and catch my breath prior to resuming the upward climb. I felt dizzy and suffocated as thousands of people constantly rushed up and down the narrow staircase.

Cantonese-speaking refugees were able to get out of the camp and find odd jobs working for local businesses. They earned plenty of good money. They looked very happy. Many of them shopped and brought to the floor—besides fruits, new shoes and colorful garments—big, newly purchased radio sets that they might have dreamed of for such a long time. After work hours and into the night, tens of new radio sets were turned on at the highest volume, creating a deafening pandemonium on the single floor. With the money they earned, they were also able to buy delicious food from the market to feed their families. Well fed, clad with new clothes, equipped with new watches, radios, and glittering jewelry, and with extra money left in pockets, some of them seemed highly satisfied, beyond their dreams, with their current livelihood.

Lacking Cantonese, My Le and I were unable to find needed work. Penniless, our family simply depended on the canned food supplied by the UNHCR. My bronchitis did not subside as time went on. My five-year-old son's measles got worse. I swallowed my misery to carry my enervated son on my back several times, via a short cut, to the nearby hospital on a hill, about a mile from where we were to have my son's illness diagnosed and taken care of.

Spotting the daily poor meals of our children, a kind refugee lady lent My Le some Hong Kong currency. Thanks to the kindness of the good-hearted lady, My Le was able to temporarily buy some fresh food for her siblings and our poor children. My Le had to walk her way ten floors up to the terrace to cook the meals for the whole ten-member family. Our eight-year-old son, Nhi Ha, was always by her side, to keep company with Mom in her loneliness and to help Mom prepare the meals for the whole group. He helped to carry the gas stove, the rice cooker, and the dishes My Le fixed, up and down the ten-story staircase. He helped Mom wash the dishes and the dirty clothes. He sang to entertain Mom in her distress.

At his young age, Nhi Ha was so sentimental. He looked so disoriented. He worried so much about Mommy's physical and mental health among a sea of unfamiliar people with antagonistic political views. He defended Mommy when refugees from North Vietnam encroached on her, such as on a staircase, in an elevator, or on the terrace where people aggressively competed for a convenient spot for cooking. In one such struggle, some guy broke the index finger of My Le's right hand. In another wrangle, an opponent yelled at My Le:

"It's by Uncle Ho's grace that you've got overseas."

Thinking this through, we would realize that what the guy had said had expressed his newly found enlightenment. When he was living behind the Iron Curtain, the propaganda taught him day by day, year after year, that the Communists were the world's super regime and the outside world was nothing but scum. The pride of being part of that super regime was fully expressed in the citations of Ho Chi Minh and the party member cards they cautiously kept, brought along when they were expelled from the country, and proudly showed to the victims of their Communist Party.

With the blind belief in propaganda, the poor guy must have suffered miserably when he had been expelled from the super regime he so much adored, and pushed into the outside scum. After actually being in the outside world for a while and realizing that the dregs of the outside society were much superior than he and his fellows had been indoctrinated to believe, the guy and his fellows must feel very indebted to Uncle Ho, who had chased them out of the Communist paradise. It was thanks to Uncle Ho that an ethnic guy had gotten promoted from the position of poor blind Communist to the position of a stateless citizen on his way to the better world he never thought of.

As for us, it was thanks to Uncle Ho that two per cent of the twenty million southerners had left their homes to get into the dreadful NEZs. Another three percent went through indefinite brainwashing camps. An extra ten percent got drowned in the deep ocean on their running away from the liberators. Additionally, while their children were being instructed to hate their own parents, ten percent of the southern population had left the country they loved to look for an unknown country where they could restart their lives. Thanks to Uncle Ho, if the lamppost knew how to move, it would go overseas as well.

In his childhood, our eight-year-old Nhi Ha did not see how great the Communist paradise was really, he simply missed the homeland of his little years. He missed so much the grandmas he heartbrokenly left behind. In one instance up on the terrace of Twen Mun camp, Nhi Ha looked far out on the horizon and murmured, "Mommy! I want to go home."

"Dear son! You want to be back in Da Nang, don't you?"

"Yes, Mommy."

"Dear son! Please tell me why?"

"I want to support lonely BaNoi."

"My poor son! I know you miss Grandma so much. But how can you support her?"

"I'll go door to door selling bread each morning. I'll sell hot tea at the train station during the day."

I could not tell how he knew me, but a fruit vendor from Yuen Long came to the Twen Mun camp, singly checked me out, and hired me to work in his store. I gratefully reported to the shop, stayed with the owner, ate meals with him, slept upstairs, and took care of the fruit shop downstairs. Staying tens of miles away from Twen Mun camp without any direct means of communication, I could not have the peace of mind to leave My Le and the children among strangers in the unknown situation. Additionally, because of my severe bronchitis, I could not help but resign after less than a month working for the kind fruit vendor.

Walking from the fruit vendor's shop to the bus stop on my way home, I spotted a private medical office in the neighborhood. A few times I thought of asking for medical help from the unknown physician. The displayed name of the doctor, which was hard to spell and remember, sounded as if he was from India. Without money in my pocket, I had to chase from my mind the intention to visit the health-care office to cure my damaging cough. On the return trip from my last day at the fruit vendor, knowing this was the last chance to pass the office of the physician, I risked venturing into the his waiting room. My heart overflowed with great concerns. Several times I stood up from the line of waiting patients to go away. What should I say when I was asked to pay for the service? It was shameful to tell him about my empty pockets. It would be more shameful to use my refugee status to beg for help.

It was late into evening. And anyway, I had set foot into his office. It was better to try than to leave. Just a couple of patients more in line. Waiting until the last patient was done, I risked talking to the physician about who I was and how severe was my health problem. Sitting at a small desk, the physician listened patiently. I did not know whether he understood my broken English or not. He did not make any comments or show any external reaction. He only told me to continue my story when I hesitated to go into details. When I had given enough information about my health status, he stood up and started carefully examining me. The physician then took twenty days' antibiotic doses from his shelves and gave them to me saying, "I'm glad that you've seen me. Else, it would have been too late to cure your pulmonary problem. Finish the doses as directed and you'll be fine."

The kind physician took me out of his office without imposing any charge. He did not even give out his name or business card when I asked for one. The kindness of the adventitious physician miraculously cured me of my deadly disease. Ever since, each time I thought of Hong Kong, the kindness of the physician was in my mind and heart.

Later on, My Le got a temporary job, on the production line of an imitation watch maker, to earn some money to feed our kids. The job site was walking distance from the building where we stayed. There was no contract but only word-of-mouth agreement. There was no training either. My Le, as well as other refugees, changed employment a couple of times with the pseudo reason of stopping work to leave for the United States. It was simply for her to land another better-paid job, maybe at a nearby building or even on a different floor of the same building.

A joint British-Canadian team of volunteer physicians came to work for the health of the refugees in the Twen Mun camp. Aunty Uyen and I volunteered to work for the doctors as interpreters. We got a reasonable stipend for such a temporary service. Aunty Uyen worked at another multistory building. I worked closely with the lady doctor Marilyn Hieatt right at the building where we lived. Dr. Hieatt was from Reigate, Surrey, in the United Kingdom. After the Twen Mun camp was closed and our family moved to Shamshuipo, I did not see the volunteer team of physicians again.

6. The song of the sea

As the flow of refugees increased tremendously, different transit camps were established in Hong Kong, such as Argyle, Cap Collinson, Chimawan, Whitehead, and Pillard Point.

On Lai Chi Kok Road in Shamshuipo, Kowloon, an old military barrack was turned into a refugee camp. The Shamshuipo camp was initially intended for one thousand refugees. Later on it was expanded to house up to ten thousand people. The Shamshuipo Transit Center camp shared a fence with the smaller Jubilee camp, and the twin camps became the Vietnamese boat people's temporary asylum. It was considered the most humane refugee center in the whole of Southeast Asia.

Our family was moved from Twen Mun to Shamshuipo in the fall of 1979.

Under the auspices of the UNHCR, Mr. Walter Smith from the Hong Kong Christian Service took over the management of the Shamshuipo camp. Refugees were provided with a three-tiered bunk bed for every nine persons.

The bed space was the bedroom, living room, and dining room for a refugee family. There was no way a refugee camp could be as cozy and comfortable as home. Camp residents must sacrifice their privacy. We were happy to have a place to lay our heads at night to sleep without the fear of being woken up in the dark to be led away. For the regular Hong Kong residents, their living space on the tiny and crowded island was so small and expensive. Refugees as we were, we had no complaint about being provided with free, jam-packed living space, which the local population had good reason to envy. We thanked the Hong Kong government for treating us in such a humane and civilized way.

Under the sponsorship of the Hong Kong Christian Services, a child-care center, a handicraft shop, and an English class were established within the camp. Refugee children were supposed to learn English at the center to become easily adaptable in their third and final destination country. The Shamshuipo open camp was in the heart of industrial Kowloon, so most of the refugee adults got some type of work in the island's market to earn some money to support their families during the transit time.

There was criticism of the Hong Kong government's policy of letting the Vietnamese refugees mingle in the economy of the island and earn a salary. Looking at the bright side, besides offering a small chance for the refugees to contribute their humble share in the prosperity of the island and preparing them for the work environment of the western world they were about to enter, the policy was a good way for the Hong Kong government to try to alleviate the financial burden that was on the shoulder of UNHCR. Moreover, the policy provided a way to ameliorate the refugee conditions while at the same time respecting the human dignity of the refugees.

My Le worked for the camp child-care center. Although she was busy the whole day, My Le enjoyed being with this young class of refugees who had lost their innocent days of childhood so early in their lives.

Our three children were also attending the classes at the transit center. Unfortunately, instead of picking up English as the center intended, our children, enjoying the company of their young ethnic Chinese refugee friends, ended up speaking Cantonese instead. Within no time, our little daughter was able to watch and find pleasure in Cantonese-speaking movies. She also was our translator when we went food and window shopping.

For the fifteen months in refugee camps, apart from working to earn a minimum living, My Le and I spent our time on useful social work to somehow alleviate the misery of our low-spirited refugee peers.

We happily made friends with several good-natured Hong Kong residents. They were so kind as to invite us to appreciate the delicacies of selected Hong Kong restaurants. We got the unique chance to attend the live show of a famous Taiwanese female singer on her tour of Hong

Kong. We went sightseeing to Hong Kong's famous Victoria Peak, went shopping at its jade market, toured its Ocean Park theme park, visited Star Ferry Pier and the Tiger Balm Gardens. We came to Hong Kong as dejected refugees but actually had the privilege of luxuriating in the life of foreign tourists to this beautiful island. The friendly world of Hong Kong greatly alleviated our homesickness and the misery of our refugee plight.

Funded by the Hong Kong Christian Service, the monthly bilingual newsletter *HOPE* came out and was distributed all over the Southeast Asian refugee centers. The air-conditioned editorial office of the newsletter was set up inside the front gate of the Shamshuipo camp. I joined the magazine and became a full-time member of the editorial staff under the editor-in-chief Mrs. Daniel, a native of India. She fervidly fought for the plight of the refugees in her monthly editorials, which might finally have cost her the position. She was replaced later by Mrs. Naomi Morris, a younger Pennsylvania native.

The refugee population from Vietnam was of all walks of life. Some of them, especially those who had been regrettably shut up behind the iron curtain for several decades, might not have been exposed to the lifestyles of western civilization. In daily life in the camps, some of those unfortunate refugees, who had customarily led a life of misery and privation, might have displayed uncivilized behaviors. Instead of fighting on the cultural front, particularly for the deplorable condition of the ethnic Chinese minorities who had been brutally expelled from Vietnam and primarily for the noble cause of political refugees in general, an unsympathetic Hong Kong moviemaking group focused their attention on some dirty details of the camp residents. They got permission from the Hong Kong government to film those sad sides of the life of the ill-starred people.

Shamshuipo Transit Center was selected by the moviemakers for their first sequence of captures. Several days earlier, a number of the female refugees had been directed by the movie producer to perform some very offensive scenes. I felt that the honor of the refugees and their righteous cause had been wronged, that they had been exploited in an offensive and inhumane way. Unable to overlook these shameful developments, I thought hard to find some effective action that could be taken to stop the filming before it was too late. Gathering friends who were earnestly committed to the good refugee cause, I strongly suggested a mass demonstration, a protest march to voice our unanimous reaction. Leaders of refugees from the twin Shamshuipo-Jubilee camps enthusiastically responded. They were advised to maneuver their camp residents to join the mass rally at the beginning of the coming week. To produce a realistically significant impact, I personally informed ahead of time the Hong Kong mass media, with whom I had a professional working relationship. I did not disclose the purpose of the rally, but only the date and time it was to take place. On the critical date, while Hong Kong mass media reporters were flocking to the Shamshuipo camp, a multitude of refugees—mostly Vietnamese southerners—from the twin Shamshuipo-Jubilee camps formed our mass line of pickets inside the Shamshuipo camp to the total surprise of the camp's management. The following day our action against the moviemakers appeared on the front pages of the Hong Kong daily newspapers. There was a rumor that the moviemakers had tried and failed to sue the Hong Kong government for damages compensation for the premature contract termination due to the refugee demonstration. After the demonstration, a Hong Kong TV station aired a short interview in which I answered various refugee-related questions.

During our time in Shamshuipo transit center, Mr. Ho Dac Ngoc and I had a good opportunity to develop a close working relationship. Mr. Ho and I did not come to Hong Kong on the same boat but shared the same destiny. We came from different parts of Vietnam but had gone through the same traumatic experiences. We shared the same perturbations and visions. We cooperated on various social endeavors in the camp. Before 1975 Mr. Ho was a renowned front-page designer for the *VAN* and several other Vietnamese periodicals published in Saigon. Touched by the miserable condition of the boat people, Mr. Ho composed seven poignant poems with illustrated surrealistic paintings. Having shared the same harrowing experiences of a refugee, and as a member of the editorial staff of the *HOPE* newsletter and a friend of his, I personally volunteered to translate the booklet of Vietnamese poems and paintings Mr. Ho had created into the English version of *The Song Of The Sea*:

> *I'm playing a concerto to the ocean,*
> *Together with the ocean*
> *My concerto sounds the plaintive lament of my motherland,*

The land of an everlasting evil fate,
The land of an indefatigable will for liberation.[29]

The translation was published by the Hong Kong Christian Service's *HOPE* newsletter in 1980.

Hong Kong was a British Crown colony. The British Government was asked by the UNHCR to give higher priority to the resettlement of the refugees from the Hong Kong camps. British resettlement organizations were openly receptive; however, the majority of Vietnamese boat people preferred going to either the United States, Canada, or Australia instead.

A native of Wellington, New Zealand, Mrs. Margaret Davis, who at the time was working in Hong Kong, had highly praised the peaceful country down under and thus indirectly expressed her intention to have my family moved to her motherland. We greatly appreciated Mrs. Margaret's sympathy. However, My Le and I had many familial and friendly ties in the United States. One of My Le uncles and multiple cousins of hers had escaped to the United States in 1975. Most of them had resettled either in California or in Wisconsin. Several priests, such as Reverends Vu Nhu Huynh, Dinh Duy Trinh, and Mai Khai Hoan, and many of our friends had come to the States ahead of us and eagerly wanted to have us join them there.

During my waiting time in Hong Kong camps, I had articles published in two Vietnamese magazines in the States: the *Van Nghe Tien Phong (Pioneer Letters and Arts)* in Washington DC and the *Dat Moi (New Land)* in Seattle, Washington. Writers Mai Thao and Nguyen Giang of *New Land* magazine through several confidential letters expressed their desire to sponsor my family to Washington State to have a better and convenient collaboration with their magazine. In lieu of going to the northwestern state, My Le and I got a sponsorship from Mr. Nguyen Buoi, the former vice president of the General Federation of Labor of Vietnam to go to the Midwest of the United States.

The sponsorship process took time. A sponsor had to go through the proceedings of either the United States Catholic Conference (USCC), the International Rescue Committee (IRC), Church World Service, or Lutheran Social Services Refugee and Immigrant Services, or any other organization while, in the camp, the sponsored refugee had to wait. During my wait time, in addition to working for the *HOPE* newsletter regarding the refugees' plight and solutions, it was a golden time for me to spend time helping our unlucky fellow-refugees in their specific individual situations. In cooperation with the Reverend Father King, I offered my services for the religious education of catechumens in the camps. Socially, some of my daily odd jobs were to voluntarily help those boat people who had not thoroughly mastered their English language skills in filling out their resettlement application forms and papers. The hardest task I undertook was putting forward responsible suggestions and comments to applicants on the pros and cons in choosing a third country for resettlement.

In the camps there were elderly refugees without accompanying relatives. There were also those who suffered from chronic diseases. And there were the disabled and handicapped. Most "third countries" did not interview these unfortunate boat people for resettlement in their homelands.

Switzerland was a very strange and unknown country in the mind of most North Vietnamese refugees seeking final asylum. Switzerland had a humane strategy of preferentially accepting these disadvantaged classes of refugees with the promise of lifetime social welfare from their government. Not many people coming from North Vietnam had ever heard of this small and humane European country. Those ethnic people living in the remote borders of Vietnam might have at some time seen the Red Cross flag but might never know the flag was shaped after the Swiss colors. When they left Vietnam for overseas, these people could never have imagined resettling in this country totally unknown to them. I temerariously approached these people in their unfortunate health circumstances, and persuaded and helped them to apply for the humanitarian programs offered by the Swiss organizations.

In my attempt to extend a helping hand to my refugee peers, I met an old and ailing ethnic Chinese lady, Mrs. Ung, who came to Hong Kong much earlier than we did. She stayed around without being picked up by any of the third asylum countries.

It was a heartbreaking situation. When her son joined the ethnic Chinese exodus, he left his sick and old mom behind in North Vietnam. The miserable lady later on was put on a refugee boat and expelled from the country by the Vietnamese government. After weeks in danger on the high seas, Mrs. Ung got to Hong Kong while her son was still there. However, the son refused to include his old mom in his family group.

He applied for resettlement to a third country but intentionally left his miserable mom out of his application for fear of being denied due to her poor health. Her plight vividly reminded me of my poor mother, whom I had heartbrokenly left behind. Unable to help my mother out of Vietnam, I made up my mind to do the best thing I could to help this abandoned mother. The forsaken lady insisted on being grafted to the same household with her son for resettlement. Her son refused. Seeing the determination of her inconvincible son, I personally talked Mrs. Ung into applying for the benefits offered by Switzerland. She was so reluctant, partly because she had no hint of the humane country and mainly because she could not suffer being away from her son. After her son left Hong Kong, with several consultations I got her interviewed by the Swiss delegation. She was easily accepted. She departed before I left Hong Kong. My prayer is that the lady and those people who resettled in this benevolent part of the world are enjoying good lives.

In 1980, with the funding from the UNHCR, the Philippine Refugee Processing Center (PRPC) was open in Bataan, Philippines. The refugees who were accepted for migration to the United States and other English-speaking countries had to consent to be transferred to the Philippines PRPC center for preliminary training. The several-months-long training was to familiarize the refugees to the new life of the asylum country, to prevent any possible cultural shock to the foreigners before they entered the refuge country of their choice. The purposes of the transit center were praiseworthy. The training was indispensable for many. However, some former military officers of South Vietnam in the Hong Kong refugee camps were strongly against the policy.

After spending so many years fighting alongside the American Allies in the hellish war and many more years of torture in concentration camps, the officer-refugees felt their former allies were ill-treating them by sending them to the camp in the Philippines. To some degree their upset was understandable. Some of them intended to refuse to be transferred to the new camp. By doing so, they would forfeit their opportunity to migrate to the country of their choice.

Dragging through the long, tedious days in the refugee camps, I had the privilege to befriend a couple of refugees in Hong Kong who were former Vietnamese military officers. Some of them got on the list to be transferred to the PRPC.

After the northern brothers had triumphantly liberated him and the whole South of ours, Mr. Phan, a former South Vietnamese army captain, had enjoyed the clemency policy of the liberators and had but a short-term brainwashing of only four years in Long Giao concentration camp. A camp warden had knocked two of his teeth out when he was caught roasting a rat to eat. Constantly hungry for food, the army captain and his co-prisoners had to eat anything that moved: snakes, scorpions, rats, earthworms—any moving creature they could catch on their way to labor. Released from the concentration camp, Captain Phan was designated to move to the New Economic Zone in Phu Quoc.

Phu Quoc is a 222-square-mile island lying thirty miles off Ha Tien Province. The island might have great developmental potential, but at the time, the largest Vietnamese island was considered a deserted area and an exile site. However, surrounded by the immense ocean, Phu Quoc was not plagued with tropical diseases. Phu Quoc NEZ would have been more livable if the newcomers to the island had been provided with initial help indispensable for survival. The NEZ program never lent any such accommodations. Captain Phan fled instead to live illegally in a hamlet near Cau Hai, north of Da Nang, and finally escaped to Hong Kong after we did. Seeing his name on the posted list of the first batch to the PRPC that morning, he fulminated:

"Damn it! Jailed by the enemy, and now the Allied sends me to jail again?"

"Don't you want to go there?"

"Go to that jail? Out of the Communist jail and into another jail? I'm not crazy!"

"It's a training camp, not a jail."

"Training camp. Reeducation camp. Brainwashing camp. Concentration camp. No difference. They're the same. Who wants to be forced to enter the camps for a life of misery?"

I was reluctant to debate with him in front of people who gathered at the information board of the camp each morning for resettlement-related news, especially when the former captain was in such a mentality. I had to find an appropriate occasion to tactfully address him as an intimate friend with the pros and cons of the situation. I felt under pressure to help in such a delicate situation. The discontentment of Captain Phan and other refugees must be resolved before the posted deadline.

The United States as well as any other third country who responded to the refugee resettlement program of the UNHCR did not do it to pay any debt they owned to their former allied veterans and to the refugees in general. Those countries, out of their own goodwill, were simply fulfilling the humanitarian covenant toward the disadvantaged. By providing the refugees with primary training, unfortunately in a less-than-favorable ambiance, to adequately and nicely fit them to the new environment, the UNHCR were doing a super job for our unlucky country fellows. In the short term, the process might be temporarily inconvenient to well-developed individuals who were more adapted to western civilization. However, for those people who did not know any word of English and were not familiar with technically developed countries, the training would be very beneficial.

It is heartrending to say, but I myself have encountered insulting attitudes shown toward some refugees of ours.

Representing a sponsoring community in Wisconsin, a pastor had come to the Shamshuipo refugee camp for a reality survey. A young refugee originally from the Vietnamese Mekong Delta was among the people being sponsored to the pastor's area. I volunteered to be an interpreter. Unfortunately I had to relay to the youth the questions the preacher asked that I did not feel it was appropriate to translate:

"Do you know how to iron your clothes? Do you know how to make the bed in the morning? Do you know how to brush your teeth? Did you ever operate an electric fan? Do you know . . . ?"

Being from Wisconsin, the pastor might know so little about the Republic of Vietnam that he could pose those survey questions. But both the youth and I felt hurt being asked the humiliating questions. The youth was the elder son of a wealthy family in the outskirts of Can Tho. The family owned several rice mills and a fleet of transportation trucks. The youth had finished his sophomore year at the University of Saigon when the debacle of the whole nation happened. During the 1975 Anti-Comprador Bourgeoisie Campaign, the youth's father was given the death sentence by the local people's court. The family's entire property was confiscated. He, his mother and sister were sent to the NEZ, where his mom died. His sister got married and fled with her husband to Thailand. The youth left the NEZ, ran to Da Nang, and fled to Hong Kong.

In the mind of the pastor and maybe of many people in the western countries, this youth and the majority of Vietnamese southerners might have been considered very low on their assessment scale. The PRPC may have been one way the western countries responded to such social evaluation of the Vietnamese refugees.

In fact, some refugees had unfortunately shown a very lamentable way of life. Having lived in chronic deprivation in the coal mines in Lang Son, Thai Nguyen, and Hon Gai, some ethnic refugees originally from these areas displayed shocking behavior in the refugee camps. As reported before, a Hong Kong filmmaker had tried to stage these uncivilized practices in a movie. The fact was that some ethnic ladies brought to their quarters dead chickens that Hong Kong families had thrown into their trash cans. The ladies brought those disease-stricken chickens home, cut them up and washed them in the ditches around their quarters, and cooked them to eat. Such practices and others were tragic and deplorable and needed to be retrained to fit the new life. For these refugees, the PRPC was a must.

For the refugees such as the above mentioned sophomore student or the Army Captain Phan, the PRPC appeared to be inconvenient and unnecessary. It was understandable that they were reluctant to accept transfer to the PRPC. However, it would have been harder to deal with each single case individually than to have a general solution for everybody. Moreover, knowledgeable refugees should have thought more of their future and long-term personal benefits and of the imminent advantages to their younger generations than of the fleeting inconveniences. Those were undeniable facts I had learned in the transit camps. I formed my argument based upon them and brought them out to convince some of my fellow refugees.

Somewhat anxious and discontent, Mr. Phan and several other people I luckily knew and shared the same unfortunate destiny of expatriation with, finally bent themselves upon my persuasions to control their initial frustrations. They tacitly accepted the unavoidable avenue of finally going to the United States via the Philippino training camp. Looking back after so many years, I pray that these people may feel happier for having unwillingly followed the intermediate steps of the refugee resettlement plan.

We were in refugee camps for seven months. The year of 1979 drew to an end. It was the time for family reunion, for commemoration of the departed ancestors, and for the angels to bring peace and good news to mankind. It was a time for heartbroken refugees to miss their separated home and lost relatives. A time for soul-soothing memories to come back and haunt everyone's heart and mind.

Our first Christmas spent in the refugee camps was so emotional. The shivery flux of wind coming from the surrounding bay turned the airspace of the island dreary and desolate on the memorable holy night. Everyone deeply felt their statelessness as they wandered in the darkness of the unknown future.

By our arrangement, the Hong Kong government had kindly provided seven buses free of charge. Nondenominational refugees from different camps on the island were bused to the Hong Kong stadium at midnight to pathetically celebrate the chilly 1979 Christmas. Refugee Reverend Fathers Trinh and Nghiem concelebrated. High on the altar were the Madonna and Child in Vietnamese dress, in a grandiose color painting by Uncle Su, she looking with her motherly eyes down on the miserable gathered crowd.

In the desolate starry night, thousands of boat people, Christians or not, young and old, joined voices in familiar Vietnamese Yuletide songs that stirred up the heartbreaking memories of the beloved relatives and the unfortunate lost fatherland an ocean far away. Peers, even unknown to each other, warmly hugged the person next to them, speechless, with arms clasped and eyes brimming with compassionate tears.

Peace on earth!
And good haven for those who lost their homeland!

EPILOGUE

Half the world away was our homeland where I had spent my childhood in the remote countryside with whistling kites flying high in the afternoon firmament. It was the land where every night my gentle mom lulled me into fascinating dreams with her sweet folk songs. It was the birthplace where I spent romantic nights under the magical moonlight. In the tranquility of the night, moonlight sparkled miraculously on the swinging green banana leaves, full of fruit flavor, in the garden.

An immense ocean away was the poor homeland My Le twice had to leave behind in search of freedom. It was the fatherland where our two mothers, My Le's and mine, shed all their tears weeping for the children who had to imperil their lives on the high seas looking for freedom. It was the land we have dreamed of contributing our services to ameliorate, but we have been deprived of the right to improve its ways of life.

In constant horror-filled dreams, the threatening words by the liberators have restlessly hunted our souls: "Puppets! You're not citizens of this country. We'll educate your offspring to hate you. Your children will have no future in this revolutionary world." It was heartbreaking; we were pushed to have no choice than to leave our birthplaces filled with loving memories. It was horrible to depart from the relatives we love so much and from the unfortunate country fellows we cherish and with whom we have shared such misery.

We miss our homeland that we left in sadness and sorrow. Our hearts ache for the miserable grandmas we could not bring along. The prospect of generations of young offspring and helpless people leading their lives in a dark future troubles our minds.

After we had anxiously waited for fifteen months in different Hong Kong refugee transit centers, on September 8, 1980, America's compassionate horizon welcomed us. In the newly given land of opportunity, we were kindly accepted and abundantly offered fully developed chances for a better life.

We were filled with deep gratitude toward the generous minds and hearts that opened wide to cordially embrace us. We love the land we are living in.

"Northeast You Will Go," an excerpt from "The Song of the Sea" by Ho Dac Ngoc, I felt deeply moved to have translated. It silently sounded to my heart as if the poet miraculously recorded the last words our mournful mothers might have whispered upon seeing us off on that gloomy night.

> *Northeast You Will Go,*
> *Where there is freedom and love,*
> *Where there is life and creativity,*
> *Where there is my soul,*
> *Which will be by your side forever.*

Do An Duc Tri
Baltimore, Maryland

Acknowledgments

D eeply grateful acknowledgments are offered to the following:

The authors and artists whose various works have been cited in this memoir.

People whose names have been mentioned. The majority of them have long gone from this world by one way or the other. The author is unable to ask these people or their families for permission to include their names in this publication. The author acknowledges the use of their names. If there are any discrepancies, please kindly inform the author for correction.

Readers of this memoir. The author acknowledges that it is but a vision from a personal angle and is based on personal experiences. The author has tried his best, but it may not one hundred percent describe faithfully every aspect of the real world. Some statements or words in this book may make readers raise their eyebrows; the author would like to sincerely apologize. The author gladly welcomes all feedback from readers.

Our dearest mothers, whose innumerable sufferings and countless sacrifices for the survival of our family were heartfelt but cannot be described in any words.

My soul mate and children, whose love, consistent encouragement, numerous miseries, and countless inputs and supports have been great driving forces pushing me to complete this work.

References

1. Mr. Bao Vo, Mr. So Vo, and Mr. Lieu Vo in Nai Cuu village, Trieu Phong District, Quang Tri Province

2. Among them were Nguyen Cao Dai, Nguyen Cao Nhan, Nguyen Cao Quang, Duong Minh Khai, Nguyen Van Niem, Nguyen Van Diep.

3. BaNgoai or maternal grandma is My Le's mother and our children's grandma. BaNoi or paternal grandma is my mother and our children's grandma. Following the Vietnamese tradition My Le and I respectfully refer to either of them as "Grandma", and address either of them as Mom, while Grandma says "Mom" to us. By the same tradition, with respect, we refer to our children's uncles and aunts as Uncle and Aunt.

4. U.S. Department of State, *"Check-List of Possible U.S. Actions in Case of Coup,"* October 25, 1963. Roger Hilsman Papers, Country File, box 4, folder: Vietnam 10/6/63-10/31/63

5. It was on the Horror Highway in 1972 that a 4-month-old baby girl was rescued by a Vietnamese Ordnance soldier from her killed mother. The soldier, carrying the baby in a conical hat, became exhausted to the point he fainted out. The baby got transferred to a Vietnamese Marine Corps Second Lieutenant, Mr. Tran Ngoc Bao, who brought her to Sister Mary at the Danang Sacred Heart Orphanage and gave her the name Tran Thi Ngoc Bich. Two months later, US sergeant pilot James Mitchell adopted the 6-month old Tran Thi Ngoc Bich on his return home to Solon Spring, Wisconsin. He named her Kimberly Mitchelle. Kimberly Mitchelle, who is a Navy lt. Colonel at the Pentagon, went to Danang Sacred Heart Orphanage, interviewed Sister Mary, and after forty one long years, in 2013, was able to track down Mr. Tran Ngoc Bao at his Albuquerque, New Mexico home.

Mr. Bao, whom lt. Colonel Kimberly addressed as Dad on the reunion day, had been brainwashed by the Communists in 1975 and came to the US in 1984.

6. Tam Toa. *Tam* means three. *Toa* has different meanings in Vietnamese. It may mean a Court, a building, an edifice, an office, or a shrine. In the old days, Tam Toa in Dong Hoi had three small pagodas/shrines or edifices while Tam Toa in the citadel of Hue was the three court houses of the imperial system.

7. John Edmund Delezen. Eye of the tiger: Memoir of a United States marine, Third Force Recon Company, Vietnam. McFarland

8. Lewis W. Walt. Introduction by Lyndon B. Johnson. Published 1970 by Funk & Wagnalls in New York.

9. Mr. Tue Duong, Mr. Long Duong, and Mr. Diem Duong

10. Mr. Niem Nguyen and Mr. Diep Nguyen.

11. Mr. Mai Thinh, Mr. Truong Cong Be, and Mr. Hoang Van Luat.

12. Lich su Kinh Te Viet Nam 1945-2000 (History of Vietnamese Economy, Volume 2, 1955-1975) by Dang Phong, Hanoi 2002-2005

13. Tho Ve Nhung Nguoi Linh Nam Xua, by Trang Y Ha, extracted and translated by D.D. Trieu.

14. Life in the New Vietnam, The New York Review of Books, March 17, 1977

15. Jose Van der Sman, interview with Vietnamese Foreign Minister Nguyen Co Thach, Amsterdam, Holland, 6 March 1982

16. Phoenix was the code name of a Vietnamese intelligence organization specializing in anti Communist infiltration.

17. The San Jose Mercury News, October 11, 1987

18. Jacqueline Desbarats and Karl D. Jackson, Washington Quarterly Fall 1985

19. acqueline Desbarats, *The Vietnam Debate*, 1990.

20. www.historylearningsite.co.uk, The Vietnam War, The Air War in Vietnam

21. Management of socialist cooperations grants high or low points to each coop member's workday theorically dependent upon the results and/or significance of the member's work. The workpoints earns the everyday living necessities for the member.

22. Lich su Kinh te Viet nam, Dang Phong, Lao Dong Xa Hoi Publisher

23. Le Thi Anh, "The New Vietnam", *National Review*, April 29, 1977

24. Nguyen Ngoc Chinh. Hoi Ky Mot Nguoi Hanoi.

25. Chris Mulin, "Vietnam Trapped by Military Priority," South China Morning Post. June 1,1980.

26. William Shawcross, "Visit to poor Vietnam." October 16, 1981.
27. William Shawcross, "In a Grim Country." September 24, 1981.
28. South China Morning Post, May 6, 1979.
29. "A Concerto For the Ocean," "The Song of the Sea," poem and painting by HoDacNgoc, *HOPE Newsletter,* 1980.